AF608059

OUT-DOORS

AT

IDLEWILD;

OR, THE

Shaping of a Home on the Banks of the Hudson

NEW YORK CLASSICS

OUT-DOORS

AT

IDLEWILD;

OR, THE

Shaping of a Home on the Banks of the Hudson

NATHANIEL PARKER WILLIS

WITH A NEW INTRODUCTION BY

EDWARD RENEHAN

AN IMPRINT OF STATE UNIVERSITY OF NEW YORK PRESS

Cover Image: Idlewood, the Residence of N.P. Willis at his Hudson River estate, Idlewild: stereoview by E. & H.T. Anthony, New York Public Library Digital Images collection.

Out-Doors at Idlewild: or, The Shaping of a Home on the Banks of the Hudson was originally published in 1855 by Charles Scribner.

Published by State University of New York Press, Albany

Printed in the United States of America

Excelsior Editions is an imprint of State University of New York Press

For information, contact State University of New York Press, Albany, NY
www.sunypress.edu

Library of Congress Cataloging-in-Publication Data

Names: Willis, Nathaniel Parker, 1806–1867, author. | Renehan, Edward, 1956– writer of introduction.
Title: Out-doors at Idlewild; or, the shaping of a home on the banks of the Hudson / Nathaniel Parker Willis ; with a new introduction by Edward Renehan.
Other titles: Facsimile title page: Out-doors at Idlewild; or, the shaping of a home on the banks of the Hudson
Description: Albany : State University of New York Press, 2021. | Series: New York classics | "Originally published in 1855 by Charles Scribner." | Includes bibliographical references.
Identifiers: LCCN 2021025111 | ISBN 9781438486239 (hardcover : alk. paper) | ISBN 9781438486246 (ebook)
Subjects: LCSH: Idlewild (Cornwall, N.Y.) | Hudson River Valley (N.Y. and N.J.)
Classification: LCC PS3324 .O8 2021 | DDC 814/.3—dc23
LC record available at https://lccn.loc.gov/2021025111

10 9 8 7 6 5 4 3 2 1

Contents

New Introduction

Edward Renehan

During the 1850s and 1860s, by the far the most prominent man in all of Cornwall-on-Hudson—indeed in all of Orange County if not New York State—was the writer, editor, and publisher Nathaniel Parker Willis (1806–1867). And nearly as prominent as the man was his Hudson Valley estate, Idlewild, where literary elites gathered and about which Willis himself wrote and published extensively.

Although largely forgotten today, Willis was a true lion of his era. The writers he worked with included in their ranks Washington Irving, Herman Melville, Edgar Allan Poe, and Henry Wadsworth Longfellow. He was, as well, a close personal friend of Charles Dickens, with whom he famously dined on champagne and oysters. He founded the magazine *Home Journal* in 1846, the name of this publication eventually evolving into *Town and Country*, still published monthly.

Willis's entire clan was highly accomplished. His grandfather, Nathaniel Willis, was the publisher of newspapers in Massachusetts and Virginia. His father, another Nathaniel Willis, founded the *Youth's Companion* magazine. Willis's sister Sara Payson Willis was a widely respected author who published under the pen name *Fanny Fern*. A brother, Richard Storrs Willis, was a noted composer of sacred music, his most lasting work being the melody for the Christmas Carol "It Came Upon a Midnight Clear." The African American writer (and runaway slave) Harriett Jacobs lived in the Willis household (Idlewild), while drafting her now-classic abolitionist memoir *Incidents in the Life of a Slave Girl*, published with Willis's help in 1861.*

* Jacobs came to the attention of Willis through his sister, Sara Payson Willis (aka Fanny Fern) who had befriended Jacobs after her escape to the North from a North Carolina plantation. In 1852, in response to the 1850 Fugitive Slave Law that enabled slave-catchers to detain and return to the South escaped slaves who had made it to the North, Willis's wife Cornelia Grinnell Willis formally "purchased" Harriet from the family that had formerly enslaved her,

In *Out-Doors at Idlewild: or The Shaping of a Home on the Banks of the Hudson* (1855), Willis chronicled the creation of his estate at Cornwall-on-Hudson (near West Point), as well as life amid its countryside. The land afforded brilliant views of the river and the mountains to the east. Calvert Vaux (1824–1895), the famed architect of both landscapes and houses, designed the elaborate and ornate Gothic Revival home that Willis named *Idlewood* (whereas he called the estate *Idlewild*), and into which the Willis family moved in July of 1853.* Willis sited the home close by a deep two-hundred-foot gorge via which what came to be known as "Idlewild Creek" cascaded down toward the river. Here, as health issues began to invalid him and confine him to home, Willis wrote a series of papers for his *Home Journal* documenting life at the seventy-acre estate; these eventually collected in *Out-Doors at Idlewild*.

With such contemporaries as William Cullen Bryant and Benson Lossing, Willis extolled "picturesque America" as represented in the works of the artists of the Hudson River School. Willis wrote a two-volume work entitled *American Scenery*, illustrated by William Henry Bartlett, in which he discussed at length the various natural wonders of the country—never overlooking the sights along the Hudson. In conjunction with such enterprises, he also strenuously lobbied on more than one occasion for the revision of names applied to elements of the countryside whenever he thought those names inadequate. Thus "Murderer's Creek" in Cornwall became "Moodna Creek" and "Butter Hill" (the massive granite mountain that forms the western edge of the great "Wind Gate" entrance to the Hudson Highlands between Cornwall and "Breakneck Ridge" on the eastern shore) became "Storm King Mountain."

> "In the varied scenery of our country," he wrote, "there is many a natural beauty , destined to be the theme of our national poetry, which is desecrated by any vile name given it by vulgar chance." Willis began dreaming up new names. . . .Willis's efforts were far from silly or trite. They accurately reflected the value placed on the scenery by the Romantics of the nineteenth century. In bestowing Romantic names on the mountains which form the northern gate to the [Hudson] Highlands, Willis captured the emotional appeal of the Highland scenery and helped assure its preservation a century later.†

thus (somewhat) assuring her safety in the North. (Harriet, born 1813, had escaped to the North in 1842.) The Willis and Jacobs families remained close friends for several generations.

* In 1857 Vaux and his younger protégé Frederick Law Olmstead commenced collaborating on the design of what would become New York's Central Park. Later, in 1872, Vaux collaborated with the Hudson River School painter Frederic Church in the design and landscaping of the latter's home Olana, overlooking the Hudson River near the city of Hudson, New York. Vaux's son, Downing Vaux (1856–1926) designed New York's Riverside Drive.

† Frances F. Dunwell, *The Hudson River Highlands* (New York: Columbia University Press, 1991), 92–93.

Willis's brick house Idlewood, which he called a "cottage," was actually quite more than that, with no less than fourteen rooms, an elaborate 13 foot by 23 foot entrance hall, high gables, and such detailed adornments as lancet windows, beautiful lattices, finials, and other accoutrements. In this design, Vaux was greatly influenced by the architect and landscape horticulturist Andrew Jackson Downing (1815–1852), a close friend of both Vaux and Willis and the author of *The Architecture of Country Houses* (1850). Downing lived in nearby Newburgh.

The agenda here was not simply decorative, but societal and cultural. D'Amore notes that Willis "wrote extensively about domestic architecture, landscape, objects, and décor in [his] magazine, arguing that attention to details in these categories would transfer a spirit of well-being and happiness to one's person and property," and that good taste in these matters would enable people of all classes to "connect with the physical spaces they inhabited in ways that previously had been available only to the elite."*

As Downing wrote:

> There are three excellent reasons why my countrymen should have good houses. The first is, because a good house (and by this I mean a fitting, tasteful, and significant dwelling) is a powerful means of civilization. A nation, whose rural population is content to live in mean huts and miserable hovels, is certain to be behind its neighbors in education, the arts, and all that makes up the external signs of progress. With the perception of proportion, symmetry, order, and beauty, awakens the desire for possession, and with them comes that refinement of manners which distinguishes a civilized from a coarse and brutal people. So long as men are forced to dwell in log huts and follow a hunter's life, we must not be surprised at lynch law and the use of the bowie knife. But, when smiling lawns and tasteful cottages begin to embellish a country, we know that order and culture are established. And, as the first incentive towards this change is awakened in the minds of most men by the perception of beauty and superiority in external objects, it must follow that the interest manifested in the Rural Architecture of a country like this, has much to do with the progress of its civilization.†

After Willis's death in 1867, his house and grounds went through a succession of owners followed by a period of abandonment and neglect—and eventually succumbed to the twentieth century.‡

* Maura D'Amore, "'Close Remoteness' Along the Hudson: Nathaniel Parker Willis's Suburban Aesthetic," *Early American Studies* 7, no. 2 (Fall 2009): 365.

† Andrew Jackson Downing, *The Architecture of Country Houses* (New York: D. Appleton, 1850), v. Downing died in July of 1852 when the Hudson River steamer *Henry Clay* caught fire and sank near Yonkers, New York, taking eighty souls with it.

‡ Some published sources say one of Idlewild's subsequent owners was the Presbyterian minister, horticulturalist, and popular novelist Edward Payson Roe (1838–1888), but this is

The house Idlewood still stands today near the intersection of Curie Road and Idlewild Park Drive, but it has been so extensively remodeled as to be unrecognizable from the home Willis knew. During the early 1900s, the two-story (plus attic) structure was taken down to a single floor. At the same time, nearly all of Calvert Vaux's unique elements were removed. All that remains is the original plan of the ground floor, the original footprint of the house, and the original basement. The place is a private family residence. As well, the elaborate grounds are no more. They've been subdivided and made into yet another outpost of American suburbia—and a distinctly *un*picturesque outpost at that.

not the case. Roe's estate, Roelands, embraced what is today the Hudson Highlands Nature Museum's Wildlife Education Center in Cornwall, adjacent to which is the small Edward Payson Roe Memorial Park, with a plaque and a hiking trail.

Mrs. A. C. Williamson

OUT-DOORS AT IDLEWILD

BY

N. P. WILLIS

IDLEWILD, SOUTHERN FRONT

OUT-DOORS

AT

IDLEWILD;

OR, THE

Shaping of a Home on the Banks of the Hudson

BY

N. P. WILLIS

"At King Kemserai's caravanserai I dismounted from my camel ; and here travelers were entertained, on condition of telling their adventures."

Eastern Story-Book.

W. H. TINSON,

STEREOTYPER,

23 Beekman St., N. Y.

TAWS, RUSSELL & CO.,

BOOK AND JOB PRINTERS BY STEAM

26 Beekman and 18 Spruce st

TO

HON. JOSEPH GRINNELL

THESE OUT-DOOR SKETCHES OF THE HOME

TO WHOSE IN-DOOR HAPPINESS HIS KIND AFFECTION IS ONE OF THE

CONSTANT BLESSINGS,

Are Gratefully and Cordially Dedicated,

by his son-in-law,

N. P. WILLIS.

Idlewild, October, 1854.

Preface.

THE following volume is a simple weaving into language of the every-day circumstances of an invalid retirement in the Highlands of the Hudson. It was written in Letters to the Home Journal, and it was expected by the author, that they would owe their interest to being plainly truthful, and to picturing exactly the life that formed itself around the new-comer to one particular portion of our country—its climate, its conveniences, its accessibilities, and its moral and social atmosphere. As it is a neighborhood to which the sick are often sent by the physicians of New York, for the nearest mountain air, which is completely separated from the sea-board, the author has thought it might add a utility to his book to give his invalid experience with the rest. In this feature of it he has aimed to serve his fellow sufferers rather than to please the general reader.

In contributing these sketches to a periodical, and contenting himself with no other formation of thoughts and events into a work, than the mere putting of the loose sketches together, the author has committed another of the offences for which he has been called to account by every genial and kind critic, as well as abused by every malicious and carping one. As this may be his last work, and it is time, perhaps, to say, what he has always felt, but neglected to say, deprecatorily, upon this point, he will venture to quote the most recent of these fault-finding passages of criticism, with a word of reply to it. Thus says the New York Quarterly Review (of July, 1854), in a most liberal and friendly criticism, written, the author understands, by a clergyman who is a stranger to him :—

"Mr. Willis is perhaps most distinguished as a writer of light, brilliant and dashing sketches, contributed to the magazines. His collected papers of this kind amount to three thick volumes. Notwithstanding their apparent absence of hard work, they have no doubt been carefully eliminated. In style they are original, artistic, and follow no previous model. * * He has that one merit—that his style is his own. There are elements in all his sketches, which, if combined in one well-compacted design, might make a sparkling novel, and Mr. Willis would better have consulted his own fame had he seized upon the retirement of five years afforded him at Glenmary, to have wrought out some works of more enduring character, where that which seems light and flippant, when we have too much of it, and liable, like loose leaves, to be blown away, might have been securely bound up in some design much safer than board covers. The mere collection and collocution of papers which have served the purposes of ephemeral magazines, into books and volumes, may enhance their chance for time—but not for eternity. There is an opportunity for Mr. Willis to do at Idlewild what he has neglected to accomplish at Glenmary. He has seen enough of the world to afford him ample material ; let him combine the qualities which sparkle along his works so that they may flash in one setting. This is good advice but it is to be observed that those who bind themselves down to the craving demands of the periodical press, soon jog along like patient horses in the traces, and forego the ambition and aspiration of authors. * * It would be better to run some of the Home Journal metal into bullet-moulds, clip over an aspiring gray eagle as it is trespassing upon his air-territory over the bounds of Idlewild, pluck a feather, nib it to a sharp point, and go to work at that novel in two volumes," &c., &c.

Kind as this is, the author feels that it implies, as do other criticisms, a misconception of both the aim and the impulse with which he has labored in his profession. It is a refusal to him of what he has never sought nor claimed in his prose writings—what, if he knows himself, he has never sufficiently wished, to give turn or color to a sentence. He could not but value "fame," if it should be thus won, inasmuch as it might give pleasure to his children ; but, TO LIVE, *as variedly, as amply, and as worthily, as is possible to his human faculties, while upon this planet,* has been his aim ; and not to be remembered after he shall have left it. Literature—periodical literature—offered him the readiest means for this—the least confining mode of subsistence, the freest access to contemporary mind and society, the most influence and power, the best habits of mental exercise and enlargement. He chose, it, therefore, *as a profession.* In it, as an editor, he found a power—over and above all power of serving himself—and upon this alone, aside from the objects just named, he has endeavored to keep a fixed purpose, suitable to the trust with which, in that power, he was charged. The reviewer above quoted, has, in one chance remark, borne testimony to his discharge of this trust—therein giving him, he must freely own, a certain "fame" which he hopes will belong to his writings while they live. He says :—

"Mr. Willis has usually minded his own business, and gone straight ahead in his literary career, without any apparent regard either of praise or blame, of appreciation, or neglect, or dislike ; * * and *he has already, by words in season, built up the reputation of a score of people as securely, at least, as his own."*

That the author has had no eye to "immortality," but has labored honestly and industriously for the wants of himself and those dear to him, and has served others whenever it was in his power, with what means and opportunities chance threw into his hands—if this, which he finds thus incidentally testified to by a stranger, be true, he has certainly achieved all his purpose in literature, and would be abundantly content with that, for all his fame.

Idlewild, October, 1854.

Contents.

LETTERS FROM IDLEWILD.

LETTER I.

THE HIGHLAND TERRACE.

[The following description, written for Mr. Putnam's very splendid work, the "Book of the Picturesque," was published immediately before the commencement of the Letters from Idlewild, and while the author was deciding upon the spot for his future residence.]

West Point is Nature's Northern Gate to New York city. As soon as our rail-trains shall equal those of England, and travel fifty or sixty miles an hour, the Hudson, as far as West Point, will be but a fifty-mile extension of Broadway. The river banks will have become a suburban avenue—a long street of villas, whose busiest resident will be content that the City Hall is within an hour of his door. From this metropolitan avenue into the agricultural and rural region, the outlet will be at the city's Northern Gate, of West Point—a gate whose threshold divides Seaboard from In-land, and whose mountain pillars were heaved up with the changeless masonry of creation.

The passage through the Mountain-Gate of West Point is a three-mile Labyrinth, whose clue-thread is the channel of the river—a complex wilderness, of romantic picturesqueness and beauty, which will yet be the teeming Switzerland of our country's Poetry pencil—and, at the upper and northern outlet of this labyrinthine portal of the city, there is a formation of hills which has an expression of most apt significance. *It looks like a gesture of welcome from Nature, and an invitation to look around you !* From the shoulder-like bluff upon the river, an outspreading range of Highlands extends back, *like the curve of a waving arm*—the single mountain of Shawangunk (connected with the range by a valley like the bend of a graceful wrist), *forming the hand at the extremity.* It is of the area within the curve of this bended arm—a Highland Terrace of ten or twelve miles square, on the west bank of the river—that we propose to define the capabilities, and probable destiny.

The HIGHLAND TERRACE we speak of—ten miles square, and lying within the curve of this outstretched arm of mountains—has an average level of about one hundred and twenty feet above the river. It was early settled ; and, the rawness of first clearings having long ago disappeared, the well-distributed *second woods* are full grown, and stand, undisfigured by stumps, in park-like roundness and maturity. The entire area of the Terrace contains several villages, and is divided up into cultivated farms, the walls and fences in good condition, the roads lined with trees, the orchards full, the houses and barns sufficiently hidden with foliage to be picturesque—the whole neighborhood, in fact, within any driving distance, quite rid of the angularity and well-known ungracefulness of a newly-settled country.

Though the Terrace is a ten-mile plain, however, its roads are remarkably varied and beautiful, from the *curious multiplicity of deep glens*. These are formed by the many streams which descend from the half-bowl of mountains inclosing the plain, and—their descent being rapid and sudden, and the river into which they empty being one or two hundred feet below the level of the country around—they have gradually worn beds much deeper than ordinary streams, and are, from this and the character of the soil, unusually picturesque. At every mile or so, in driving which way you will, you come to a sudden descent into a richly wooded vale—a bright, winding brook at bottom, and romantic recesses constantly tempting to loiter. In a long summer, and with perpetual driving over these ten-mile interlacings of wooded roads and glens, we daily found new scenery, and heard of beautiful spots, within reach and still unseen. From every little rise of the road, it must be remembered, the broad bosom of the Hudson is visible, with foreground variously combined and broken ; and the lofty mountains (encircling just about as much scenery as the eye can compass for enjoyment), form an *ascending background and a near horizon* which are hardly surpassed in the world for boldness and beauty. To what degree sunsets and sunrises, clouds, moonlight, and storms, are aggrandized and embellished by this peculiar formation of country, any student and lover of nature will at once understand. Life may be, outwardly, as much more beautiful, amid such scenery, as action amid the scenery of a stage is more dramatic than in an unfurnished room.

The *accessibilities* from Highland Terrace are very desirable. West Point is perhaps a couple of miles below, by the river bank ; and, though mountain-bluffs and precipices now cut off the following of this line by land, a road has been surveyed and commenced along the base of Cro'nest, which, when completed, will be one of the most picturesque drives in the world. A part of it is to be blown out from the face of the rock ; and, as the lofty eminences will almost completely overhang it, nearly the whole road will be in shade in the afternoon. To pass along this romantic way for an excursion to the superb military grounds of West Point, and to have the parades and music within an easy drive, will be certainly an unusual luxury for a country neighborhood. The communication is already open for vehicles, by means of a steam ferry, which runs between Cornwall Landing (at the foot of the Terrace), and Cold Spring and the Military Wharf—bringing these three beautiful spots within a few minutes' reach of each other—Morris the song-writer's triple-view site of "Undercliff," by the way, overlooking the central of these Highland-Ferry Landings.

It may be a greater or less attraction to the locality of the Terrace, but it is no disadvantage, at least, that three of the best frequented summer resorts are within an afternoon drive of any part of it—the West Point Hotel, Cozzens's, which is a mile below, and Powelton House, which is five or six miles above the Point, at Newburgh. For accessibility to these fashionable haunts of strangers and travellers, and the gaieties and hospitalities for which they give opportunity—for enjoyment of military shows and music—for all manner of pleasure excursions by land and water, to glens and mountain-tops, fishing, hunting, and studying of the picturesque—Highland Terrace will probably be a centre of attraction quite unequalled.

The river-side length of the Terrace is about five miles—Cornwall at one end and Newburgh at the other. At both these places there are landings for the steamers, and from both these are steam ferries to the opposite side of the river, bringing the fine neighborhood of Fishkill and Cold Spring within easy reach. Newburgh is the metropolis of the Terrace—with its city-like markets, hotels, stores, trades and mechanic arts—an epitome of New York convenience within the distance of an errand. Downing, one of our most eminent horticulturists, once resided here, and Powell, one of the most enterprising of our men of wealth, lives here still ; and, along one of the high acclivities of the Terrace, are the beautiful country seats of Durand, our first landscape painter, Miller, who has presented the neighborhood with a costly and beautiful church of stone, Verplanck, Sands, and many others, whose tastes in ground and improvements add beauty to the river drive.

To the class of seekers for sites of rural residences, for whom we are drawing this picture, the fact that the Terrace is *beyond suburban distance from New York*, will be one of its chief recommendations. What may be understood as "Cockney annoyances" will not reach it. But it will still be sufficiently and variously accessible from the city. On its own side of the river there is a rail-route from Newburgh to Jersey city, whose first station is in the centre of the Terrace, at "Vail's Gate," and by which New York will eventually be brought within two hours or less. By the two ferries to the opposite side of the river, the stations of the Hudson Railroad are also accessible, bringing the city within equal time on another route. The many boats upon the river, touching at the two landings at all hours of day and night, enable you to vary the journey to and fro, with sleeping, reading, or tranquil enjoyment of the scenery. Friends may come to you with positive luxury of locomotion, and without fatigue ; and the monotony of access to a place of residence, by any one conveyance—an evil very commonly complained of—is delightfully removed.

There is a very important advantage of the Highland Terrace, which we have not yet named. It is *the spot on the Hudson where the two greatest thoroughfares of the North are to cross each other*. The intended route from Boston to Lake Erie here intersects the rail-and-river routes between New York and Albany. Coming by Plainfield and Hartford to Fishkill, it here takes ferry to Newburgh, and traverses the Terrace by the connecting link already completed to the Erie Railroad—thus *bringing Boston within six or eight hours* of this portion of the river. Western and Eastern travel will then be direct from this spot, like Southern and Northern ; and Albany and New York, Boston and Buffalo, will be four points all within reach of an easy excursion.

To many, the most essential charm of Highland Terrace, however (as a rural residence in connection with life in New York), will be the fact that it is the *nearest accessible point of complete inland climate*. Medical science tells us that nothing is more salutary than change from the seaboard to the interior, or from the interior to the seaboard ; and between these two climates the ridge of mountains at West Point is the first effectual separation.

The raw east winds of the coast, so unfavorable to some constitutions, are stopped by this wall of cloud-touching peaks, and, with the rapid facilities of communication between salt and fresh air, the balance can be adjusted without trouble or inconvenience, and as much taken of either as is found healthful or pleasant. The trial of climate which the writer has made, for a long summer, in the neighborhood of these mountainous hiding-places of electricity, the improvement of health in his own family, and the testimony of many friends who have made the same experiment, warrant him in commending it as a peculiarly salutary and invigorating air.

We take pains to specify, once more, that it is to a certain class, in view of a certain new phase in the philosophy of life, that these remarks are addressed. For those who must be in the city late and early, on any and every day, the distance will be inconvenient, unless with unforeseen advances in the rate of locomotion. For those who require the night and day dissipations of New York, and who have no resources of their own, a nearer residence might also be more desirable. For mere seekers of seclusion and economy it is too near the city, and the neighborhood would be too luxurious. But for those who have their time in some degree at their own disposal—who have competent means for luxurious independence—

who have rural tastes and metropolitan refinements rationally blended—who have families which they wish to surround with the healthful and elegant belongings of a home, while, at the same time they wish to keep pace with the world, and enjoy what is properly and only enjoyable in the stir of cities—for this class—the class, as we said before, made up of Leisure, Refinement, and Luxury—modern and recent changes are preparing a new theory of what is enjoyable in life. It is a mixture of city and country, *with the home in the country.* And the spot with the most advantages for the first American trial of this new combination, is, we venture confidently to record, the HIGHLAND TERRACE, ENCIRCLED IN THE EXTENDED ARM OF THE MOUNTAINS ABOVE WEST POINT.

LETTER II.

HIGHLAND TERRACE CONTINUED.

[This Letter also preceded the commencement of the regular series of Idlewild Papers.]

DAY before yesterday, a cold and raw snow-storm kept us housed by the fire. To-day, the flies were troublesome to my horse, and the shade of the Sontags of the woods—(the maples, still full-leaved and only more beautiful with autumn)—was refreshing to both of us. It is, as I write, a summer's evening—crickets iterating, mosquitoes reconnoitering, wasps stretching their legs, and evidently reconsidering their premature givings-over, the ground fragrant with the twilight dew, and—my pen embarrassed. I had prepared to give you a picture of the Tropics, thinking you might like it as a contrast to stave off the first rudeness of winter. But in Broadway, to-day, it must have been as hot as Hayti—and of Hayti, therefore, you would rather read when it is cooler. What shall I write about ?

October and Webster have left us—one gone to the Past, the other to the Future—but the parting of both, like a Sabbath of midsummer. What a day was Sunday, the 31st !—tranquil, balmy, genial, beautiful. I spent its "service-time" with Nature—not irreligiously to myself, though I fear it seemed so to my neighbors. Let me describe it to you (even if there seem little to record), for the apparition of beauty, in face, or mountain, weather or flower, grows to be more and more of an event to me. Standing aside and letting the world crowd on, as I have done of late, the sense of what is fair and excellent has rallied, like the quality which the pressure had most overborne, and I am most moved by what the day brings to admire. Is this a change to be sad about ? We should have a sweet word, like "sunset," for departed health—the clouds so brighten with it.

As I was saying, October's dying day was a Sabbath of profound beauty. (You may have realized it in the city, as the prisoner hears the music of the band marching under his window.) I drove along the Hudson, a mile or more—taking wife and children to church—and, with the last note of the bell, stood tying my horse to the fence. (You know the church. It is that pretty structure of stone which is the gem of this ten-mile Terrace of the Highlands. The bell, in its turret you remember, sends its echoes into the elfin haunt of Drake's poem—the wild home of the "Culprit Fay.") Just across the road lay a broad lawn, with a skirt of noble trees on its farther edge, and the river lay below. Ah, thought I, as I looked around, that little church is but a chapel within a vast cathedral—the Hudson a broad aisle, the Highlands a thunder-choir and gallery, Black Rock a pulpit, and a blue dome over all—and lo ! Nature, in her surplice of summer, ready to preach the sermon ! Why not do my worshipping out of doors ?

I have always found it easier to be devout when pacing slowly, than when sitting still. I should pray better, even in a church, if I could walk the aisle, instead of remaining motionless in a pew. "The groves were God's first temples," and it was, perhaps, because men could there walk and pray that the early saints were more pious. The more the body is pent up, the more thoughts wander, is a common human experience, I believe—truer even of pews than of prisons.

Nature, as you know, seldom repeats herself, even in an every-day morning, but seems to keep sky and weather in an eternal succession of new experiments. I had never seen the Hudson look as on this last day of October. It was strange as well as beautiful. The Terrace Bay (that broad sheet spread below the ten-mile lap of the Highlands, on a knee of which sits Newburgh), was all one breathless surface, but half of it was in shadow as dark as polished steel. Water so silvery bright and so inky black I never had seen together. Of every mountain there was a mirrored reflex ; but one was copied in light, one in darkness—like truth in reputation. And the sails of a fleet of becalmed vessels dotted this far mirror like snow-flakes lightly fallen. Nothing moved. Nature seemed to have bid even the un-Sabbath-keeping keels to stop and let the scene look holy.

Up and down under the trees edging the high bank of the river, I paced out the service-time, hearing every note of the organ, hymning it on the other side of the lawn, and eloquently preached to, by Nature—the theme God's wondrous works, and our many blessings in open air. It was a sermon I shall remember. My heart was warm with it as I met the congregation coming from the sermon in the church, though probably they, and the preacher I had not heard, set me down for a vagrant, profaning the day. My mention of it, as you will understand, is partly vindicatory. Die who will, in these days, the obituary notices strive mainly to prove that he was pious.

LETTER III.

Lessening the Brook—Pig-Prophecy—Nearing of the City with Spring—the City Eye, as felt in the Country—Telegraph Wires, Æolian.

April 2d, 1853.

THE Brook of Idlewild, like myself, is beginning to lessen its individualism, at the approach of summer visitors. With the preparation for coming back of the leaves, the torrent, so lonely and loud in winter, begins to hush to a brook little heard ; and its foam-clad cascades and rapids show but for common rocks, blest only in the pleasant shade that comes with their renewed insignificance. So it is ! Take summer from us—stream or man—and, "with the winter of our discontent," comes a strengthening of the floods within us, these again stilling and lessening with the return of more genial surroundings. Come, brother brook ! let us murmur contented along ! What we lose in one season we gain in another—the lonelier and colder around, the louder and prouder in ourselves—the bleaker, the stronger—the drearier, the more clothed with music and majesty of our own.

Spite of the pig-prophecy in December, we have had plenty of snow ; the frost, of course, having little chance at the ground, and the freshets abundant—both hasteners of Spring. Yet it was a sensible old woman of our neighborhood who brought me the report. She went to the pig-killing, as usual, to beg the *pig's melt* for her cat. And this layer of unwholesome fat—Nature's preparation against cold, like an inside blanket for the bowels of the pig—she assured me was, "this year, next to nothing, and a sure sign of little or no snow." I hired a sleigh instead of buying one, upon the strength of it—of course a loser by putting my faith in pig's bowels and their prophetic preparations for the winter.

With the disappearance of ice from the Hudson (so that we can cross regularly to the railroad), and with the reappearance of the steamers on the river, we are shoved down to a suburb once more. The rattling monster plying along the shore opposite, with its smoke-tail high in air, was in New York an hour and a half ago. Broadway is within reach—shops and picture-galleries, lions and lectures, calls and confectionery, friends and fashions, dust, dandies and omnibuses—all within the goings and comings of a day. Yet we have been country-folks for six months—so remotely buried behind mountains and dilatory mails, that the city seemed a perpetual yesterday, impossible to sympathize with or make use of. The Highland Terrace (the ten-mile lap of mountains on whose knee we sit, overlooking the river) is the Switzerland of summer visitors from New York ; the place to bring families to, for change of air ; the paradise of scenery and farm boarding-houses with little to pay ; no gaieties except pic-nic-ing and horseback-riding, and no champagne or "fashion," except what you bring with you. Half the population of the neighborhood, therefore, drops away with the autumn foliage and returns with the violets and strawberries. But it is droll what a double sort of place it makes, to have the society thus deciduous. Where the trees and farm-houses shed their leaves and lodgers together, it curiously intensifies "the seasons" for those who stay on with the evergreens.

No ! judging by the "teams" and people on the road, you would scarce believe yourself in the same part of the country, *before* the "first cold snap" and *after*. City lingerers stay on till then. But when a fire to breakfast by is no longer a deniable necessity—and, with some particularly frosty morning, there is a general radiation, towards the steamboat landing, of loads of trunks, children's chairs, bathing-tubs, servants and side-saddles—the *feel* of the city eye is, by common consent, suddenly taken off. For the first time in six months, it is obvious that everybody passing has dressed for the neighbors only. Even the few wealthy people who occupy the beautiful sites upon the river, lay aside their fine carriages and begin to do their driving in light wagons. The farmers, however,—the "regular bone and sinew," who would scout the idea of being subject to anybody's criticism of their appearance—betray, by a unmistakable eruption of old hats, shabby coats and rusty harnesses, that the disease of human vanity is epidemic ; that they had been all summer "sitting for their pictures" to the strangers among us ; that the neighbors, who know all about our crops and acres, are not to be so carefully dressed for ; and that, now the pretty girls are gone from the roads, with their broad-brimmed straw hats and blue ribbons, even the riding behind a team is a different matter—horses, somehow, to be less curried, and shaving every day not so absolutely necessary.

To being affected by the season, however—to being less susceptible to winter than to summer wind—there is one delicious exception. With a November blast as with a June breeze, *the news passes to music !* Whether country folks or city *belles* listen, the Æolian harps strung along upon the telegraph poles, play perpetually the same. To the strange beauty of this music (little noticed or valued) I have become quite wedded, in my life out of doors, for the last winter. It is more varied and beautiful than people think. You can always hear it—if not as you walk upon the road, at least by laying your ear against the poles—and, by selecting one that stands near a running stream, you may hear a duet of breeze and brook, a capricious out-singing of each other alternately by wind and water, that is as heavenly to muse by as a voluntary of Nature well could be. The poles differ very much, both in the quantity and quality of sound—partly, perhaps, from difference of size, or kind of wood, or tightness with which the wire is pressed by the leaning—but, by stopping in your walks, you get to know these with their variations, and you may thus choose your standing-place, and have music fainter or louder to suit your mood. There is one telegraph post, by a little bridge which crosses Idlewild Brook, where I have heard a great deal of waking-dream accompaniment. Stopping there with the glow of exercise in the blood, there seems a kind of fellowship in the instrument's being, like oneself, independent of the wintry air. The invalid's nerves, too (as much more susceptible to pleasure as to pain), are ready for harmony in its most delicate caprices. What news was going past on those wires—what death or marriage, love or business, was being told in those varied vibrations—I did not lose romance by trying to guess or discriminate. The same tune seldom carries the same language to any two hearts. But there it was, murmuring day by day, in changeful contention with the brook, always somewhat audible when closely listened for, and often as loud as a love-whisper, and as changefully expressive, and I must own to have grown habituated to it as a luxury. How many good things we may have, in this mercenary world, after all, without paying for them ! "Telegraphing is expensive," but here is its greatest advantage (per *my* use) and nothing to pay. I trust the stockholders will not take the hint, however, and put sentry-boxes around the posts, to be let out for roadside operas !

LETTER IV.

Slight of Small Streams in the Landscape—Character of Idlewild Brook—Legend and Name of our Nearest Village.

April 16, 1853.

Among "the neglected of this world," I have always thought, are the streams under the river size—those that have valleys of their own and can turn a mill, but are not navigable and scarcely "down on the map." The way travellers go up the Hudson,—expatiating on its scenery and glorifying it in prose and rhyme, but pass, without even a look of inquiry or recognition, the outlet-openings of numberless "runs," brooks, "creeks," and "kills," which are tributary to that noble river, but as beautiful in degree and much more varied and secluded is, like the treatment of the lesser poets, a thing to be protested against, if only to show that, of such servile Cæsar-or-nobody-dom, such unenlightened worship of mere bigger-ness, one is not, oneself, a part.

My own experience is, that it must be a small stream to be enjoyed, both sides at a time. From the deck of a steamer on the Hudson, its two shores are so indistinct as to be only admired for what beauty of outline they may have. The slopes, dells, jutting banks, rock-shadows, caprices of curve at water's edge, verdure and foliage, are confused by the distance into a wall of grey. Hence the disappointment that is sometimes expressed by the steamboat passenger, at a first view of the river of whose beauty he has heard so much. Landscape-loving is more affectionate than reverential. One wants just enough of it. That key-word to happiness, *competency*—what one is competent to appreciate and no more—may be applied as aptly to water-courses as to wealth. Though living upon the bank of the Hudson, therefore, and admiring it boundlessly in the labyrinth of Highlands through which it winds away from my daily view, I shall be tender-hearted only to the brook hidden behind me. The glen of Idlewild is but a morning's ramble in extent—a kind of Trenton Falls for one—but, its stream falling over a hundred feet within our own gate, and sometimes a cataract that would bring down a sloop or a lumber-raft, it has varieties of charm that will at least occupy what loving I have time for. I have a chance sympathy with it, in one point, moreover. The salable uses to which its power has been put—its "water-privileges"—are now of little or no value. A miller near me, even with plenty of water, finds it cheaper to grind by steam. A "mill-seat" and a poem are things getting less and less likely to "pay." We are becoming mere ornamentals, Idlewild and I. What poetry I may write upon irresistible impulse, and what vagaries of water there may be, from snow-melting or summer freshet, will be for those who idle near us, or for such occasional appreciator as chance may send along.

My windows—some two hundred feet above the Hudson—overhang, on one side, the meeting of our lovely brook with a respectable creek ; which two tributaries, immediately after, glide blissfully together into the great river, and (like many a beau and belle, famous while separate, but who marry and are heard of no more) pass the remainder of their fresh-water life in swelling the general stream where they are useful and forgotten.

The "creek" I should redeem from the English interpretation of the word. It is not an "inlet" or "corner in a haven," but a rocky and rapid stream, coming down by a noble aisle from the mountains, and as large as half the celebrated rivers of England. Its name is a matter of some doubt. The common people call it "Murderer's Creek," which the more intelligent of the neighbors say is a corruption of Moodna's Creek—Moodna* having been the name of an Indian chief whose tribe lingered long by its secluded waters after the coming of the white man.

My next neighbor up stream, Mr. Philip Verplank (between whose noble promontory lawn and our own Highland eyrie these two streams have their meadow-meeting and united forthgoing), gives me the following as a tradition which may possibly contain the etymology. It is a slip from an old newspaper, and I copy it as it stands :

> "Little more than a century ago, the beautiful region watered by this stream was possessed by a small tribe of Indians, which has long since become extinct, or incorporated with some other savage nation of the West. Three or four hundred yards from where the stream discharges itself into the Hudson, a white family of the name of Stacey had established itself in a log house, by tacit permission of the tribe, to whom Stacey had made himself useful by his skill in a variety of little arts highly estimated by the savages. In particular, a friendship subsisted between him and an old Indian called Naoman, who often came to his house, and partook of his hospitality. The Indians never forgive injuries or forget benefits. The family consisted of Stacey, his wife, and two children—a boy and a girl—the former five, the latter three years old.
>
> "One day Naoman came to Stacey's log hut, in his absence, lighted his pipe, and sat down. He looked very serious, sometimes sighed deeply, but said not a word. Stacey's wife asked him what was the matter, and if he was sick. He shook his head, sighed, but said nothing, and soon went away. The next

* Still others say that the word is *Merdner*, and that this was the name of the first English settler.

day he came again, and behaved in the same manner. Stacey's wife began to think strange of this, and related it to her husband, who advised her to urge the old man to an explanation the next time he came. Accordingly, when he repeated his visit the day after, she was more importunate than usual. At last the old Indian said—

" 'I am a red man, and the pale faces are our enemies—why should I speak ?'

" 'But my husband and I are your friends ; you have eaten salt with us a thousand times, and my children have sat on your knee as often. If you have anything on your mind, tell it me.'

" 'It will cost me my life if it is known, and the white-faced women are not good at keeping secrets,' replied Naoman.

" ' Try me, and see.'

" 'Will you swear by your Great Spirit you will tell none but your husband ?'

" 'I have none else to tell.'

" ' But will you swear ?'

" 'I do swear by our Great Spirit I will tell none but my husband.'

" 'Not if my tribe should kill you for not telling ?'

" 'Not if your tribe should kill me for not telling.'

"Naoman then proceeded to tell her that, owing to some encroachments of the white people below the mountain, his tribe had become irritated, and were resolved that night to massacre all the white settlers within their reach. That she must send for her husband, inform him of the danger, and as secretly and speedily as possible take their canoe, and paddle with all haste over the river to Fishkill for safety. 'Be quick and do nothing that may excite suspicion,' said Naoman, as he departed.

"The good wife sought her husband, who was down on the river fishing, told him the story, and as no time was to be lost, they proceeded to their boat, which was unluckily filled with water. It took some time to clear it out, and meanwhile Stacey recollected his gun which had been left behind. He proceeded to the house and returned with it. All this took up considerable time, and precious time it proved to this poor family.

"The daily visits of old Naoman, and his more than ordinary gravity, had excited suspicion in some of the tribe, who had accordingly paid particular attention to the movements of Stacey. One of the young Indians who had been kept on the watch, seeing the whole family about to take their boat, ran to the little Indian village, about a mile off, and gave the alarm. Five Indians collected, ran down to the river side, where their canoes were moored, jumped in and paddled after Stacey, who, by this time, had got some distance out into the stream. They gained on him so fast, that twice he dropped his paddle and took up his gun. But his wife prevented his shooting, by telling him, that if he fired, and they were afterwards overtaken, they would meet no mercy from the Indians. He accordingly refrained, and plied his paddle, till the sweat rolled in big drops down his forehead. All would not do ; they were overtaken within a hundred yards of the shore, and carried back with shouts of yelling triumph.

"When they got on shore, the Indians set fire to Stacey's house, and dragged himself, his wife and children to their village. Here the principal old men, and Naoman among the rest, assembled to deliberate on the affair. The chief among them, stated that some of the tribe had undoubtedly been guilty of treason in apprising Stacey, the white man, of the designs of the tribe, whereby they took the alarm and well-nigh escaped. He proposed to examine the prisoners, as to who gave the information. The old men assented to this, Naoman among the rest. Stacey was first interrogated by one of the old men, who spoke English, and interpreted to the others. Stacey refused to betray his informant. His wife was then questioned, while at the same moment two Indians stood threatening the two children with tomahawks in case she did not confess. She attempted to evade the truth, by declaring that she had a dream the night before which had alarmed her, and that she had persuaded her husband to fly.

" 'The Great Spirit never deigns to talk in dreams to a white face,' said the old Indian : 'Woman, thou hast two tongues and two faces. Speak the truth, or thy children shall surely die.' The little boy and girl were then brought close to her, and the two savages stood over them, ready to execute their bloody orders.

" 'Wilt thou name,' said the old Indian, 'the red man who betrayed his tribe ? I will ask thee three times.' The mother answered not. 'Wilt thou name the traitor ? This is the second time.' The poor mother looked at her husband, and then at her children, and stole a glance at Naoman, who sat smoking his pipe with invincible gravity. She wrung her hands and wept ; but remained silent. 'Wilt thou name the traitor ? 'tis the third and last time.' The agony of the mother waxed more bitter ; again she sought the eye of Naoman, but it was cold and motionless ; a pause of a moment awaited her reply, and the tomahawks were raised over the heads of the children, who besought their mother not to let them be murdered.

" 'Stop !' cried Naoman. All eyes were turned upon him. 'Stop !' repeated he, in a tone of authority. 'White woman, thou hast kept thy word with me to the last moment. I am the traitor. I have eaten of the salt, warmed myself at the fire, shared the kindness of these Christian white people, and it was I that told them of their danger. I am a withered, leafless, branchless trunk ; cut me down if you will. I am ready.' A yell of indignation sounded on all sides. Naoman descended from the little bank where he sat ; shrouded his face with his mantle of skins, and submitted to his fate. He fell dead at the feet of the white woman, by a blow of a tomahawk.

"But the sacrifice of Naoman, and the firmness of the Christian white woman, did not suffice to save the lives of the other victims. They perished—how, it is needless to say ; and the memory of their fate has been preserved in the name of the pleasant stream on whose banks they lived and died, which to this day is called Murderer's Creek."

But this indifference, as to name, seems to grow upon its banks. One of the most picturesque and lovely little villages in our country lies nestled in the bent arm of its outlet—*and without a name !* The inhabitants cannot tell you where they live. To be sure, it is so in the bottom of a well—so down in the deepest cleft of the Highlands, that a bird would almost fly over without seeing it (buried in trees, too, for the gentlemen residing there have charmingly respected them) ; but still newspapers and letters must come ; and theirs are addressed to the neighboring *and smaller* village of New Windsor. It is to this place without a name, as the nearest to my home, that I must, henceforth, properly belong. If it were but the beginning a little earlier to be forgotten altogether, one might ex-paragraph thither to be "lapt in elysium"—but while still liable to "obituary notice," the lack of that ever-third word, "Died at ———," might imply a careless disrespect. Shall we have a name to our village, dear Postmaster-General ? It is at the meeting of three streams of different magnitudes—Hudson River, Moodna Creek, and Idlewild Brook—and Moore's "Avoca" has become an understood designation for a meeting of waters. May we call it AVOCA ? It would be descriptive as well as musical—useful too, for that sweet song might well embody a tempting spirit of inhabitiveness. I will leave the suggestion upon echo.

LETTER V.

Reasons for Neighbors moving Off—Morals of Steamboat Landings—Class that is gradually taking Possession of the Hudson—Thought-property in a Residence—Horizon-clock of Idlewild—Society for the Eye, in a View.

April 23, 1853.

I MET one of my neighbors yesterday, seated in his wife's rocking-chair, on top of a wagon-load of tools and kitchen utensils, and preceded by his boys, driving a troop of ten or fifteen cows. As he was one I had always chatted with, in passing, and had grown to value for his good sense and kindly character, I inquired into his movements with some interest. He was going (to use his own phrase) "twenty miles farther back, where a man could afford to farm, at the price of the land." His corn-fields on the banks of the Hudson had risen in value, as probable sites for ornamental residences, and with the difference (between two hundred dollars the fancy acre, and sixty dollars the farming acre) in his pocket, he was transferring his labor and his associations to a new soil and neighborhood. With the market for his produce quite as handy by railroad, he was some four or five thousand dollars richer in capital, and only a loser in scenery and local attachments. A Yankee's pots and kettles will almost walk away on their own legs, with such inducement.

There is another "alluvial deposit," however, besides Taste and Wealth, which helps to drive the farmer from the banks of the river. The steamboat landings occurring every few miles, are nests of bad company, and constant temptations to the idle curiosity of laborers and children. It is a gay sight—at least contrasted with plough and barn-yard—to see the "day boat" sweep up with twice as many inhabitants as the nearest village ; crowds of city-dressed people, leaning over the balustrades, and the whole a gaily painted and confusedly fascinating spectacle of life and movement. Then the "evening boat," with her long line of lights, her ringing bells, and the magical glide with which she comes through the darkness, touches the wharf, and is gone ; the perpetual succession of freight-boats ; the equipages from the surrounding villages ; and all the "runners," coachmen, porters, and "loafers," who abound upon the docks, swarming the bar-rooms in the intervals of arrivals, contribute to keep up an excitement, within reach of which a farmer's customary reliances are made vexatiously uncertain. He would scarce need more than this to make him seek a different neighborhood. But for once, the "money down" also pays virtue's expenses, and it is not surprising that the migration of the river farmers to both cheaper lands and a more moral atmosphere, is general and lively. The "opening down the middle" of the Empire State's robe of agriculture, will soon be edged with velvet, and, for its common cloth, we must look to the sides and skirts, broad back and towering shoulders. *A class who can afford to let the trees grow* is getting possession of the Hudson ; and it is at least safe to rejoice in this, whatever one may preach as to the displacement of the laboring tiller of the soil by the luxurious idler. With the bare fields fast changing into wooded lawns, the rocky wastes into groves, the angular farm-houses into shaded villas, and the naked uplands into waving forests, our great thoroughfare will soon be seen (as it has not been for many years) in something like its natural beauty. It takes very handsome men and mountains to look well bald.

Yet the mover-back from the banks of the Hudson soon finds, probably, that he has sold more than he meant to sell. The *farm that belonged to his thoughts* has gone with the other farm. He has parted, unintentionally, with what he was daily in the habit of looking for, measuring time by, thinking about, and finding society in—the rail-trains and steamers, schooners and barges, sloops, yachts and lumber-rafts, of one of the most lively thoroughfares in the world. Stupidly enough, he had included all this in the "scenery"—the mere trees, hills and running water, of which he expected to find plenty where he was going ! But a mere landscape—and a landscape alive with moving objects of beauty and interest—are very different places in which even to be yourself solitary.

It is to this blindness as to the *un-fenceible property in a spot*, that Idlewild owes its name. It belonged to a valuable farm ; but it was a side of it, which, from being little more than a craggy ravine—the bed of a wayward torrent—had always been left in complete wilderness. When I first fell in love with it, and thought of making a home amid its tangle of hemlocks, my first inquiry as to its price was met with the disparaging remark, that it was of little value—"*only an idle wild* of which nothing could ever be made." And that description of it stuck captivatingly in my memory. "Idle-wild !" "Idle-wild !" But let me describe what belongs to Idlewild, besides its acres of good-for-nothing torrent and unharvest-able crags, and besides the mere scenery around them.

To begin with a trifling convenience, it supplies *a clock*, gratis. From the promontory on which stands my cottage, I see five miles of the Hudson River Railroad, and two miles of the Newburgh and Erie—a clock rimmed round with a mountain horizon, the loveliest of landscapes for a face, and half-mile streaks of smoke for the fingers. Once learn the startings of the trains, and every one that passes announces the time of day. The smoke-fingers serve also as a barometer—more or less white and distinct, depressed or elevated, in proportion to the dampness of the atmosphere. It is something of a luxury also to be *daily astonished* ; and I feel no beginning, at present, of getting used to seeing a rail-train slide along the side of a mountain—the swift smoke-tails of the Newburgh and Erie cars slicing off the top of Skunnemunk several times a day, at an elevation of two hundred feet above the Hudson, and often, when there is a mist below or above it, looking more like a meteor shooting along the face of a cloud, than a mechanical possibility in which a mortal may take passage or send a parcel. To have these swift trains perpetually flying past, one on each side of the river, and meeting at right angles where the ferry-boat is seen continually to cross, varies a man's walk, even at the tail of a plough.

But the two railways, though the most wonderful features of the *movement* in my landscape, are the least beautiful. The spread of the river above the pass of the Highlands (upon which I look immediately down), might be a small lake of four or five miles in extent, embosomed in mountains. This would be fine "scenery" to be solitary amidst, though the birds and the tree-tops were the only stirrers. But to be just as picturesquely secluded, as to personal remoteness, and still see the lake beneath my lawn traversed daily by a hundred craft of one sort and another—steamers, tow-boats, sloops, rafts, yachts, schooners and barges—makes, as I said before, a different thing of solitude. I presume five thousand people, at least, pass daily under my library window ; and as one looks out upon the crowded cars and flotillas which bear such multitudes along, it does not require poetry, in these days of animal magnetism, to express how the sense of society is thus satisfied. A man mingles in a crowd, or goes to the play, to satisfy the social craving which is irresistible—but he need not speak or be spoken to, to get rid of his lonely feeling altogether. He must have a certain amount of human life and motion within reach of his eye. And, just how near or distant these moving fellow-beings must needs be, to magnetize companionship into the air, would vary, probably, with each man's electric circle. Across the river and over to Skunnemunk is near enough for me.

LETTER VI.

Evergreen Independence of Seasons—Nature's Landscape Gardening—Weakness as to Reluctance in Planting Trees.

April 30, 1853.

We are not particular about the coming of spring, at Idlewild. It is impatiently waited for among shrubberies and fruit-trees, and on gravel-walks only shaded in summer. But, lose yourself (as you may) in our waterfall wilderness, and you would not know April from June. It is a little seventy-acre world of rocks, foam-rapids, and pathless woods, the ground carpeted with unchanging mosses and ferns, and the thousands of evergreen trees—hemlocks and cedars, white pines and yellow pines, balsam firs, laurels and cypresses—in such majority that falling leaves are scarce missed. What with this, and a labyrinth of glen-depths where the windy gusts never reach, we only know winter by the snow—late autumn and early spring differing little from summer, or mainly in temperature more inspiriting.

It is, perhaps, additionally local, this nine-month summer at Idlewild—owing partly, that is to say, to the precipitous wall of mountains which partitions us off from the seaboard, and sends the east wind clean over our heads without touching, so that the Boston flayed-alive-ishness* is no part of our climate—but I was trying to draw a picture, which, even without this, might be usefully suggestive. An out-of-doors where there is no windy weather and no naked trees—a *fir-glen*, such as may be found, little valued, almost anywhere hereabouts—makes a *home for an invalid*, with "the north" very materially softened. The eye needs its medicine.

* This local experience is, perhaps, worth making another comment upon. There are those who may be interested to know that there is a mountain wall, so near the city as this, under shelter of which the sour and penetrating *East Wind* of the sea-board is never felt. It was the knowledge of this, by the eminent physician whose advice first brought me to this place, which induced his successful prescription. I have passed a whole winter on this Highland Terrace, daily on horseback, and riding constantly over its ten-mile surface, without once feeling anything like the depressing and searching east wind so poisonously uncomfortable at Boston. The information may be of use to invalids.

Surrounded by evergreen woods, we look out from our cottage windows, for instance, upon perpetual summer, as to foliage ; and it is healing, even to the lungs, in December, to need reminding, half the time, that it is not June. Half the time, too, *it is* (if the newspapers are to be believed) "remarkable weather for the season." Two days out of three, in our usual winters, would be taken kindly by the ripening oranges of the tropics. Live but near a sheltered fir-grove—where the sun draws the perfume from the resinous bark, and the air is unreached by the wind—and, though a delicate invalid, you may pass half your January noons out of doors. Yet most persons choose exposed situations for country residences, and surround the house with elms, oaks, and maples—trees naked half the year. With a latitude of too many wintry months, but with a capricious climate, whose summer days, departed by the almanac, may be, any morning, back at our door, it is surely best, if possible, to be ready, at short notice, to *realize* them—to let it *look* as well as *feel* like summer—to see verdure and breathe perfume, as well as glow with the warm air that commonly keeps perfume and verdure company.

I am making an experiment at Idlewild—seeing how far a place can be improved by originating nothing—taking advantage only of what Nature has already done. I began by setting down my cottage amid an old wood, upon a site otherwise perhaps second best, instead of waiting twenty years for shade upon a spot with a better view. With groves all around us, and a half-mile avenue of hemlocks extending from the water's edge upon the Hudson to the gate up the brook, I have not yet planted a single tree. We go to *them* so much easier than they come to us. Here and there it begins to look rather expensively terraced—but those curious levels, in the precipitous sides of the ravine, were Nature's own spread of her lap, and we have only smoothed down her gown. In the wildest rock chasms of our torrent brook, we have, now, two darkly-shaded lakes—cascades pouring into them, waterfalls pouring out of them—and you would scarce believe how little finishing it took to complete Nature's intended damming-up of the approaching crags at the outlets. For one great advantage, a road up the glen, we are indebted rather to accident—a former proprietor having built it at some expense, in a project to quarry slate—but, upon the edges of a track roughly hewn through underbrush, forty years ago, there are now rows of noble trees which look like large investments of time and money. Perched on a hillside, we have a fish-pond, of crystal clearness, which you would also take for an expensive caprice, done with lead pipes and much round-about digging ; and that was a natural spring, of singular and unfailing abundance, known to all the vagrant boys of the neighborhood as the coolest and best water to be anywhere found, and which it needed but little work to "puddle round and stone up." With a tract of uneven surface, which has been left a long time idle and wild, it is surprising how you may thus need to strike but the thousandth blow, in the determination to complete only what Nature has struck nine hundred and ninety-nine at, before you. You get such large effects with so little labor—a consideration, where a shovel at a dollar a day moves dirt so slowly.

I said, just now, that I had not yet planted a single tree at Idlewild. This is half a betrayal of a weakness that I feel growing upon me ; and, having been reminded to-day of what I have once put in print from quite an opposite feeling, I may as well make a clean breast, and so, perhaps, get the better of it. In our current of life we have eddies of these quiet side-weaknesses—a string of them. At fourteen we begin to be secretly nervous lest our beard should be belated. Whiskers pretty well outlined, there awakens an unconfessed wonder and indignation that the world does not seem ready for our particular genius. Soon after, we are mortified that even our guardian angel, reading our hearts, should know how hard it is to smile with contempt because papas do not think us "a good match." The struggle of life comes ; and, with the current swifter and deeper, there is an interval, perhaps, when the eddies of secret weakness find no slack-water for play. But, that past, we begin to be sensitive about our age and our first grey hairs ; and when that is scarce over, there comes another feeling—the weakness that I speak of—the secret reason (though scarce before recognized and brought fairly to the light) why I have been two years moulding Idlewild into a home, and have not yet set out a tree.

We dread being reminded of what is going to do just as well without us. The time of life for this feeling may be sooner or later, but it comes. We outlive it—for we see old men very fond of planting trees. But, with every willingness to look *forward*—death a gate to which we see our steps turning, and still go tranquilly on—the look *backward* has its pangs—pride-pangs—over and above the partings of affection. What we prize and admire that will not miss us—what will come to its beauty after we are gone—what will not need us to appreciate or point out its splendor, but will be looked at and loved as well when we have been long forgotten—of this we are reminded, oftener and more bitterly than we always like to own. We do not set up memorials of this kind without a sigh. To plant a tree is to do this—its growth slow, its maturity delaying, its full promise far off, while *we* are loosening hold, conscious of uncertain stay, sure to be soon gone beyond its shading. But I will try to-morrow. Trees should be growing here and there at Idlewild—whether or not I shall be here to see them in their beauty.

LETTER VII.

Earlier City Migration to the Country than usual—Peculiar Dignity-plant—Object of Country Farmers in taking City Boarders for the Summer—Suggestion as to City and Country Exchange of Hospitality.

May 7, 1853.

OUR nominal summer, in this region, dates from the period when the farm-houses receive their city boarders for the season ; and I find, by conversation with my neighbors on the road, that it is to commence this year a month earlier than usual. The engagement of rooms from the first of *June*, instead of the first of *July*, is so general as to be quite the leading topic of interest and curiosity. It is attributed partly to the rise of provisions and other expenses of living in New York, and partly to the growing taste of mingling country and city life. Differing from England in nothing so much as in the less value we set upon *the individual home*, there is a wonderful proportion of our respectable families who pass the winter at hotels and boarding-houses, and to whom rural migration is an easy and agreeable change. They have no residence to lock up or let. They strike tent as willingly as the Arab, whose nomadic taste the American seems to share. From pavements and operas, omnibuses and heated rooms, the change to green fields, quiet, and fresh air, is but the paying a bill and packing a trunk.

But in this neighborhood—this Highland Terrace, ten miles square, lying in a half-bowl of mountains—"taking boarders" is not exactly what it is elsewhere. The difference is worth explaining—for it shows that dignity is a plant which may grow differently in one place and another. I have already complimented the locality, for its being so chance-formed, geographically, as to be entirely exempt from the sour east wind. Downing compliments it, in his horticultural writings, because the *arbor vitæ* (the flat cedar), the most rare and curious of evergreens, is here the commonest shrub by the wayside. As the only climate where thrives a peculiar dignity-plant—the different feeling I speak of, as to taking boarders—it is, I think, equally to be complimented.

"Board" and "hospitality" differ, here, in nothing but the equivalent. For the entertainment given by our farmers to families from the city, during the summer months *money is taken*, instead of the usual return of similar hospitality, or the incurring of a debt of civility. In all other respects, it is an interchange of advantages between equals in social rank. The charges for board are very moderate—pecuniary profit not being the acknowledged or main inducement on the farmer's part. He does it, ostensibly *and allowedly*, to give his family the advantage of more extended intercourse, to see the world near-to, to dispose of his superfluities, and receive superfluities in return—to furnish fresh air, beautiful scenery, fruits, flowers, and cordial welcome, without charge, and take for equivalent, such new notions of dress, views of passing topics, and observations of city manners and character, as may be gathered from the entertainment of city society under his own roof. *For the greater expense it is to one party than to the other*, in the carrying out of this agreeable interchange, a small rectifier is thrown in, in the shape of a bill.

In other parts of the world—perhaps it will be granted—the taking of boarders, in some greater or less degree, involves the personal dignity and position. It is understood usually, as an admission of "reduced circumstances." The host and hostess preside at table rather to attend to the wants of those who sit with them than to share the meal. They are not included in the daily arrangements for amusement, do not enter a guest's room without some more definite reason than to lounge or chat, would not venture to nick-name or be playfully familiar, and, in all respects, preserve those formalities of language and manner which imply a barrier not to be overstepped.

That all this is very different, in the Highlands between West Point and Newburgh, any one who has passed a summer here will readily admit. The families that receive from ten to thirty boarders are among the most respectable in the neighborhood—farmers who do not, confessedly (nor probably in fact), depend materially on taking boarders for a livelihood. The common price, indeed, would hardly be thought to clear expenses, if time and rent were taken into the account. But, while no pains are spared to make the visiters happy and comfortable, it is done with the joyous and cheerful stimulus of hospitality—the first comings in spring looked forward to with eager pleasure ; the parting adieu in autumn received with whatever friendly regret the guest's character and manners may have inspired. In the arrangements for excursions, in walks and drives, the family is as much included as their own wishes and circumstances of mutual convenience would naturally bring about. At table and in the parlor, in doors and out of doors, there is as much social equality as between the boarders themselves. In the society of the country around, it is rather an addition to the dignity than otherwise, to take boarders in the summer—showing competency to entertain and accommodate, and implying, of course, a polish from intercourse with strangers.

Now, this really seems to me, I must say, a *social novelty worth transplanting* and propagating—worth copying, even in the city. How many families there are in New York who have house-room to spare, and who, *if their dignity and position were not involved or lessened,* would find both profit and pleasure in opening their doors to "boarders !" They might receive only such as came properly introduced or recommended. The chances of agreeable friends and "good society" might be as fair as in the ordinary course of forming acquaintances. House and furniture already provided, as in country board, there would be a profit at half the price charged at hotels. Why, New York is a wilderness of unoccupied attention and unoccupied apartments, on which pride alone turns the key. Yet, if the hospitality *for money* were a little too startling at first, how many independent families there are who have country houses, between whom and those who have city houses *hospitality might be exchanged*—three months of summer board for three months of winter—and no pride hurt, but health, pocket, and love of change materially and reciprocally accommodated !

LETTER VIII.

Ownership in Nature worth Realizing—Thumb-and-finger Nationality of Yankees—United Experience of Many, as expressed in a Common-minded Man's Better Knowledge—Lack of Expression and Variety in Gates—Pig-tight Gates.

May 14, 1853.

SPRING is a beautiful piece of work ; and not to be in the country to see it done, is the not realizing what glorious masters we are, and how cheerfully, minutely, and unflaggingly the fair fingers of the Season broider the world for us. Each April morning, to drop the reins upon the neck of your horse, and look, charmed, around, seeing that Nature did *not* go to bed, used up and tired, the night before, as *you* did, but has been industriously busy upon the leaves and blossoms while you were asleep—so much more advancedly lovely than yesterday—is, somehow, a feeling that has in it the bliss of *ownership.* The morning seems made for you. The fields and sky seem *your* roof and grounds. The air and sunshine, fresh colors and changing light—all new, and not a second-hand thing to be seen—nothing to be cupboarded and kept over for to-morrow, or for another guest—gives a delicious consciousness of being the first to be waited on, the one it was all made and meant for. A city April, in comparison, is a thing potted and pickled, and retailed to other customers as well.

And—speaking of green leaves—I have been vexing myself to-day over a thumb-and-finger nationality that we have. The Irish laborers, at work upon our cottage grounds, during the earlier season, have gone to and fro, without damage, intentional or unintentional, to what did not belong to them. They respect one's property in a tree as well as in a wall or a door. But, with the opening season, the mechanics—Americans, of course—have resumed *their* labors on the unfinished building ; and the marks of their passings in and out are very different. They board among our neighbors around, and either way from the public road, on the river or the village side, the approach is through a long avenue of fir-trees. You may track them (seeing any day whether they have gone to dinner or not) by the broken twigs of fresh-green tassels upon the ground. They never pass near one of my beautiful hemlocks or cedars without refreshing the memory of their American thumb and finger as to its being a free country—breaking off a branch, slapping it once or twice against the leg as they walk along, and throwing it away. If it were grass, and only missed in the crop—or if their "bosses" milked them when they got home—I should say nothing. A trespass on pasture at least benefits the owner of the cow. But the disfiguring of trees, whose every graceful spray, from the ground up, is part of an outline of proportion—destroying what nothing can restore, from a mere wanton non-recognition of any man's property in more than the fuel of a tree—is a thumb-and-finger Fourth of July which I must venture to wish somewhat abated. The young gentlemen, of course, intended no special annoyance to me. I would have spoken to them on the subject, but they would have understood it as an economy of firewood. The liberty they take is part of a national habit of mind. It is a pimple on the nose of the Republic, which must be reached by physicking through public opinion—not so rudely picked by any one individual as to make a pock-mark memorial of his name.

* * * * * *

I daily acquire respect for an uneducated person's better knowledge of some things. In almost any practical matter, it is a great saving of time to go first, and get a common-minded man's view of it. I wasted a good deal of thought and contrivance, lately, even on a matter of taste, by neglecting my usual first reference to this two-legged dictionary. I had been troubled about a *gate*. Architectural literature, somehow, seems strangely behind-hand and benighted on this subject, or perhaps there is some work which treats of it with more particularity, and which I have not fallen in with—only I see no gates on the road, or in landscape embellishments, which would indicate the existence of such better authority. There is no *variety of appropriateness* in them. It seems to me that a gate should not only be absolutely convenient, but it should tell the story of what it leads to—and tell it modestly, like a place's speaking of itself to the passer-by. Gentlemen's gates in our country are very apt to brag. There is not near so much meat in the kitchen, or wine in the cellar, as they talk of. But there is, besides, an *individualism wanting*, in the construction of gates. We might well copy Nature. The expression of the mouth—Nature's gate to the stomach—grows out of the character. Architecture should do the same thing—be able to furnish a man a plan for a gate to his house, on his sending a daguerreotype of himself. But, while there are thousands of kinds of people, there are only two or three kinds of gates—a poverty of adaptedness, which, as I said before, is behind the omnificent age we live in.

I am straying from my point, however—having started only to speak of a working-man's better knowledge than mine, as to *convenience* in a gate. I had taken pencil and paper to bed (with a cough which keeps me sitting upright half the night, and which I turn to account by working as a cough-power to turn a waking-wheel on any subject that perplexes me)—and had spent hours in the combination of lines and curves to express what I wanted the entrance to my cottage to say. An autobiography that would latch and swing upon a hinge, was the amount of it—and I soon found that it was a kind of rehearsal of a gravestone, that would require more study than I had thought for—but I went to sleep at last, over one that seemed tolerably successful. It looked well by the cool light of the next morning ; and, making a clean drawing of it, I walked down into the glen and showed it to a laboring man by whose opinions I usually take the measure of my own. "Yes, sir," said he, after looking at it a moment, *"but it isn't pig-tight !"* I had quite forgotten that it was to keep out pigs as well as let in friends. It was too open at the bottom. The beauty of my frame-work—as long as pigs run loose—would be misplaced on a public highway.

Of course I took back what I had thought disparagingly of other people's gates. They may have had reasons—*pig-tight* reasons of convenience—for doing as everybody else did. I gave up the idea of letting my own gate tell any particular story, and applied to the architect who built my house, for a plan of one. He drew it, as he does everything, well—but it does not look at all as if it led to *me*. There it stands, however, leading to Idlewild. Friends will understand where it promises too much.

LETTER IX.

Private Performance of Thunder-storms—Nature's Sundays—Marriage of Two Brooks—Funnychild's Deserted Bed.

May 21, 1853.

QUEEN VICTORIA has private theatricals at Windsor—but I have a private performance of storms at Idlewild better worth coming to see. These players of Nature thunder over my two dams in the ravine, for twenty-four hours after pouring their deluges upon the mountains ; and water, foaming down through sunshine, and listened to without need of an umbrella, is as much more charming than when performing where previously heard and seen, as a play is made more charming by the sunshine and privilege of a queen's presence.

Nature, like love, costs money to appropriate and make the most of ; but I was musing, to-day—as I stood looking at the swollen sheet of last night's heavy rain, plunging over the closed-up chasm of one of our precipices—on the difference of value received for investments nominally equal. The building of the dam which changed those rapids into a waterfall of twenty feet, cost from twenty to thirty dollars—the price that will be paid for a private box, next winter, to see Cerito dance the Bayadere. But that is the last of Cerito's legs for *that* money, and here is my waterfall, as lively as ever, after six months of dancing day and night, and nothing extra to pay, either, for the "chorus and ballet" added to the performance by every thunder-storm that comes along. The cataract, moreover, after its twinkling feet have quivered in the air, comes down into the meadow and gives a drink to my horse and cow (an afterpiece you will not get from Cerito) ; and I go to see it when I like ; on foot or on horseback ; in the morning mood of hope, or the evening mood of sadness ; with friends, or without them ; at dawn, or by moonlight ; all winter and all summer, and with the promise of the same performance for as many more winters and summers as come round to Idlewild and me. A private cataract for a lifetime, or a private box to see a pair of legs for an hour—both performers dancing to music, but Niblo and Nature the two managers, and both got up "with no regard to expense"—price twenty dollars for either. What would a newly-arrived angel think of a world where these two money-worths were set down as equal ?

But the morning has been, in many ways, one of interest to me. The clearing off, after last night's heavy thunder, gave us a sunrise fit for Eden. There are such days—days when boys should be let out of school—the deliciousness of the weather amounting to a Sabbath—and this has been one of them. It was a happiness to live only. Mere breathing and seeing has been full of surprises. So *new* seemed the world ! Everything out of doors looked irresistibly bent on a holiday—birds merrier, leaves fresher, blossoms gayer-colored, sweet-smelling plants joyously prodigal of their fragrance. In the seasons when the leaves are on the trees, this kind of Sunday of Nature comes around once in about seven days, I have observed, though not with the exact regularity of the week in the almanac. And I think, too, that one's natural spirits instinctively follow this same rotation—the weary and cloudy Saturday of the soul coming round, followed by its bright Sunday of repose and Monday of better courage. We are all happy, sometimes, we know not why. May we not oftenest put it down to this inward seventh day's rest, and renewal of the joy of existence, keeping time with Nature ?

To marry two brooks was my errand out of doors this beautiful morning. The meadow-lawn, two hundred feet below our cottage-windows, is the junction-porch of two converging glens—Idlewild and Home-shut—and each has its brook, brought from far-apart sources, but joining lips within our fence upon the Hudson. Both glen-openings being included in one tangled domain, the road out, towards Newburgh, makes a bend around the meadow, crossing below the projecting promontories of the two ; and, as we must needs, of course, traverse their two streams, it was desirable to bring them a little sooner together, and span their united waters with one bridge. It required some digging and damming—Funnychild (the other brook), after all manner of noisy vagaries in its own glen, coming out to coquet capriciously with the swells of the meadow, and shieing Idlewild just where Nature intended they should meet to part no more—but we made the new bed some days ago, and only waited for a thunder-storm, it being an object to remove the barrier just when the swollen flood might give a more natural turn to their meeting. I should mention that Home-shut, though directly opposite my study window, is a glen so intricately out of the way that no chance foot would ever cross it ; and, from its close-wooded entrance of hemlocks, the demure stream, so sunny and merry the moment after, comes out like a veiled nun out of the dark porch of a cathedral—Funnychild being also a rivulet of capricious stay, and disappearing (gone to the *springs*, perhaps), for two months of the year.

But we brought the two together—breaking down the barrier—with the startling celerity that makes one gasp at most weddings—though, from the way they took to each other's bosoms, you would have thought they had never been anywhere else. The long bother of our preparations, indeed, seems to have been time wasted. Away they went, along Idlewild's every-day track, astonishing the old trees, no doubt, with the freer fingering of the banks by the rising ripples, but making everything look brighter and fresher. It will be a happy union, I think. Idlewild staying all the year, Funnychild will not be so much missed in her summer absences. Only her deserted bed looks a little melancholy—but that we must cover and forget. I shall remember this glorious morning and its pretty bridal, I am sure, as long as I haunt hereabouts.

LETTER X.

Making a Shelf-road—Character shown in Wall-laying—By-the-Day and By-the-Job—English Literalness and Yankee "Gumption."

May 28, 1853.

In the making of a shelf-road around one of the precipices of Idlewild (something like the way to a hanging-bird's nest when we began, but, at present, the winding and easy access to the cottage from the Newburgh side)—we have had a larger amount of *wall-laying* than has entered into my previous out-door experience ; and I have taken a lesson in it, of which, perhaps, I can say an instructive word or so. My friend, the builder, will not take the alarm, I hope. I would not rashly invade his art and mystery. I refer, not to mason-work proper—such as is done with trowel and hammer, plumb-line and spirit-level—but to such laying up of loose stones by the hand as is done for common day wages, though usually by the smarter class of laboring men.

My study of the matter was by way of understanding the preferences of two of my "hands" who seemed equally industrious—one wishing to work by the day, however, and the other to be paid by the rood. As they were both old at the business, I thought it must be rather a difference of natural character than of skill or profit—in either case, a difference worth understanding—and, as the weather was of the kind that throws us upon ourselves for amusement, I put on my mittens, and, as the farmers say, "took hold" with my men.

Our way, that morning, lay through a group of large hemlocks ; and, by the inexorable level of carriage-road grading, the noblest tree was undermined on the lower side. To soothe the old monarch—build a wall that would hold up the fresh earth once more around the exposed roots—I took for my first experiment at stone-laying. It may not deepen the shade of the old tree, perhaps, to have done this myself ; but I shall enjoy it more from having made sure of my welcome to it.

One is a better judge of most work by having had some little apprenticeship at it, and, by what I found difficult or easy in my own handling of the material, I soon began to see the difference between my friends By-the-day and By-the-job. By-the-day worked much the hardest. He lifted two or three stones before he got hold of the right one, held this between his knees while he decided where he would lay it, and twisted it round two or three times after he had got it in place. By-the-job was a little longer looking at the fresh cart-load before making his selection, but the taking the stone up, and setting it in its place, was usually but one movement ; or, he gave it a turn in the air with his upward lift, brought the proper face of it to the front with one effort of mind and hand ; and, once dropped into the line of the wall, *that* stone was done with. If it was not a fit (though it generally was), he had given it its proportion of look and lift, and the next one must remedy the defect—prop or overlay it. He built as good wall, on the whole, as the other man, seemed to be taking it very easy in comparison to the other's hard work, and got on a trifle faster. The difference, I saw, consisted in thoroughly deciding on every movement before it was made, making it promptly, and wasting no time in reconsiderings. If I had been a casual observer, I should have thought By-the-day was the more industrious and better man. By-the-job would be my preference, after thus seeing them closer.

But I must record my own success in wall-laying—rounding the corners of the rough-edged apology to the old hemlock. "He who exults in himself," says the elder D'Israeli, "is at least in earnest ; but he who refuses to receive that praise in public for which he has devoted so much labor in his privacy, is not ; for he is compelled to suppress the very instinct of his nature." I must record, therefore, that I was praised by both my fellow-workmen—By-the-day and By-the-job. They agreed it was a neat piece of work. And (to unbutton a little more towards where it touched me) it is very delightful, after one's biography is written (and the Rev. Dr. Cheever wrote mine twenty years ago), to discover that one has a talent that has been entirely overlooked—a superiority that, in the hurry of life, has lain dormant and unsuspected. My next biographer will please mention, that, with proper advantages, I should probably have been a first-rate layer of stone wall.

* * * * * *

And—talking of working men—I was amused, a few days since, with a contrast as to treatment of obstacles, between two who were working for the same wages—worth describing, because it illustrates with some truth the difference between the common American mind and the common European. We were preparing to throw our bridge across Idlewild Brook. A quiet little narrow-shouldered American, with my horse hitched to a drag, was drawing stone for the road-way beyond, and a broad-shouldered fellow from the old country was digging earth to fill in. As I stood looking on for a moment I saw a thrifty little cedar, which had been partly uprooted ; and, requesting the digger to set it upright, and shovel some dirt around it, I walked on. Returning a few minutes after, I saw my cedar erect enough, but its roots still exposed. "Why didn't you cover it with dirt ?" I asked. "Sure, sir," said sturdy Great Britain, with a look of most honest regret that he had not been able to oblige me, "you told me to *shovel* it, and I had no shovel." He was working with a *spade !*

It was not ten minutes after this, that I saw my little Yankee dollar-a-day unhitching the horse from the drag. "What are you going to do ?" I asked. "Why, there is no more stone to be got on this side," he said, "and that carpenter don't seem to be coming along to fix this bridge. I thought I'd step over and get What's-his-name's oxen and snake them timbers up, and then haul 'em across with a block and tackle, and put on the planks. I could draw stone from the other side, then." Here was a quiet proposal to do what I looked forward to as quite a problem, even for a professed mechanic. I had bespoken a carpenter for the job, three weeks before. There stood the two abutments six feet high and twenty-five feet apart, and a stream swollen by a freshet and hardly fordable on horseback rushing between : and how those four immovable timbers, thirty feet long, were to be got across, without machinery and scaffolding to span this chasm of twenty-five feet, I was not engineer enough to see. It was among the "chores that a man with common gumption could do, easy enough," however, as my little friend said, and it was done the next morning, with block and tackle, rollers and levers—he going about it as naturally and handily as if he had been a bridge-builder by profession. There being no higher price, for day-labor with *his* amount of "gumption" and day-labor such as *the other man's*, who could not conceive how a spade might be used for a shovel, shows how common a thing ingenuity is, in our country, and how characteristic of a Yankee it is to know no obstacle. It was worth recording, I thought.

LETTER XI.

Plank Foot-bridge over the Ravine—Its Hidden Location—Value of Old-man Friendships—Friend S.—His Visit to the Bridge—His Remembrance of Washington—Tobacco Juice on Trees to Prevent Horse-biting, &c., &c.,

June 14, 1853.

I TOOK a jump, to-day, the full length of a quiet observation made to me by a venerable old man, and the startling effect upon my imagination reminded me how rarely we do this—how seldom we are eager or ready for a thought that is presented to us, willing to fly where it leads the way, understand fully all it points to, and see it fairly home again with a responsive look or word before half forgetting it. Of such listening, it is true, every soul liable to be saved is not equally worthy, even in a republic ; but my friend's remark and its bearings (like much that he daily looks and says), are worth more than my best attention ; and I will venture therefore to weave this and what belongs to it, into my chronicle of everyday happenings.

Over a part of the ravine of Idlewild hitherto almost wholly inaccessible—a winding chasm between two sheer precipices, tumultuously filled below with a succession of foam-rapids—I had felled a couple of trees ; and, with bits of rough board, formed a passable bridge, to which, by dint of pick-axe-ing, I had ridged a pathway, aslant down the face of the rock. As no strolling foot would ever find the tangled way thither without a guide, I kept it for such visitors as I thought loved nature well enough to appreciate its covert wildness and beauty ; and, for the eight months past, this flying bridge has been my finger-twist of free-masonry—the secret of Idlewild, which I revealed to those on whom my heart turned no key. So enchanced was the beauty of this by the snows and swollen torrents of winter, that I kept a pair of high-legged water-proof boots (as my friend Pike of the *Tribune* will remember), in which I embarked any beloved visitor who I thought should see it, *weather* or no ; and though these were not many, the path was usually traceable—a kind of out-door memorial that the snows of the wintriest storms will show the footprints of friends.

My neighbor S—— would have been one of the first to be taken to a haunt thus confidential ; but, as he is eighty years of age, and the path rather a giddy one, I had deferred it till some bright day should find us together near the spot. I may mention perhaps (feeling to-day, somehow, as if the world were to be trusted), that he is one of those Providential gifts in a country neighborhood, an old man at leisure for a friendship. This is a luxury, that, through life, I have looked for and found delightful. Sunsets and sunrises glow alike. The heart is warm after life's day's-work is over, as before it begins—after the harness of manhood is laid off, as before it is put on. The love generally felt for genial and kindly old men, with their unselfish sympathies, their tried judgment, and their half-mournful tenderness towards those they are soon to leave, has not been enough remembered in poetry. Their calm and reliable affection is the Indian Summer of our friendships.

Strangers *will* tie their horses to the trees from which I can least spare the bark they eat off while their masters are rambling about, and I had just been washing the trunks of two or three evergreens with tobacco-juice (said to be a six-months' disguster for the worst kind of crib-biter), when neighbor S——, with his white locks flowing over his shoulders and his calmly genial face beaming from under his broad-brimmed hat, drove down the avenue—a moving picture among the beautiful cedars and hemlocks that made them more beautiful than before. As it was one of those inspiriting days of May, with adolescence in the leaf-coaxing breeze, I thought it a good time to tax my friend's knees of fourscore with a scramble to my hidden bridge, the path to which opened from the thicket near by. He readily assented. We tied his horse to one of the tobaccoed cedars (which the fine animal, a splendid bay, opened teeth upon, and immediately backed off to the length of his halter, taking an attitude of repugnance in which we found him on our return), and then successfully made our winding descent to the chasm.

As he stood upon the bridge, the old man was the unconscious centre of a *tableau vivant* of great beauty. The rapids came down in four or five foaming leaps, apparently from the sky above—flew, in a glassy and glittering sheet, beneath his feet—and, with another twisted foam-jump below, dashed into a dark lake almost walled in from the reach of the sun at noon. There is not a spot of wilder loveliness in the world ; and the venerable figure and presence of him who stood silently in its midst, gave it the soul for which the landscape-painter invents figures, thus centralizing the beauty of the scene.

"I was here once before," said the old man, waking from his reverie, "It was when I was sixteen years old. We lived in the village above, and a freshet carried away some of our machinery. I remember climbing along this wild chasm in search of it."

The double picture thus suddenly presented to my mind—that same person standing there sixty-four years ago, a slight stripling then ; and now a white-haired old man, bent and venerable—chance-brought to the same spot once more—*his memory at the moment, looking at the scene through the vista of a life-time*—was a strong call upon the imagination. The two currents—the wild one beneath him, and the life-blood at his heart, had met before and parted to meet again after so long a lapse of years—each, meantime, forgetful of the other, fulfilling its vicissitudes of fulness and feebleness ; but *his* lessening now and preparing to change its channel and flow through eternity ; while the other, rejoicing now in strength undiminished, is to cease when the world shall end—the slender thread of that old man's existence to outlast the thundering torrent by myriads of ages—what a parallel for the fancy to follow through ! Yet the half-musing remark which stirred it might have been lost upon attention carelessly given—might have been drowned in the noise of those deafening waters. What interminable aisles of thought and instruction thus open upon our commonest pathway, the dim doors of which we scarce notice as we pass !

Mr. S—— is my next neighbor up the Valley of the Moodna ; and, along the road that runs between his house and the woods of Idlewild, he once overtook a slow-pacing horseman, who, with bridle dropped before him, was lost in thought. He was himself a small boy, going to mill with a bag of corn ; and, as his horse gradually outwalked the other, he had full leisure to study the looks of the slow rider. Boy as he was, the face and mien of that fellow-traveller on the same common road made an indelible impression on his memory. It was General Washington, then making the house which Mr. S—— now occupies, his head-quarters. Forge Hill, as it was called—the smithy of the army—was just in the rear, and the house occupied by General Lafayette was a little farther up the stream. Beyond the hill, stands the picturesque old mansion where General Knox was, for some time, quartered, now occupied by Mr. Morton. Our neighborhood is, historically, most interesting—Mr. S——'s reminiscences of his boyhood, and its every-day contact with the movers in that great drama, are so simply and truthfully told as to have a wonderful reality. His description of Washington, as he appeared to his boyish eyes—(looked upon with a certain strange awe and reverence, he says, by the inhabitants and people around)—would be an invaluable portrait of the great Father of his Country, if it could be copied from those gentler tones by pen or pencil. The gallery of memory at Idlewild will be graced by many of these word-pictures, sketched by this venerable old man—pictures lasting in the minds that receive them, but untransferable, in their full beauty, to others.

LETTER XII.

Foliage and its Wonders—Caprice of Tree-living—Auto-verdure of Posts—Hemlock, the Homestead Emblem, &c., &c.

June 11, 1853.

I HAVE hitherto known June as rather a belated month—seldom out in its full bulk and beauty of leaves till the second or third week. We have had it now, in what would pass for its sufficient glory, since the middle of May. As it was to decide some of my experiments of taste, I have watched it more closely than usual, and its early advent was particularly welcome. The thinning of groves and clearing out of underbrush—work at which I was busy for a great part of the winter—seemed sometimes to have impoverished the woodland beyond its power to rally. It is hard to keep up one's faith in foliage, during its absence. The bare trees looked as if a miracle alone could re-clothe them as abundantly as they certainly were clothed by the last summer, and one's cuttings and loppings seem to have needlessly lessened the probability. Who ever looked through the scattered branches of a tree in winter, and understood how it could be so close-leaved in June as to be the mass of shadow that it becomes—impervious to sight, almost impervious to sunshine ? Nature is, certainly, wonderfully prodigal in her fulfillings. The promise of spring is kept beyond all expectation—a season of astonishments—morning after morning—the more startling from its contrast with the short-coming-dom that reigns in most else. One hurries out of bed at daylight, living in the country in such a season as this, eager to see what changes have taken place overnight in the landscapes growing beautiful around.

But Nature is a little wilful withal. She seems determined that Idlewild shall stay the wilderness that she made it—owing no tree, at least, to my planting. And, after a half-dozen vain attempts, I have let it alone. There are trees enough. Some of them do not stand quite where landscape gardening might fancy. But I believe I will keep it to say, that Nature had her own way about it altogether. Some of her caprices are curious. In laying a plank, last November, from the fork of a willow to a crag on the other side of our torrent-brook, I sawed off a limb of the tree, perhaps thirty feet long, and left it upon the rocks. Strolling through the glen, in the early spring, I noticed that this amputated branch was budding from one extremity to the other—touching the earth nowhere, but drawing moisture from an elbow-bend in one of the branches which had fallen across a tuft of moss in a fissure of the crag. There were my hemlocks, which, with men and oxen, I had transplanted, roots and all, dying in the moist and genial bed I had made for them ; and here was this stray waif, that nobody asked to live, and with no reasonable means of living, as lively, after six months, as the tree it was cut from ! I showed it to Morris, my brother quill, the other Sunday that he was here ; but, though he is a man to find an excuse for almost any perversity, he could only shake his kindness-box uncomprehendingly over this. In some cart-loads of chestnut posts I find the same auto-verdure embedded in stone wall, with only one end standing flat on the surface of the ground ; half of them are in full leaf, along the river-side, at this hour ! Sap, like love, seems "bent on steering with its cargo to consignees not named in the papers for that voyage."

With this fertilizing May—the best mixed succession of rain and sunshine for many a year—the deciduous trees so jumped into leaf, and were, all of a sudden, so prodigally massive and shady, that I began to think I had over-valued our wilderness of firs, declaring Idlewild, as I did, to be independent of changing foliage in the preponderance of its woods of evergreen. The maples and chestnuts, oaks, dogwoods, and willows, quite smothered us with their Spring-burst, I must own. But June, with its new dress for my slighted hemlocks, has brought me round again, and (till taken again by surprise, at least) I shall be inconstant no more. Hemlocks are our pride at Idlewild. How wonderfully beautiful they are now—every finger-tip of their outspread palms thimbled with gold, and every tree looking as if all the sunsets that had ever been steeped into its top were oozing out of it in drops. Of all Nature's renewals, I think this is the fairest. The old foliage forms such effective contrast for the new. The child-blossom and its predecessor are heightening graces, each to the other—neither so beautiful alone, and both finding room enough and enjoying the same summer together. Parent and child are one glory. The home-tree was not stripped and deserted for the new comer. Of that most precious of our wayside religions—the homestead-hallowing—it seems to me that the hemlock should be the chosen emblem.

LETTER XIII.

Noon Visitors to Scenery—The Bull-Frog at the Gate—Inconvenient Opening of a Spring—Frog Curiosity and Intelligence—Process of Animal Progression, &c., &c.

June 18, 1853.

I LONGED to invest a bull-frog with an office to-day. The stone he sat upon should have been my porter's lodge, and he should have explained, to a carriage-load of gentlemen and ladies, that Nature, at *that* time of day, was "not dressed to receive company." Why, it was *just upon noon !*—and there drove up a party of strangers, in a Newburgh hack, who had come over to see Idlewild. Not a shadow on the landscape ! Hillside and meadow, precipice and plain, blanketed alike with one glare of sunshine, flat and reliefless. Idlewild was there, it is true, every tree and every rock ; and so is "Childe Harold" in a pocket dictionary—every word of it. And the poem may be appreciated by fumbling the dictionary wherein are all its words that *might* be put together, as well as scenery by being visited when its lights and shadows are all unlinked. Nature (does everybody know it or not ?) pours out her champagne of beauty twice a day—at morning and evening—and at noon it is stale. Yet how fashionably timed an excursion is—getting away comfortably an hour or two after breakfast, and returning to dinner—leaving alone all the dawn and sunset, the starlight and moonlight, to *enjoy scenery from ten till two !*

* * * * * *

The frog I was in company with, at the moment when these visitors passed in, had taken refuge from the mid-day sun, by squatting directly under my new gate—the perpendicular shadow of the latch-beam just making a square coverlid for his back. The gate being quite an architectural affair, and of a style somewhat beyond my worldly condition, I was swallowing the inevitable Æsop of finding this classic emblem of over-ambitiousness seated *just there*—but I was interested, at the same time, in speculating on the instincts of my croaking friend, in connection with the circumstances which had evidently brought him to the spot. He was on a visit of inquiry. A phenomenon had occurred which had excited his curiosity. I knew the frog well. His remarkable size had attracted my attention early in the spring ; and as I had invariably seen him on passing the pool at the side of the road, thirty or forty rods below, where he habitually resided, I could not well be mistaken in his identity. The event which had brought him away from home was curious in itself ; though I do not know that I should venture to describe it with such particularity if it were not for the grounds it furnishes in Natural History, in support of the "progressive theory." *This* frog *reasoned*—and is, of course, on his way to down with his thighs and swing his arms like a gentleman.

In shaping the entrance to Idlewild from the Newburgh side, I had thought it worth while, at some cost of digging, to go in behind a magnificent cluster of fir-trees—not only because the main gate on the river would be thus set in a picturesque frame of evergreens, but also because, over the shoulder of the hill, the road would descend into a grove, old and beautiful, giving the visitor and his horses a welcome of shade. After several days' working into the steep sand and gravel—(a dry and obstinate old hill, it seemed to me, to be part of a planet that moves through space so easily)—my Irish persuaders came suddenly to a stand-still. The slope they were pick-axe-ing began to tremble like a jelly. A little shovelling, right and left, and the quicksand broadened and grew softer—water began to run—the dry soil caved in from above, and a large mass of liquid earth commenced a slow procession down hill. We had intercepted an abundant water-course, which has its natural issue on the other side of the road, forty or fifty feet below. Nothing could be more agreeable, of course, than a hill which would walk away of its own accord—provided it went in the right direction. But my destiny, in all matters of mere dirt, is perversely ordered. Base things have the charge of my not loving the world too well. My charming new road was, in one night, entirely choked up and smothered in mud—a new wire fence unsettled and sent tumbling down—gateway obstructed, and every sign of no end to it. Patches came down, as large as a breakfast room, with young trees all standing, and grass growing—part of them, too, from my neighbor's lot, across the line. It occurs to me, as I write, by the way, whether I should have put my neighbor's trees in the pound, for trespass. Or, if his land moves over the line by locomotion of its own, does it become mine ; or, if not, is he bound to come and take it away ? There are nice questions for law, in these land-slides.

But—we managed, at last, to get the better of our Water-wilful—decoying its flow around the bend of the road by a "blind ditch," and walling up its outlet of quicksand behind a solid embankment. It is a fine "capability," thrown away—for, issuing from the over-hanging acclivity just within the gate, its plentiful and bright water might rain over the lip of a sculptured vase—a charming first feature for the entrance to an Italian villa, or to a cultivated garden, but too artificial for a rocky wilderness like Idlewild. I have given it a sprig or two of weeping willow, to moisten into curtains for my gate—(a little job of upholstery which a running brook takes but a year or two to do)—and, when the pendent branches droop luxuriously enough to call the attention of the passer-by, other minds, even less observing and inquiring than my neighbor the bull-frog, will wonder at signs of water on a promontory so high and dry.

Yes—and I believe Neighbor B—— (bull-frog) *did* observe the new phenomenon ; and *did* wonder ; and certainly *did* make an express journey, three or four hundred yards along a dry and un-amphibious-able road, up a hill and on a warm day, to look into it, for his own merely intelligent satisfaction. He crossed from my gate to the new mud-puddle in the corner (as I saw him do)—dropped into his contemplative angle of forty-five degrees, and sat reflecting in the very centre of the sloppy ooze for perhaps half an hour (as I thought it worth while to stop and see), and, returning home towards evening (as I happened to be there to make sure of), made himself into an easy-chair with his knees high up and his stomach for a cushion (as no other gentleman animal of my acquaintance can), and sat in his accustomed place, among his lively little family of tadpoles, probably speculating (as an old magazine editor might do over *Putnam),* on the effect this higher breakout might have, in intercepting the flow of *his* circulation. It was a wonderful new issue, but it might be a more elevated tap of the supply, for *his* puddle, after all !

To return to the science of the matter, there really seems to me to have been, here, sufficient proof that a frog can observe, is capable of curiosity, and will, though driven by no instinct of immediate necessity, take pains to be better informed on a subject that interests him. Why, to have gone thus out of his element, and by such use of his limbs as shows them to the least advantage—ascend a dry hill where probably a frog was never seen before—visit a new moisture-land, and return the same day—it was Columbus-y ! I cannot shut my eyes to such proof of enterprise and intelligence in a neighbor. It cannot be that reason so advanced can stop there—or that such a frog is not on his way to become a man. Neighbor B—— is, in my opinion, one of a series—perhaps the "first number" of an angel—at all events, as suggestive of progression* as many a man that

* It is in the structure and physical development of the frog, by the way, that we have the most encouraging and interesting proof of progression as a law of Nature. No other animal has such wonderful changes in his actual body and in a single stage of existence. It is hard not to be sceptical as to the disposal of a monkey's tail, for instance, if he is to become a man capable of salvation, or as to the changes that must take place in some men before they can be any way passable as angels—yet how much easier it is to conceive what improvements may take place in the worst and ugliest of us, when we read in Natural History that "the tail of the tadpole is gradually absorbed?" Thus says science :—

"The young frog, which is called a tadpole, is, at first, furnished with a long fleshy tail, and a small horny beak, having no other apparent limbs than little fringes on the sides of the neck. These disappear in a few days, and the hind feet are very gradually and visibly developed ; the fore feet are also developed, but under the skin, through which they subsequently penetrate.

votes for President. I respect him. I commend him to the notice of visitors to Idlewild. He sits upon a stone, by a small pool of spring-water, on the meadow-shore of the Moodna, just where you turn Sloop-Hill, and get a first view of my cottage chimney. He dives usually towards noon It gets too warm. But he seems to have the same feelings as I, that Idlewild is in its beauty with the sun is the East (the meadows and slopes velveted with dewy shadows), and you would scarce fail to see us both, B—— and me, by driving that way an hour after sunrise. I should like to compare *his* impression of Idlewild with that of the visitors who passed us both by, going to see it at *noon !*

THE TAIL IS GRADUALLY ABSORBED. The beak falls, and discloses the true jaws, which, at first, were soft and concealed beneath the skin. *The eyes which, at first, could only be discerned through a transparent spot in the skin, are now visible with their* THREE *lids.* There are but four toes to the anterior feet ; the hind ones frequently exhibit the *rudiment of a sixth.* Tadpoles reproduce their limbs when cut off."

To the maimed, the deformed, the crippled, the amputated, the unlovely—this is surely an analogy with comfort in it. That which is Unheavenly about us, is to be "gradually absorbed."

LETTER XIV.

Canterbury Rowdies—Pianos and Porkers—Unwelcome Visitors—Penalty of Pounding—A Public Benefactor.

June 25, 1853.

THE corner of the Highland Terrace, which forms our neighborhood (a cluster of three rural villages, cut off by Moodna Creek and its toll-bridge from the city-reach influences of Newburgh), is charmingly primitive and rural. With no pine-apples for sale, no frequentation by the gentlemen and ladies, who make twenty-four-hour excursions from New York, no billiard-table and no newspaper, it is an eddy of still life, left behind in unrippled simplicity by the current of progress. Delightfully unaffected and farmer-like as life hereabouts is, however, *we have a class of rowdies*—rowdies with a twist to their tails—and they overrule the law as effectually as the rowdies of New York, and by the same sort of tacit admission in the mind of the public. *The pig-interest is too strong to be meddled with.*

But the way in which the "higher law" is openly claimed for these rural rowdies, in the very heart of our pretty village of Canterbury, for instance, is very curious. Out of any one of those nice white houses along the street, will come the most dainty-looking young ladies, fresh from tasty parlors, and mammas that take a magazine. The pretty white fence incloses a little garden, with flower-beds, edged with box, rose-bushes, and lilacs. Door bells, or brass knockers, of course. *Inside* the gate all is "genteel." *Outside* the gate, however—in the street, on the sidewalk—right before the front door, and under the parlor windows, stands *the family pig-trough.* The family pigs have the run of the village during the day, and at night and morning they come home for their own particular swill—eaten, in the evening, perhaps, while the piano is playing on the other side of the pretty white fence. In dry weather, when there is no bed of mud in the carriage-track, in the centre of the street, the gentleman pig stretches himself across the sidewalk to sleep ; and, on your way to the post-office, you may walk round a score or more, or take the middle of the street. You respect pig. You see pig. You smell pig. But beautiful young ladies sit in the windows, just over the fence.

The cottagers in the country around would be less particular, of course, if there were a way to be so, than the more genteel villagers, but the pig-trough, outside the gate, is the unvarying feature. And these gentlemen outlaws know the country, and take long walks. Leave a bar down, or let your visitors from curiosity (as happens to me every day) forget to shut your gate as they enter, and the pigs are all over. They rooted up, for me, yesterday, a green slope, covered with laurels, upon the beauty of which I had particularly set my heart, cherishing it for a foreground to a picture some artist will paint for me—and it took me and my man an hour to get the unpunishable defacers out once more on the highway. They get in at night. Here and there one climbs a wall like a clumsy boy, dragging it after him as he goes over. The religious bearing of this "hard trial" is perhaps the only one that can be safely dwelt upon. One does not say his prayers near so easily, I find, after driving out pigs morning and evening, nor begin very immediately again, to "love his neighbor as himself."

It is against the law, everybody knows, for pigs to be turned loose on a public highway. Any one of my daily trespassers could be *lawfully* driven by me five miles to the nearest "pound"—I could then *lawfully* take pains that the sheriff gave notice to the owner that his pig was there—*lawfully* see that the poor animal was kept from starving for the several days before he might be taken away—*lawfully* go four or five miles to attend the justice's court and appear as prosecutor—*lawfully* pay my own expenses for this two or three weeks of trouble, travel, and vexation—and *lawfully* make an enemy for life of the owner of the trespassing swine, who would, perhaps, have a dollar of fine to pay, in consequence of my persecution of him. All this it costs to follow up *one* trespass by *one* pig. Pig endurance costs less.

But the village of Newburgh, only four miles from us, has outlived this stage of progress. Pig-vagrancy has been put down in its beautiful streets—owing, however, to the resolute public spirit of a single individual. DOWNING, to whom the country owes so much for its advances of refinement and embellishment, undertook to suppress pig at Newburgh, where he resided. He was told it was Quixotic—that the time, money, and trouble it would cost might ruin him—that his grounds would be disfigured, his trees girdled, and his garden of precious plants torn in pieces by the infuriated people—that the poor had no place to keep their pigs, and there was much to be got by a smart pig on the public highway. His self-interest and pity for the pig proprietor were both appealed to. He persevered, however, patiently and long—and succeeded.

Now we want such a pig-apostle at Canterbury—some public-spirited, generous and kindly man, who will make himself remotely beloved and remembered by such a crusade of unpopularity against the rowdies at our gates. We wait for him, as New York waits for *her* pig-apostle. Let us make ready to give their advents a welcome.

LETTER XV.

Trouble in Gate Designing—Letter from an Unknown Correspondent, on Gates—Invisible Society at Idlewild—Correction of Error as to Hemlocks—Handsome Irishman's Mistake in Felling Trees, &c.

July 2, 1853.

My *gate trouble* at Idlewild seems to draw in light from a distance—we candles of authors burning darkest at the wick. A friendly subscriber to the *Home Journal*, who signs himself "parochially Yours," sends me a pencil-drawing of a gate that is both "pig-tight" and beautiful ; one, indeed, which I should have pounced upon as a treasure of modest usefulness and elegance, had I seen it in time, but which, now (my gates being built), I can only reserve for the next brother-suitability who nestles a cottage hereabouts. The letter which accompanies it, by the way, has a verbal description, which may enable the appreciative to take possession of the model without seeing the drawing ; and, for this reason, and because the writer touches instructively and charmingly on one or two other points, I will copy the most of what he says :

* * Your *gate difficulties*, as recorded in a late number of the *Home Journal*, will meet with sympathy as far West as civilization has made picket-surroundings necessary. An application to our village carpenter, a man of skill and taste, for the invention of a new gate, resulted in one, of which his inclosed pencil-sketch will give you some idea. The construction is simple and inexpensive ; while the cappings of the gate posts are particularly new and becoming. The form of the main part of the cap, as you will see, is that of a truncated pyramid, with a projection of about four inches, and supported by two brackets on each side of the post. The top rail of the gate is supported (or rather finished) by light *open* brackets between the pickets ; and the top rail of the fence by *tight* brackets between the pickets. Both gate and posts look well when built. At the left of the sketch is another sort of fence and post which I am now having built. The post is octagon in shape, with the cap to match, and the moulding "broke around it," as the carpenters express it. The gate used with the octagon post is similar to the other, but both gate and post are adapted to a lighter fence.

You say you sought to make your gate an index to what was behind it. Allow one familiar with your writings to suggest either of these gates, particularly the first, as proper to carry out your design. I could go on and reason comparatively and logically in extenuation, convincing you that a man is no more a correct judge of his own mental character than he is of his own portrait ; but I forbear, for which I expect your thanks. If the gate and its belongings do not suit you, however, throw it aside, and give me credit for desiring to please you.

I once passed through a door-yard gate which did, though unintentially, give an indication of the designer's character. The gate was a common one, shut by a chain and ball. But the *post* to which the inner end of the chain was attached, *was carved and painted in the likeness of a negro, with one hand raised to his cocked hat, and the other extended to welcome you in.* As you opened the gate towards you, in going in, the negro post-porter bent towards you by a joint in his back, and fairly bowed you in. Upon letting the gate go, a spring in his back "brought him up standing" again, ready for the next comer. This faithful fellow performed the amiable for his master for many years, without reward, except now and then a new coat—of paint ; and finally died of a rheumatic back, contracted in his master's service.

I can corroborate the phenomenon of the sprouting of your chestnut *fence-posts.* I lately saw a row of willow cross-stakes used to support the top-rail of a "Virginia," or "Snake-fence," which had leaved out profusely while performing their new duties ; and they presented a very singular appearance, too.

I thank you for your good word in favor of my old friends, the *"hemlocks."* In this hemlock town, they are of little account. My carpenter, who hates hemlock as a cat hates water, calls it "devil's pine." He says his trade have a tradition that the devil undertook to make a pine tree ; but found it so shaky that it had to be pinned together with long, hard knots ; which knots, in lumber, are a carpenter's abomination. * * *

Of the invisible but gay society at Idlewild—(very tangible, very enjoyable and very sufficient, for me, though many would think it differed little from a hermit's loneliness),—this letter is one note of the music, overheard. The consciousness of readers so thoughtful of us—friends at a distance who partake of one's daily existence, and respond, silently or verbally, to its key-records, as given in these Idlewild Papers—peoples the wood-path, that looks to the stranger lonely. There is no solitude in thoughts that are waited for. Oh, how many there are—kind and indulgent as friends need be—who walk with me by the brook !

But there is now and then one who catches me tripping, and reads me a little lecture ; and I have one, referring to the "hemlocks" spoken of just now, which I will quote for the setting right of one of my chance mis-quotations. If the reader remembers, I supported my experience of the anodyne effect of hemlock woods, by giving an account of the tree, from an encyclopedia. I turned to it in haste, when wearily closing a finished letter, and, it appears, copied a description of the wrong tree. Thus talks my viewless companion to me, on the subject :—

* * From long revolving in your sphere through the medium of your writings I have come to feel a sort of personal familiarity with you and yours. Having, therefore, noticed a mistake in your last letter from Idlewild, I take the liberty of pointing it out. In a note to the mention of "hemlocks," you evidently confound the beautiful *coniferæ* which overshadow your cottage, with the *"unbelliferous"* water-hemlock, wherewith our friend Socratcs dismissed this world from his presence. A potation known to me in some part of my experience as "swipes," is manufactured, I believe, from the leaves of *our* hemlock tree ; and, if the Athenian sage had solemnly drank but a decoction of this hemlock, his digestive organs would have suffered no farther disturbance, probably, than that which is necessarily consequent upon imbibing a glass of inferior "spruce beer."

Yours in all friendliness.

Another nameless friend sends me a valuable explanation of my failure in the transplanting of two or three of these same "hemlocks." He writes thus, from Boston :—

* * I notice by your last letter that the hemlocks, of you own setting out, are dying. They were probably transplanted out of season. *Now* (June 15), is the time for transplanting evergreen trees, and it is the only time of year when it can be done successfully. At least, from now to the fifteenth of July is the most favorable time, though I have done it with perfect success as late as the first of August. This was at Dorchester, but perhaps your season is a little earlier. The President of our Horticultural Society told me he thought July the best month. Remove the tree without injuring the roots, but, *except the bucket of water after setting it out, do not continue to water it for the week or ten days following, unless there is a drought.* * * *

The danger of too much watering, for transplanted trees, is a new suggestion—one at least, which I had not found in the books on horticulture—and my kind friend may have thus given us one of those precious little un-previously-printed truths which are getting so scarce, now-a-days. Mine, which died, were watered daily—a loyal devotion which I had thought seldom thrown away upon a tree. And my care and admiration of this, the most beautiful of my surroundings, has, in another way, proved equally disastrous. I must tell the story. It will be a kind of obituary notice of the lost trees. But, it may be useful, also, as a caution to the lovers of such things.

The working men who drift along through the country, are of all sorts of personal appearance. My neighbors, however, not selecting, as I do, with an eye to the effect they will have, as figures in the landscape, while they work—(and the humblest and most stumpy getting employment the easiest)—I have a kind of first choice of them, as to looks. If there is a man on the road who is unconsciously or saucily picturesque—either from his uppish bearing, his rough beard, or that peculiarity of appearance, handsome or otherwise, which raises mistrust against a new comer—he is pretty sure to bring up at Idlewild, where he is hired to dig like any other man ; but where he performs also an additional service of which he is not very laboriously aware. It is easy to locate him very much as a painter would do—if he is to chop up a heap of brush, for instance, to "dump" the load and his chopping-log at an angle of the brook or under a slope of the hill—and he gives life to the scene by action in just the right place, charmingly effective in his shirt-sleeves and his easy unconsciousness. One of my men, who has been with me for several months, has the brow and bearing of a knight-templar, and a beard of which Domitias Ahenobarbus might be proud ; and, as he works among my trees and precipices, he is often the most centralizing and effective point of the view—the offset to a waterfall here or a rock there—and embellishing wonderfully the otherwise uninhabited landscape. He has little idea how many fine pictures he has helped to make, that are stored away in my reverie-loft—but I was about to speak of one whom I remember with less satisfaction.

In the depth of an almost impenetrable wilderness, four or five noble young hemlocks guarded a spring ; and I was thinking of clearing away the underbrush from these, and so making an easier approach to my hidden Egeria, when a man applied to me for work. He had a bad face, but he was otherwise magnificent. So straight a back, so slight in hips and waist, a neck and head with so graceful an uplift, chest so expanded and limbs so moulded for lithe elegance and power—he was a Paddy-Apollo. He looked as if his body knew it, and stood and moved accordingly—though his brain was too dull to comprehend it.

I engaged him at once—gave him an axe—and directed him to the spring, where he should go and wait for me, after his dinner. Some one called and detained me an hour or two, but I finally mounted my mare, and rode to the glen, thinking what a fine combination it would be—such a figure as that, at work under those magnificent hemlocks. I reached the spot. There stood my man. And there *lay my trees ! He had cut them down—all four*. What my exclamation was, I could scarcely venture to try ink upon. But I remember that I found very little Christian resignation in his excuse :—*"You didn't come, Sir,"* said he, *"and I thought I'd better go at something."* Four beloved hemlocks, shading a spring, lost by appreciating the beauty of a man !

LETTER XVI.

Laurel-blossoming—The Imbedded Stone, and Jem's Neglect of his Countryman's honors—Sabbath stop to our Running Water, &c., &c.

July 9, 1853.

NATURE, it seems to me, has her "calico and haberdashery." The hanging out of the "Spring goods" along the Bowery was never more gaudy than the laurels now in flower hereabouts. The blossoms are too much, for they smother the leaves—the sea-green, massive and glossy leaves, which are as beautiful as the flowers. Everybody exclaims (it is true), at this gaudy glory of the laurels—a bushel of blossoms on every stem, and the colors in confused heaps, like "the worsted" for a rainbow—but I observe that the slighter and rarer beauties of shade and water are, meantime, lost on them. Once familiar with the tangle of a little wilderness like this, it is as curious and interesting to see what strangers will pick out to admire, as for a painter, who left a pulse in every stroke of the pencil, to listen to critics as they pass. Open to air and sunshine as it all is, there are secrets of beauty at Idlewild. And these are easily missed ; though, like the blood-drop of his own life, which the poet hides in a fiction, it seems strange, that this is not alone read and the rest forgotten. One walks on, beside stranger or friend, and leaves an overlooked loveliness unspoken of—for it spoils a charm to be obliged to point it out and explain it—but one cannot help fretting, now and then, over favorites unseen and neglected. And it is not much consolation (strange to say) that one *owns* more of a minute by seeing more, and enjoying more, in it—*owns* more of any sweet spot by appreciating it better—*owns* more of life, more of beauty in people, more of sunrises and sunsets, more of books and of music, by having an eye truer and deeper, a sense keener and fonder. There *is* a gold—life's purest and most precious ore, too—which we are impatient (this would prove) not to share with all comers.

* * * * * *

And, *apropos* of laurels and appreciation, I had a smile, a day or two ago, which I believe I will not keep to myself, though I must record a disparagement of a friend, by telling the story of it.

There is a tree in the avenue to our cottage on the inland side, which has taken up a flat piece of rock, as a cobbler takes a lapstone between his knees. The bark of the trunk having grown around it, the stone (of the size of the bottom of a chair) has been gradually lifted, till it is now about two feet from the ground, solidly imbedded, and as level and comfortable a seat as a carpenter could contrive. Strolling along the grounds with us, not long ago, out friend, Judge Daly, seated himself here ; and it has ever since been called "the Judge's Bench."

But the Judge is an Irishman, and so is my magnificent Jem, with the Crusader's beard—a beard with two things behind it which I very much prize, viz :—a strong back and a constant and hearty performance of what he undertakes. We were at work upon the road, soon after the Judge's visit ; and a superb and luxuriant laurel standing in the line of one of the curves, I saw that its removal was inevitable, but told Jem to take advantage of the opportunity to pay an appropriate compliment. We had made his countryman a Judge in America, and the least he could do, as a brother Emerald, was to grace the bare bench with this luxuriant laurel. We selected the spot, while I pronounced the Judge's official eulogy, and Jem (I thought) listened cordially, and promised to transplant the shrub with great care, so that it would flower in a week or two at his worship's elbow.

Jem forgot all about it ! And it was the first order, in eight months, that he had not executed to the letter. I was away from home the morning following, but, passing where the road had been graded, the second day after, I saw the uprooted laurel thrown into the hemlock thicket, on one side. I called to my man. "Faith !" said Jem, rubbing his head with the most honest embarrassment, "I wholly *dis*remembered it, sir !" He immediately and eagerly set to work, and dug a hole and planted the neglected laurel, however ; and, though a shrub which oftenest dies with transplanting, it flowered superbly ; almost cushioning the Judge's Seat with its exuberant spread. But it was natural, in Jem, after all, to have paid little attention when his countryman was praised. An American in Ireland would have done the same. We are ready to glorify the foreigner for the very qualities to which we are dull, in our countrymen. Jem's was an every-day verification of the old proverb, but being his first inattention in almost a year of service, I thought the smile it stirred was worth sharing, perhaps.

* * * * * *

Nothing could well be wilder or more lawlessly picturesque than the Brook of Idlewild—the two hundred feet of sudden descent which it performs for our fenced-in and private admiration, being a wholly untameable ravine of rock and rapid—but it is subject to the restraints of piety and industry to a degree of which the admiring, stranger is not always aware. Our city friends oftenest passing Sunday with us, and the wooded solitudes of the glen being an inviting temple for rambling converse and meditation, it would be pleasant if the waters, on that day, were even less restrained than on a week day—grander in their beauty and louder in their anthem of accompaniment. But, on that day, the channel is dry ! The friends who walk where should be the torrent we talk of, find but rocks, shadows, and silence. Spite of our wishes to the contrary, the brook makes the Sabbath a day of rest.

Yes—for the five mills, above us on the stream, shut their sluice-gates on Saturday night, to start with full ponds on Monday ! In the summer, when the springs are comparatively low, it takes the twenty-four hours to fill all these industrial reservoirs ; and, on the first working-day of the week—when our friends have just left us—the loosened waters come down and the cascades are in their glory. The washerwomen, perhaps, think it a special Providence, contrived though it be by mortal millers ; but we wish that "washing-day" would bring our visitors also to the brook. Charming on Monday, we are, on the other five days, subject for our beauty to the caprices of the clouds—modified to a certain degree, it is true, by the miller next above us, who may shut his gate morning or evening, and stop off our loveliness till his dam runs over. Those who come to Idlewild, day after day, may forget or remember, as they prefer the romantic explained or not, that the wild torrent by which they stray depends somewhat on whether our neighbor has corn to grind.

LETTER XVII.

Effect of clearing out Underbrush from a Wood—Praise Disclaimed—Horror of Bloomerized Evergreens—Neglect of departed Great Men—Carrion Nuisance, &c., &c.

July 16, 1853.

To place the columns of a temple and let angels build the roof, might be thought to realize the Millenium which we all hope to come back and see—but it is very much the experience of one who clears a wood of underbrush in the winter, and then sees it leafed over in June. I daily walk through an avenue which we cleared in December last, and feel as if I had been helped by a miracle. It is an aisle under a dome of emerald. An atmosphere so dim with contemplative shadows, yet so living with the flecks of light, made tremulous with the stirring leaves, seems to me an outdoing of Gothic windows and painted glass. So to contrive beauty and exercise power—to begin a work which is so followed up and completed by Nature—is as good as to be a king and build a cathedral.

But I (the stray cows and I) must enter a disclaimer at some praise that has been bestowed upon the trees of Idlewild. A stranger, who has been here, writes kindly and enthusiastically to the editor of the *Newburgh Gazette*, and sums us up in a sentence : "The view not to be surpassed, *the trees beautifully trimmed* and plenty of them ; rapids, falls and ponds." And to this the editor himself adds a confirmatory and charmingly written half column, but repeating the partial error which I, and the cattle of Neighbor Loosepig, cannot justly leave unmodified by an explanation. Thus writes Mr. Allison (who I hope will honor his brother-craftsman with his acquaintance when he next drives over) :—

> "Our correspondent does not over-estimate the beauties of 'Idlewild,' it is, truly, a delightful spot, as a recent excursion to its cool shades and gurgling waterfalls convinced us. It is in all respects a delectable abode—delightfully located on the west bank of the Hudson, about five miles below Newburgh. The road leading to it is charmingly picturesque, and we know not a drive that can more agreeably occupy an afternoon. We were fairly lost in the wildness of, its solitudes. Were we an afflicted Rip Van Winkle, we know of no other spot where we would sooner sleep away our troubles. Nature holds out an alluring pastime to the wanderer along its solitary walks—its serpentine streams—its

wild waterfalls ; your ears are continually saluted by the music of miniature torrents and cascades, where the wild waters are precipitated over ledge and precipice, as they rush boundingly on to the Hudson. *A beautiful variety of trees, judiciously improved by the hand of Art,* increase the picturesqueness of the scene. Mr. Willis has here a country seat in all respects calculated to surround a literary life with the very inspirations which it needs. After seeing it and roaming for several hours amid its exquisite scenes, listening to its murmuring waterfalls, and fanning ourselves in the breezes that loiter in its sylvan recesses, we no longer wondered, etc., etc., * * The feelings which the spot spontaneously inspired, were aptly expressed by a lady of our party, who wrote upon the artificial railing, which assisted us across the stream just below the principal waterfall—*'Second edition of Paradise Regained—Illustrated.'* It is truly a miniature Eden—as near an earthly Paradise as Nature and Art can make it."

This is charming praise, but for its intimation as to my "improving trees by the hand of Art." If, by "trees beautifully trimmed" is meant trees of which the *cow-twistings* have been cut off, I consent to the fact thus gracefully mystified. Neighbor Loosepig's cattle have heads full of fleas ; and when they break in, after sundown, and pass the night between grazing and twisting their horns into the lower branches of the cedars and hemlocks, they spoil, of course, such foliage as they can reach. Perhaps our visitor had the removal of these un-mend-able small-tooth combs of breachy cattle in his eye when he wrote. But, if he supposed there was a single tree which had been despoiled of its lower branches for beauty only, he does my love of Nature an injustice. Oh no !—trees despoiled of their lower drapery there may be—but those Bloomerized evergreens had torn petticoats to begin with. The legs to be seen are of those whose covering was not worth preserving. I have Downing's horror of tree-trimming—let me here record it.

* * * * * *

Of cows I have one more local mention to make—one that will, perhaps, be delicate to handle—but I must venture upon it, and try in some other way to patch up my popularity with my neighbors.

We are neglectful of our dead, as a nation. Mount Vernon, upon which England would have piled a hundred Westminster Abbeys, if there were room, is just sold to the highest bidder. The columns to our statesmen and our hero-Presidents rise with galvanized spasms. Near by to Idlewild (a Spirit of Glory and a Spirit of Beauty, whose once belonging here gives pride and grace to the air about us) are the unmonumented graves of Duncan and Downing. We seem to resent greatness, and pass it eagerly behind us into oblivion.

But (if I may be pardoned for having stumbled over a sadness when in search of a smile) I was about to speak of the other extreme of this posthumous forgetfulness. On the romantic banks of the Hudson we do not even bury our cows ! Since last August, almost a twelve-month, the carcass of one has lain at water's edge, within stone's throw of the lively village of Cornwall ; and within a mile of Newburgh lies another (and *has lain* for the three months since warmer weather forced its claims on the nose of posterity, and how much longer I know not)—and, of the lesser dead, cur and grimalkin, there are daily comings and goings, their insignificant weight giving them a blessed buoyancy upon the tide through which they are no sooner detested than forgotten.

Now—after the subject's being suggested daily by the shie-ing of my mare, or the call for camphor by those who are driving with me—there have occurred to my mind three remedies for the evil, one of which must come into effect, it seems to me, with the first step of our glorious country beyond the mere prosperities of civilization. Either each family should be taxed with the honors to its own dead, from the chance carrion that drifts upon its land, to the chance greatness that was rocked in its cradle ; or they, neighbors or others, whose comforts or interests, safety or sense of beauty, are, or have been, affected by the unhonored one, should contribute as they pass ; or, the Public should recognize duty to the dead among its governmental functions, and appoint its officers accordingly. The latter, after much reflection (assisted by camphor and compulsory attention and remark), seems to me the remedy most efficient and desirable. In its full extent—justice to *all* the dead—it would be sanguine indeed to believe its going ante-Millenially into operation. But there is hope in beginnings. The new office would, with even limited funds and functions, be welcomed in every village upon lake or river, and find candidates enough. And when the new functionary—(Esq. and Coroner of Dead Cow)—shall have done justice for a while to the chance un-salt-ed on brook and river, may we take a step onward towards a shadow that is now dwarfed in the distance before us—the country's duty to its unhonored for deeds and intellects !

LETTER XVIII.

Summer of Even Weather—Lightning-Rods falling into Disuse—Filling of Country Boarding-houses—Luxury of Rural Remoteness—Viewless Peopling of a Spot—Wallace the Composer, and his Tribute to Alexander Smith, &c., &c.

July 23, 1853.

THE summer, hitherto, has been one of singularly even distribution—rain and sunshine, coolness and heat, breezes and thunder-storms, alternating, with the punctual iteration of meal-times. Of thunder and lightning we have had more than used to be a monthly allowance ; but as these imposing phenomena of weather come around with more common-place and familiar regularity, while, at the same time, the lightning "strikes" more seldom than formerly, we are in want of a theory to account for it. Has the republican principle impregnated the exhalations, so that any superiority of one storm over another is yielding to a democratic equality, in cloud-land ? Or, does the increasing net-work of railroad iron and telegraph wires divide and scatter the otherwise untapped accumulations of electricity ? Of the two causes, it would seem to be rather owing to the spread of the popular principle, judging by simultaneous phenomena—the Theodore-Parker-slaught upon the glory-cloud of Webster's memory, for example, and the lament of the *Tribune* over the galleries of valuable pictures "buried in the private houses and parlors of the English aristocracy," being somewhat corroborative. Whichever the cause, moral or physical, thunder-clouds, like English noblemen, are becoming mainly industrial in their action on the atmosphere around us—the conservative exclusiveness of lords and weather alike losing force—and, even in my small way, I can acknowledge having profited by the change. There is a proudly democratic trifle in my pocket, the price of a lightning-rod, that would have been necessary to my new cottage, but for thunder-and-lightning's having become of no consequence.

* * * * * *

With the advance of the summer, the usual change has come about, in the character of our population. The farm-houses are peopled with city-boarders—butter scarce ; horses in great demand ; a tree an exception, which has not a nurse and baby under it ; and the roads, at evening, quite hollyhocked with young ladies in gay ribbons. Near as we are to two of the most fashionable summer resorts of the country, we charmingly preserve our rural habits, as a neighborhood. At a mere biscuit-toss over the ridge of the Highlands sits West Point ; but the row-boat communication around the bluff, is so tedious as to be an effectual barrier. Newburgh, with its gay and crowded "Powelton House," is but four miles off, but the two toll-gates, between, seem to fence off their gay equipages from our lovely lanes. Were it not for the proposed railroad on the Hoboken side of the Hudson (which will at once thoroughfare us into the featureless come-at-a-bleness of the rest of this valley of hurry), we should remain a rare shelf of country-life still untainted—domestic and economical ruralizing still to be found, here, for quiet families and lovers of unceremonious seclusion. We may last simple, for yet a while, it is true—but I cannot help croaking over the inevitable foreshadowings of "improvement in the vicinity," however much my neighbors may rejoice at the prophetic dollars it adds to the prices of their lands. With no deliberate leisure—no contemplative repose to strengthen the inward structure of character, and mortar into proportion the broken edges of events—life becomes a mere scaffolding of destinies unbuilt, loosely incomplete, and unworthily slight and temporary. I dread more industry hereabouts. I would patriotically oppose any more stir, any more hurry, any more of what would call for larger shop-signs, fresh paint and "business enterprise." But let us enjoy the benighted repose of our little corner, yet a while.

* * * * * *

Idlewild is getting fast peopled with the viewless crowd that will make haunted ground of it. Knowing what we do of Nature, it would be illiberal to suppose that a shaded walk is the same, whether fair forms have trod it or no—that the brook-music of a wild glen is the same, whether or no bright intellects poured thoughts upon its inarticulate echoes. Uhland's ferry-passenger, who paid triple price because he had thought of his wife and child in crossing—

("Take, oh boatman, thrice thy fee,
Spirits twain have crossed with me")—

was a conscientious acknowledger of peopled air. Of the many who come to Idlewild, some stay on, unseen. It is half why now and then another, who comes after, finds the air strangely enchanting.

But I will add ink to a quaint compliment thrown on the air of Idlewild, a day or two ago, for the new poet, Alexander Smith. The one who said it is an entrapper of those lightning-fancies which it takes genius to arrest in their flash, and his music is full of them—the "Clock Waltz," for example, where the dance stops while the clock strikes twelve. It was WALLACE, the composer, the violinist, the pianist—a king in this realm of ear-witchery, but quite as subtle in his originalities of thought and language—and we were dangling our legs over the brook, together, sitting on the bridge and wiling away the summer noon with gossip and idleness. I should premise, by the way, that Wallace is the most unconscious sayer of good things whom I have ever fallen in with—not knowing, apparently, his own utterance of the strangest thought from the expenditure of the same amount of breath in a respiration. He was speaking of some one whose name he could not remember. After looking for a perplexed moment into the foam dashing below—"Call him John Smi——" (*Smith*, he was about to say, but, arresting the word between his lips, when half pronounced, he straightened himself, lifted his hat, and looked around as if to acknowledge a sudden presence)—"Smith is a name, now," he continued, "a poet, by Jove !—Alexander Smith !—But, as I was saying, this man—call him Jones"—and he went on with his story, though not till after a musing half-instant, in which he evidently was recalling to his voluptuous memory a delicious book in which he had (un-professionally) found a revel for his fancy. I do not think he ever, knew whether I heard his queer parenthesis, or not. But "Smith" would have been pleased to hear it—and will find it in the air, if he ever come to Idlewild.

LETTER XIX.

Neglect of Personal Appearance in Country Seclusion—Unexploring Habits of City People—Dignity of Un-damage-able Dress—Thoughts on Cooper's Mansion being turned into a Boarding-house—Suggestion to Authors, as to turning their Influence to better Account—Letter from Cooperstown, &c., &c.

July 30, 1853.

THE dashing surf of city population which ebbs to our ocean of green leaves in June, reminds us of the bubbles on sidewalk shore—the dress and fashion, at high tide, which we had well-nigh forgotten. It is one of the little restraints (or little wholesome reminders—which you please), of living "within city reach." I caught myself growing shabby, by the aid of its inevitable comparison ; and I had really been quite insensible of the change as it had come about. One begins to be neglectful of dress as soon as "folks'-eyes" are taken off by the Autumn departures. And, from that time to Summer again, the comfort of dress that may be forgotten with one's breakfast, becomes a habit difficult to unlearn. It is hard to take boots and hats once more in, among things to be thought of. The overcoat that has been worn six months for a body-coat, seems the tightest thing that is any way rational—but it would look Diogenes-tub-y to persist in wearing what would make strangers stare. Boots of which the owner is but twice conscious—their first day's wear and their last—seem to use up quite enough of an immortal soul's amount of the attention to be given to things on this planet ; but such boots as have two *soles* to be saved, besides the *soul* of the wearer (considerably more than a trebling of one's grudging attention to what is to be saved)—must be worn where ladies come and go. A cravat that can be tied while watching a sunrise, must be displaced by one that takes as much time and thought as the reading of, at least, two chapters of the Bible, "with hymn and doxology"—but the loose tie (to the eyes of the world that never asks how the time gained by the neglect may have been differently applied) looks "hardly respectable." Not that I would say a word against such "personal appearance" as is graceful and becoming. Wives take more pride in us—children respect us more—common people think better of us, and dogs are less likely to bark at us—for a "genteel exterior." But all things have something in the opposite scale. And, for instance, with a horse saddled at the door, and a glorious morning going on in the fields and woods around, I declare I find it very difficult to lose the half hour or more which the difference of dress requires. One gets sensitive about *losing mornings*, after getting a little used to them with living in the country. Each one of these endlessly varied daybreaks is an opera but once performed—a light upon a stray cloud at sunrise, perhaps, being like a wondrous passage of music that may never be repeated—and is this to be lost for the tie of a cravat ?

I daily see parties of young gentlemen and ladies who are summering in the country about us. They would enjoy it, of course, to the best of their knowledge and convenience. But the slopes—the rocks in the fields, the eminences within a half-hour's scramble—are the points from which the delicious scenery around them is best seen ; and yet they walk only upon the common road. Our own ravine of Idlewild—a gem of scenery, in its far-down depths, which people might well take journeys to see—was scarce known to exist, by summer boarders within half-a-mile of it, till we made it promenade-able with smooth paths. It is a very simple problem, the glorious enjoyment of all Nature has to show, in one scale, and a pair of patent leather shoes in the other. As these gentlemen unconsciously price it, scenery is proved to be dear at the cost of a shoe-scratch. It is the dread of damage to sidewalk-y boots and shoes (which English customs declare to be wholly out of taste as well as out of place in the country), that keeps daintily-shod city gentlemen from exploring the points of view in these magnificent Highlands of the Hudson. And they are willing to lose grace and freedom of movement into the bargain. It is a thick shoe alone that treads fairly and firmly on a country road. The gait that spares patent leather is constrained and unmanly. I saw an over-dressed youth jump from a wall, a day or two since. He had been sent into the adjoining field, by the lady he was with, to gather a flower or a blackberry. But, as he came to the ground, there was an anxious three-dollar-fifty-tude in the way of dividing a shock among his joints—an effort to spare his boots—which must have given a ludicrous turn to the impression he was making on the mind of the lady. Would it not be good policy as well as good philosophy—would it not "pay," even for city folks—to dress plainly and *un-damage-ably* when out of town ? I wish it could be brought about. To *think* for oneself, if one pleases, but to *look* like other people whether or no, is the law of a republic ; and I unwillingly conform to our great All-alike-dom's superfinery in the country.

* * * * * *

I have been half sad, half merry, to-day, musing over a letter I received. I will add it below, that it may be read merely for its information, if the reader prefer. It is dated at "COOPER HOUSE, Cooperstown"—the homestead of our Pioneer Imagination, our Early-day Fame and Glory—converted, at his death, into a *summer boarding-house*, as the public knows. There are two feelings stirred by this—or rather a feeling and a consideration. The spirit of the family-proud gentleman—for that he was, and a patriotic republican, too—would look mournfully back from the shadows of Memory-land, at this putting of waiters' aprons upon his household gods, and setting them to answer bells and take sixpences. His home and its ancestral atmosphere of dignity were his passion—indulged, perhaps we may say without disrespect, with imprudent costliness, since their barriers were to be broken through at his death. I was impressed with the prominence of this feature of his mind, in walking with him through his grounds and over his house, a few summers ago. He was cherishing and embellishing the estate—the manorial centre of *Cooperstown*—as if it were never to pass from his family.

But, this is a country where the horse Pegasus is not admired unless drawing a cart, and where the Muses are most respected at the wash-tub. We will not weep over it (unless we can set up a soda-fountain with our spare tears)—let us take a business view of the matter.

Should not the *authors themselves* turn a penny out of this national disposal of literary fames ? Should not Irving and Prescott "charge" for having hotels named after them ? Would not Sunny-side "pay" to be got gradually ready for a boarding-house, and the *post-mortuum* sale anticipated by Geoffrey Crayon himself—transferable with furniture and associates, thirty days from his death. Longfellow, is a long-lived customer, but his mansion at Cambridge would make such a "splendid place to drive out to and eat strawberries," that it might "do" to cut down those "Washington elms," and be laying out the beds. Morris, at Undercliff, I trust, has "too long to run." Hawthorne should have a cottage to return to, that would be more "permanent stock" than his Consulate. I will build one for beloved Theodore Fay, in a dell of Idlewild, with the first symptom of his bringing home the honors of his Foreign Embassy to grace its value. The younger poets and rising authors are a California mine undug—if they did but know it. Would not a company in Wall street "make a good thing" by hiring Curtis and the rest to go and live on "places"—the "stock" to rise or fall as the forthcoming and future celebrity of these men of genius should make their homes valuable for boarding-houses ? It is quite time that American genius recognized the nature of the soil their laurels are planted in. Fame "pays" over here. Let other countries raise monuments and statues to great men—a silly waste of stone, *we* say, unless they can be Macadamized—though, by the way, we clipped a passage from the last month's English Review, which reads a lecture to Poets on this very point of not turning themselves to account. Thus says the writer :—

"The contempt of practical men for the poets is based upon a consciousness that they are not bad enough for a bad world. To a practical man nothing is so absurd as the lack of worldly shrewdness. The very complaint of the literary life, that it does not amass wealth and live in palaces, is the scorn of the practical man ; for he cannot understand that intellectual opacity which prevents the literary man from seeing the necessity of the different pecuniary condition. It is clear enough to the publisher who lays up fifty thousand a year, why the author ends the year in debt. But the author is amazed that he who deals in ideas can only dine upon occasional chops, while the man who merely binds and sells ideas, sits down to perpetual sirloin. If they should change places, fortune would change with them. The publisher, turned author, would still lay by his hundreds. The publishing author would directly lose thousands. It is simply because it is a matter of prudence, economy, and knowledge of the world."

And now for the letter from our friend, the lodger at Cooper House :—

"After pursuing a most erratic course for the last two months, jogging about hither and thither, sometimes on pleasure, oftener on business, jaded, bruised and worn thin in steamboats, railcars, and stage-coaches ; alternately feasted and starved at good, bad, and indifferent hotels, I have finally, partly through accident, anchored in Cooperstown, and now date from the fourth story of the Cooper House, where I shall tarry long enough at least to shake off the dust, grow cool, take a long breath, and look around me. Well, a word or two, respecting my present harbor. This Cooper House is, indeed, a fine affair. Purchased by an enterprising gentleman from New-York, it has been, this spring, most expeditiously converted into a spacious, airy, elegant hotel ; the proprietor displaying an admirable taste and tact in leaving the two lower stories of the building in their original state, exactly as when occupied by their late distinguished possessor, J. Fenimore Cooper. These apartments, so sacred to his memory, by retaining their identity, throw an additional charm and delight over the whole house, while a peculiar zest and local interest are yielded to the 'Deerslayer,' and the 'Pioneers,' when perused in the unaltered, identical library of their departed author ! The grounds are also untouched, and are wild and extensive—bewildering one in a perfect labyrinth of serpentine walks and miniature forests ; a tastefully constructed flower-garden, forming a pleasing supplement. Indeed, as a summer retreat, this hotel, for beauty of situation and classic association, cannot be surpassed. At all events, the view now gladdening my vision from this window, can rarely be excelled by one more lovely or diversified. How I wish I could paint, draw, sketch, scrawl, or even scribble you a portrait ! To the north stretches the lake—beautiful, and calm, and bright with the gorgeous hues of the setting sun—surrounded by a perfect amphitheatre of hills, of a bold, undulating outline, creating a scenic effect truly picturesque and romantic. A perfect landscape—one of Nature's own masterpieces, which your pen could adequately portray and eulogize. Mine is feeble, and only in the most prosaic terms can it express my heartfelt admiration. This lake is indeed a gem—capital for fishing, admirable for sailing, perfect for pic-nics, exquisite for moon-light *tête à têtes !* Why, in the name of all that's charming and delightful, are you not here this moment ? Quit your Idlewild, or any other wild, and only truly rusticate in and around the groves and mountains of 'Leather Stocking' memory ! Your muse would here be nobly inspired. Imagination and Fancy, holding high carnival in your brain, a volume of poems alone could satisfy and appease the revellers !

"Refreshing my memory with the 'Deerslayer,' a few days since, I was seized, of course, with an irresistible desire to visit 'Natty Bumpo's' cave ; so, making all needful inquiries as to the route, I sallied forth, and, in due time, reached the spot. The ascent to the renowned cave is a terrible one, and only after losing my hat, my breath, my courage, and nearly my neck, did I gain the summit, and fairly plant my foot, on classic ground ! But the view here obtained, I found surpassingly beautiful, and fully compensated for my break-neck scramble. Seated upon a rock, the cool breeze fanning my face, I abandoned myself to all the luxury of a fairyland illusion—my delighted eye ranging over an unbroken succession of mountain, hill, dale, and valley, well cultivated farms, and rich fields of waving grain,—the complete compass of the lake including the rise and graceful sweep of the Susquehanna. Rousing from my reverie, I clambered down from my dizzy height, and explored the interior of the eave, which is of no great magnitude ; found it rather damp and solitary, so I lighted a cigar, by way of cheering myself, dedicating the curling smoke, as a sort of grateful incense to old 'Natty's' memory ! Finally, retracing my steps homeward, I arrived in time for dinner ; myself rather fatigued, my coat slightly torn, my hat much battered, and my stomach a perfect vacuum ! All of which evils were soon remedied ; and light indeed did I esteem them when compared with the pleasures which accompanied their infliction. But I weary your patience with my raptures. My praises of this mountain country, however, are justly due. My admiration continues unsated, and 'scenes must be beautiful which, daily viewed, please daily.'

"Hither repair, recruit your health, 'and indulge the dream of fancy, tranquil and secure.'

"Yours, sincerely,

PHIL."

LETTER XX.

Timely Seasons and Untimely Age in America—Wild Glen so near the Hudson—Finding of Water Lilies—Anchoring a Lily in a Brook—Name of Moodna, &c. &c.

August 6, 1854.

THE frequency of our thunder-claps, of late, seems to have acted on the seasons like an *"encore"*—for this July is but June over again. The wonderful increase of bulk in the trees, since the time when they usually stop enlarging and multiplying their leaves, is a subject of general remark among the farmers. The foliage has come in crowds and processions. The streams, too—commonly losing their fulness at this season—are now in the loveliest plumptitude of Spring. Ah, could this sweet re-*June*-venescence of stream and foliage be copied by our country's flesh and blood—a country in which people grow old faster than in any other, and where, instead of repeating our June of youth, we Autumnify in Summer, and Wintrify in Autumn, omitting seasons with a diseased hurry in which there is no justice to fruit or seed ! And, as to the "Indian Summer"—green old age—it blooms in Europe in every homestead, though denied to *their* climate. *We* have it in our climate—but we have no second summer of parents and grandparents, blooming in vigorous and hale renewal, tranquil and venerably beautiful, after life's stormy equinox of care ! When will old age, in America, be the long-cherished honor and comfort to its children, the fruition and happiness to itself, that it is in other lands ?

My cottage, at Idlewild, is a pretty type of the two lives which they live who are wise—the life in full view, which the world thinks all, and the life out of sight, of which the world knows nothing. You see its front porch from the thronged thoroughfares of the Hudson ; but the grove behind it overhangs a deep-down glen, tracked but by my own tangled paths and the wild torrent which they by turns avoid and follow—a solitude which the hourly hundreds of swift travellers who pass within echo-distance affect not the stirring of a leaf. But it does not take precipices and groves to make these *close remotenesses*. The city has many a one—many a wall on the crowded street behind which is the small chamber of a life lived utterly apart. Idlewild, with its viewless other side hidden from the thronged Hudson—its dark glen of rocks and woods, and the thunder or murmur of its Brook—is but this every wise man's inner life "illustrated and set to music."

One of the most plain-spoken and practical of our lady-neighbors was giving me a direction, the other day, for the safe imprisoning of a flower in this hidden ravine ; and it was couched in so sweet a phrase, that it would seem as if the glen could only be spoken of—as the inner life it resembles can only be written of—in poetry. I had come in, rich and happy, from a ride—rich in the discovery of a passionately-loved fragrance tributary to the air of Idlewild ; one, the dreamy deliciousness of which I remembered from boyhood, lamenting its absence, here, among a wilderness of sweets more prized. *I had found water-lilies near by*—a pond full of them, in the very midst of the nameless village,* just around the bend of the valley. They looked at home, though the water which embosomed them lay between two factories ; for no rural village of old England is more picturesque and lovely than this ; and, under the shade of the old trees, is seen, after working hours, as well-dressed and joyous-looking a population as could easily be found—rural scenery and happy industry combining to form the whole type of the village, it seems to me.

It was, of course, a first thought to transplant one of these lovely lilies to the Brook of Idlewild—broidering its banks with those slender and delicate white leaves, as if with the spread hands of infants scattering fragrance. But, to be the home of anything so delicate, the brook is too wild, at times. With the chasm through which its gentlest flow or its most swollen freshet must alike come—a succession of plunging cascades, with a descent of two hundred feet—it would be rough work for a lily in the pond below. And it was the expression of this dread, to the lady I speak of, which drew out her remark. "Oh," she said, "the lily is delicate, but *it will stay if you anchor it well.*" I was simply to lay a fragment of the rude rock upon the roots of the fragile flower—but the expression had so sweet an inner rainbow of similitude—the delicate love that can be so transplanted and "anchored," to bloom safely and fragrantly in a torrent's path ! It was one of those poems, in a word, which are sometimes uttered so unconsciously in ordinary conversation.

* Why not name it after its mother—the "creek" that turns its mills? MOODNA is a good honest word ; and so peculiar, withal, that it would avoid mail blunders, and work well. A village with two hundred children should surely be providing them with a name to say where they came from. As it is the nearest village to Idlewild, I belong to it myself ; and I claim to be spokesman for the children, as one who suffers, with them, from the prolonged deferring of a baptism for our whereabout. As for me, I must have *some* token to give of where I belong—some name of a place to date a letter from. I have once before proposed "Avoca" (the meeting of waters)—three streams meeting below the village ; but we soon heard of several Avocas. MOODNA, the traditionary word which belongs to the stream it depends upon and graces, is a better name ; and, till the Postmaster-General gives us another, I shall venture (with your permission, dear neighbor villagers !) to make use of this. *Idlewild, near Moodna*, must be my date for letters—though it is a strange country where such auto-geography should be necessary in a village of five hundred inhabitants.

LETTER XXI.

Avalanche or Storm-King—Idlewild Ravaged by the Flood—Accidents to Persons and Destruction to Property—House Laid Open—Rareness of such Phenomena, &c., &c.

August 13, 1853.

I DO not see, in the *Tribune** or other daily papers, any mention of an event which occupies a whole column of the outside page of the highest mountain above West Point. An avalanche of earth and stone, which has seamed, from summit to base, the tall bluff that abuts upon the Hudson—forming a column of news which is visible for twenty miles and seen by every traveller on railway or steamer—has thus reported a deluge we have had—a report a mile long and much broader than Broadway, of which (I say again) there is no corresponding mention in any other journal.

Seriously, however (and it is scarce kind or in good taste, perhaps, to commence so triflingly the mention of what has been a severe calamity to our neighborhood), we have had a deluge in the valley immediately around us—a deluge which is shown, by the overthrown farm-buildings ; the mills, dams and bridges swept away ; the well-built roads cut into chasms ; the destruction of horses and cattle, and the imminent peril to life, to have been a phenomenon quite beyond the warnings of previous experience. Covering so comparatively small a space—a mile or two in breadth—its results would hardly be much heard of, or thought credible by the country around ; yet, by the tenants of the cottages swept away, and by the many heavy sufferers, in property, along the courses of the streams, it is thought that few natural events have ever happened, more startling and calamitous. It occurred three days since (on the evening of August 1st), and a walk, to-day, down the valley which forms the thoroughfare between

* Begging pardon of the *Tribune*—since this was written, *Thursday's* paper has come to hand, containing the following paragraph :—

> "There was a great freshet in Orange County, on Monday afternoon. Extensive damage was done to buildings and farms on the margins of streams. Canterbury and Cornwall were the principal sufferers. In many places on the hillsides the roads were washed away, gullies to the depth of some twelve feet being made. The country in various places presents the appearance of having been torn with an earthquake. From the steamboat in the neighborhood of Crow's Nest, the banks of the river had a striking, grand effect ; the water rushing from the summit of the hills like a cataract, and dashing into the Hudson."

Cornwall Landing and Canterbury—(or rather a climb and scramble over its gulfs in the road, its upset barns and sheds, its broken vehicles, drift-lumber, rocks and rubbish)—would impress a stranger like a walk after the Deluge of Noah. Idlewild has suffered severely in its beauty—bridges, dams and embankments swept away ; green meadow-glades covered with loose rocks, logs and gravel ; paths effaced, and noble old shade-trees barked and peeled by the drift-wood, or half-prostrated and uprooted—but the first sympathy, of course, is with the destruction to what is *useful*. Let us leave for a moment, the damages to what is merely ornamental, and speak of perils to life and interruptions to business.

The flood came upon us with scarce half an hour's notice. My venerable neighbor of eighty years of age, who has passed his life here, and knows well the workings of the clouds among the mountains, had dined with us, but hastened his departure to get home before what "looked like a shower"—crossing, with his feeble steps, the stream whose strongest bridge, an hour after, was swept away by the torrent. Another of our elderly neighbors, the principal merchant of Cornwall, had a much narrower escape. The sudden rush of water alarmed him for the safety of an old building he uses for his stable, and which stood upon the bank of the small stream usually scarce noticeable as it crosses the street at the landing. He had removed his horse, and returned to unloose a favorite dog, tied in the inclosure ; but, before he could accomplish it, the building fell. The single jump with which he endeavored to clear himself of the toppling rafters, threw him into the torrent, and he was swept headlong towards the gulf which it had already torn in the wharf on the Hudson. His son and two others, who chanced to see him, plunged in at this critical moment, and succeeded in snatching him from destruction. Still another of our most venerable citizens, the portly and honored Judge of the district, was riding up from Cornwall to his residence, when the solid and strongly-embanked road was swept away, before and behind him, and he had barely time to unhitch his horse and make his escape, leaving his carriage islanded between the chasms. A man who was driving, with his wife and child, along our own wall on the river-shore, had a yet more fearful escape—his horse suddenly forced to swim, and his wagon set afloat and carried so violently against a tree, by the swollen current of Idlewild Brook, that he and his precious load were thrown into the water, and with difficulty reached the bank beyond. In one of the houses, the front of which was swept away, were four women with two or three children. They fled from the toppling doorways, and took refuge under a tree which was, immediately after, so surrounded by the torrent, that they feared to leave it. A passing neighbor rescued them, after a trying period of suspense. There are vague reports of other similar escapes and risks, but these are all which have yet come definitely to my knowledge ;

and though horses and cattle were drowned, there happily seems to have been no human life lost, among the varied accidents.

Of lesser incidents, every passer-by has something to tell. A party of children who were out "huckleberrying" on the mountain, were separated from home by the swollen brook, and one of them nearly drowned in vainly attempting to cross it. Their parents and friends, out all night in search of them, suffered painfully from anxiety. An aged farmer and his wife, who had been to Newburgh, "shopping," and were returning with their two-horse wagon well laden with goods for themselves and neighbors, attempted to drive over a bridge as it unsettled with the current, and were precipitated headlong. The old man caught a sapling, as he went down with the flood, the old woman holding on to his coat-skirts, and so they struggled until their cries brought the neighbors to their assistance. A gentleman's horse and wagon were over-whelmed by the torrent, close to the Cornwall Landing, and swept into the Hudson.

The flood was at its highest as night came on ; and, quite unaware, myself, of what its ravages had been in the brook-valley parallel to ours (of which Cornwall Landing is the foot), I started for my usual early ride on horseback the next morning, supposing Idlewild to have been the principal sufferer, and deferring the survey of my ruins and desolations till exercise and breakfast should brighten hope a little. The sight of the new and tremendous gulf which seemed to have split open the side of the mountain beyond, drew me in that direction, but I was soon stopped. The road, our smoothest and most travelled one, was crossed by a chasm, impassable except by climbing on foot ; and, down the descent of the valley lay a succession of overthrown barns and sheds, broken vehicles, mill-wheels, boards and logs, the largest building on the way to the village completely disembowelled, and the stream still coursing violently between its two halves of ruins. I was stopped, as I scrambled along the gorge, by a curious picture for a common highway. The brick front of the basement of a dwelling-house had been torn off, and the mistress of the house was on her hands and knees, with her head thrust in from a rear window, apparently getting her first look down into the desolated kitchen from which she had fled in the night. A man stood in the middle of the floor, up to his knees in water, looking round in dismay, though he had begun to pick up some of the overset chairs and utensils. The fire-place, with its interrupted supper-arrangements ; the dresser with its plates and pans, cups and saucers ; the closets and cupboards with their various stores and provisions were all laid open to the road like a sliced water-melon. Expression of faces and all, it would have made a subject for Hogarth.

Of the scene at Cornwall (the mouth of the gorge where the torrent found its outlet), I must defer the description until I am able to speak with more certainty of the extent of the heavy damages to property—but nothing could well be more picturesque (if one may admire picturesque disaster) than the inhabitants of the village, that morning, picking out their furniture and fixings from the overset buildings and from the bed of the subsiding waters. Every one, as he waded and worked, had his thrilling story of escape or risk to tell in a sentence ; and, losers as all were by the visitation, I could not help remarking that there was a keen excitement which amounted to a suppressed relish of its adventures. "That man," said one of my neighbors, pointing to a stout, laboring Yankee, of the invincible cut, "was taken off his legs last night." "Yes," said the man, with a look of no-you-don't, "but not hurt, Mister ! I can be carried down stream, like any other man—but I can't be melted nor drowned, nohow !"

By this storm and flood, common life and long experience were, for once, taken entirely by surprise. The "oldest inhabitant" does not remember such a deluge ; and it was probably a chance phenomenon that might not again happen in a lifetime—the aggregation of extensive masses of clouds into what is sometimes called a "*water-spout*," by the meeting of winds upon the converging edge of our bowl of Highlands. The storm for a whole country was thus concentrated, and broke upon the summit of a single mountain. Old Butter-Hill was swept of a covering of soil and rocks, unstirred before since the Biblical Deluge ; and the two glens of Cornwall and Idlewild—ravines which have been channelled out by the wear of waters for ages, but which, since memory, have been the freshet-and-drought-varying beds of small brooks, well studied and thought manageable by millers and farmers—were filled in one hour, as if by the return of long-past powerful rivers to beds which, in their immemorial absence, had become cultivated valleys.

LETTER XXII.

Gentleman towing a Cow—Daughter taken out in the Storm to see the Freshet—The Power of a Flood—Lofty Bridge Swept Away—Extent of Desolation, &c., &c.

August 20, 1853.

THE Idlewild experiences, during the one-hour flood which came back like an old love, last week (like a re-awakened river, that is to say, rushing madly back to a deserted valley, where its return had been long thought impossible), were of mingled sublimity and inconvenience. My first intimation that there was anything uncommon in the brook, was the sight of a gentleman in a boat, towing a cow across the meadow, under our library window—a green glade, seldom or never flooded, and in the centre of which our own cow had been all day, tethered and grazing. Our neighbor's evening's milk had been evidently rescued from a torrent ; but where it came from (as it had just begun to rain), or what had become of the member of my family who had been thus subjected to a restraint that made no provision for extraordinary circumstances, I was puzzled to conjecture. The roar from the foaming precipices of the glen had been heard by us all, but thought to be thunder. So sudden a disappearance of cow and meadow, everything under water except the trees, was a startling change to take place between two looks out of the window.

The Opera, of which this was the overture, was too attractive to be missed. The nested birds, who could look down from their private boxes, and my little daughter, with her opera toilette of India-rubber cape and short petticoats, were all of the audience except myself, probably, who were likely to appreciate the acting and music—though "the million" were there, in the shape of rain-drops as big as thimbles, filling gallery and parterre in crowds somewhat unceremonious and uncomfortable.

But—what a drawing-up of the curtain, as we made our way along the overhanging lobbies of the glen ! The rocky chasm—in which the brook, with any freshet I had heretofore seen, was still only a deep-down stream—seemed, now, too small for the torrent. Those giddy precipices, on which the sky seems to lean, as you stand below, were the foam-lashed sides of a full and mighty river. The spray broke through the tops of the full-grown willows and lindens. As the waves plunged against the cliffs, they parted and disclosed the trunks and torn branches of the large trees they had over-whelmed and were bearing away ; and the earth-colored flood, in the wider places, was a struggling mass of planks, timber, rocks, and roots—tokens of a tumultuous ruin above, to which the thunder-shower pouring around us gave but a feeble clue. With the unyielding and confining sides of the glen—two hundred feet of descent even within the short space of our own cottage grounds, all walled in with precipices of sheer rock—the swollen deluge seemed infuriated to madness. With all my memories of swift Trenton and slow Niagara, I had never before received such an impression of the power of a flood. A heavy-limbed willow, which overhung a rock on which I had often sat to watch the freshets of spring, rose up while we looked at it, and with a surging heave, as if lifted by an earthquake, toppled back, and was swept rushingly away. One old tree, dead for many a winter, but whose tall and leafless trunk stood like a steeple against our most giddy cliff—its roots apparently never reached by the crest of the most swollen freshet—was playing backwards and forwards among the trees that overhung it, lashed like a willow-twig by a child's hand. The twilight was closing in too fast for me to await its downfall, but it was doubtless near. There was no trace of it, nor of the mingled earth and rock in which it was imbedded, the morning after.

In throwing a rude foot-bridge across one of the rapids of our cascades, I had given it (by the advice of an old resident) what was thought to be rather an imaginary elevation—some ten feet above the highest remembered surface of the stream. But, as my little companion turned the corner of the rocky shelf-path which leads around the cliff to the ledge on which the bridge rested, I drew her suddenly back. The foam was plunging against the upper limit of the precipice, the body of the flood high above where the bridge had stood, and every vestige of it, of course, long since swept away. Over the dams and embankments, paths and rock-seats upon which I had expended love, money, and labor for a year, the heaviest body of the flood now poured, uninterrupted. The glen which I had made passable and habitable, was the wilderness of a torrent scarce approachable ; and, to-day, with the flood fallen, and the grandeur of its desolation embellishing it no more, it is indeed a desert to my eye. The green spots are covered with loose stones and drift-wood ; the noble trees, stripped of their bark, are already withering in their massive tops ; rocks that were velveted with tendrils and moss, are now bare or bleak with leafless stems, and the broad meadows below are wastes of gravel and flood-rubbish. The stars are still above us, the mountains still around us, the brook singing as if nothing had happened—but it will take years to make Idlewild as beautiful again.

LETTER XXIII.

Young Lady killed by Lightning at our Neighbor's House—Another Paralyzed—Careless General Attention to such Fearful Events, &c., &c.

August 27, 1853.

A STARTLING calamity breaks in upon this limited history of what happens at a home. Close to our gate—at the door of one of our nearest and most valued neighbors—a lovely girl was yesterday struck dead by lightning. A friend who stood with her at the moment, a young married lady whom she had come to visit, was a greater sufferer, in being prostrated by the same flash, and paralyzed from the waist downwards—her life spared at the cost of tortures inexpressible. It is hard to make a record of this—fitly, I mean—for the saddened reading of those around us, and the careless reading of the public at large. It was paragraphed in the city papers, and read this morning by thousands who have already forgotten it. Yet to us, who saw the flash and trembled at the thunder—to us, who, but just before, had seen the victim, surrounded by friends, happy and admired—the hush and gloom of the calamity now brooding around us, and a feeling as if we must still grasp and fold our own precious ones shelteringly to our bosoms—it is an event for which common and passing mention is not enough. Strong words crowd up to tell it, though, to the hurrying world, with the claims of new and present moments beckoning them on, this mentioning of an "accident" again is but repetition—a recalling of what was flung to the Past with yesterday.

The household from which this finger of lightning plucked its victim, numbered, at the time, as many as fifty-six persons ; and they were mostly in sight, grouped about upon the grounds in front of the house, the sultry heat, at the close of the Sabbath afternoon, having brought every one out of doors. The venerable mansion, opened in summer to boarders, has been the residence of the same family almost from time immemorial. It is a large-spread and picturesque old house, so buried in trees and vines that you can hardly see a corner of it, and its aged but active and beloved mistress (a widow of eighty, and sister of the venerable friend and neighbor of whom I have before spoken) was seated under the willows which form the avenue to the front porch, and fell backwards with the shock of the fatal flash. The troop of children, several of her own grandchildren among them, who were around her upon the benches and greensward, had been, but a moment before, out upon the grassy hillock where the stroke fell, but were sent towards the house to avoid the coining shower. The telegraph-wires, which collected and pointed the stroke, hung in a relaxed curve within six feet of the summit of this hillock (a favorite play-ground for the children), and the fluid here entered the ground, though the adjoining posts and wires for half a mile were shivered and torn apart.

The sky was darkening, but scarce a drop of rain had yet fallen. Miss Gilmour had been chatting with a handsome boy-admirer, but left him to take aside the confidential friend whose guest she was, that she might read her a letter. It was from her mother (a widow with this only daughter), and related to some visit about which the moment was seized for a girlish taking of counsel. They passed out of the gate, crossed the road to be out of hearing, and stood under the telegraph-wire, where the letter was opened. Her lips were scarce parted to read, when the flash came—an arrow of intense light, shooting along the wire and blinding those who stood watching them. A scream of piercing agony arose with the crash of the thunder. A look towards the glare—one of those whom they had seen a moment before, lying prostrate, the other upon her knees with hands struggling wildly upwards—and the truth was revealed. From joyous life, health and beauty, every pulse beating with the promise of as happy a morrow, that young creature had been summoned in an instant.

So complete an extinction of life in an instant is doubtless a merciful sparing of the usual pain of death. The countenance of Miss Gilmour showed no suffering. Faint purple streaks followed the veins upon the left side, and the skin was slightly broken upon the left hand and the left foot ; but the person was not otherwise disfigured. A recovery from a partial injury by lightning, however, is probably as severe pain as could well be endured. The escape of the electric fluid from the body suddenly surcharged with it, is described by the surviving companion of Miss Gilmour as a fierce and scorching issue of fire from every pore. With what power of thought remained to her she imagined it to be the sudden beginning of the anguish inconceivable of another world. The paralysis of her limbs, though complete for a while, yielded ultimately to medical treatment, and she is likely to regain the use of them, partially at least ; though the nervous system is doubtless shattered beyond remedy. How difficult it must be, through the tears of such suffering and sorrow as are crowded together by an event like this, to see where those recompenses are, which, philosophers tell us, make human allotments equal !

LETTER XXIV.

Dilemma as to Placing Settees—Double Service of out-of-door Seats—Difference Between Appreciation of Landscape by Men and by Women—Right of all Strangers to enter Beautiful Grounds—Favor of being Figures on the Landscape—&c., &c.

September 3, 1853.

WHETHER to be beautiful or to control beauty—whether to be admired or to enjoy that which is admirable—are questions I have been puzzled to settle this morning, not for young gentlemen and ladies commencing their destiny, but for a half dozen out-of-door settees[.] The angel of arrangement who decides it for *us*—(making some of us plain and obscure but blissfully appreciative, and some of us conspicuous or beautiful and that is all)—was never more bothered than I, nor ever wished more heartily that the unconscious beginners had sense enough to make the choice judiciously for themselves. On *one* spot of my lawn, the seat would itself be a picture ; on *another* spot, it would itself be almost out of sight, but would command a good point of view for those who should sit upon it.

Half the dilemma is in the unusual beauty of the settees. As when an Earl and his Countess play ushers to the goods and merchandise which England sends to the Exhibition, one is terribly be-Sedgwicked to know how to dispose of so unaccustomed a feature. It is the edge of a new epoch, however—the useful enlisting the ornamental—and the Berrians are teaching us, with their vast warehouse of similar wonders, that utility and beauty may be linked in everything. Lady Ellesmere and 601 Broadway are on the crest of the same wave of progress.

Rural seats, I find, may be made to perform double service. They are sign-posts saying, "Stop here, where the view is beautiful"—giving the stranger, at the same time, a chance to repose. And this need not be credited altogether to a spirit of accommodation. One gets jealous for the beauty of grounds he has laid out, and landscapes to which views have been opened through his trees and shrubbery. As I sit writing, now, at my window (a covert one, crowded in between an astonished hemlock and a yellow pine), I see a party of ladies from one of the boarding-houses in the neighborhood. They are taking their usual stroll after breakfast—their broad straw hats, flowing dresses and gay parasols embellishing the foreground of my prospect with an effect that Kensett's pencil could scarce improve. They are of course "charming women" (judging by charming ones I have known who were similarly dressed), and I could not sit patiently here, if there were any probability that they would pass those three openings in the lawn, without stopping to look out upon the river. But, thank Heaven, there is *no* probability of it. Thank Heaven, there is scarce such a thing as a woman insensible to the beauties of Nature. Men are—often I have had curious opportunity to observe the difference, living where I do. Fifty strangers a day, perhaps, ramble through this open-air gallery of pictures ; and, knowing every turning of a path where they should stop to see a landscape, I observe easily whether they are walking with Nature or with themselves only. One *man* out of three strolls past the different openings to the glen and river without turning his head ; while, in the whole summer, I have scarce seen one *lady* pass them, who did not loiter, lift her hand to point into the distance, or make some exclamation of pleasure. Such love of beauty is a getting ready for Heaven, I more and more believe. Women are better than we.

I may as well take the opportunity, by the way, to say a word, here, upon a point that seems to be variously understood in our new country. Strangers, coming to Idlewild, often send to the cottage-door, to inquire "whether a stroll through the glen would be any intrusion." A beautiful boy—so beautiful, that, as he stood upon a rock by one of the water-falls, he left a picture there which the sight of the rock will always recall to me—said he had "often wanted to stroll through the glen, but that his uncle, with whom he had driven past the gate, would not go into any man's grounds with whom he was not acquainted." Why, my sweet fellow, it would be time for a new deluge, if any bright spot on the surface of the world could be so shut from you ! No ! no ! There is no such "right of property" possible in a republic. Fence out pigs, we may—if we know how, and nobody leaves the gate open—but, to fence out a genial eye from any corner of the earth which Nature has lovingly touched with that pencil which never repeats itself—to shut up a glen or a waterfall for one man's exclusive knowing and enjoying—to lock up trees and glades, shady paths and haunts along rivulets—it would be an embezzlement by one man of God's gift to all. A capitalist might as well curtain off a star, or have the monopoly of an hour. Doors may lock, but out-doors is a freehold to feet and eyes.

And—it seems to me—the favor is on the other side The figures in a landscape are half its beauty. "Grounds" are embellished by groups, and by waving dresses and moving forms, to a degree a painter well understands. Idlewild (I am eager to say) is never so lovely as when its tangled wood-paths, and rocky labyrinths, lawn-walks and avenues, meadow-glades and rustic seats are alive with the boys from the school near by, and with the gentlemen and ladies, nurses and children, of our neighborhood so populous in summer. I look from my window, or from the crags and terraces which give glimpses of the glen, and see pictures which these uncostly statues and graceful moving objects endlessly vary. The gain is mine.

LETTER XXV.

A Wet September—Effect on Trees—Freshets—Dam-building—Nature's Lesson in Water-power, &c., &c.

September 10, 1853.

By the almanac, September is upon us—but the trees seem quite confused as to the time of year. So much wet weather has brought back April again. The elms, at least, are putting out, for a second time, their demonstrations of tender green—a midsummer budding which I had thought denied to all nature's productions except well preserved gentlemen and ladies. How these faintly verdant and scarce developed new leaves, which are thus venturing out from the edges of the old branches, are to encounter the rough handling of the October frost that will soon be upon them, I have some curiosity to see. Will they pinch and wrinkle up with a sudden paralysis, or will they brighten into the gloomy colors of Autumn, and die off gracefully' and by willing gradations, like leaves that have properly observed times and seasons ?

I notice that the hemlocks have also had a second budding. The evergreens, generally, have thriven beyond all remembered precedent, with the continued wetness ; and the white pines, particularly, have spread their new tassels into such enormous brooms as to be the subject of common remark among the farmers. There are trees which need more sunshine, however. The chestnuts and oaks have not attained more than half their usual thickness of leaves this summer. The butternuts are prematurely withering. Maples and birches look like November already. Half the inhabitants of the woods at least need something warmer than water, occasionally.

* * * * * *

Freshets do a great deal of work ; and it has been rather surprising to me, this summer, living for the first time on the edge of so tempestuous a torrent-path, that the taming and getting of this irregular but most efficient power into harness, is not more studied by those who suffer so severely by it while unsubdued. The flood, of which I recorded the ravages a week or two ago, is estimated to have injured property, in the two glens through which the water-spout discharged itself, to the amount of twenty thousand dollars. Yet it did what one of my neighbors calls "a five-hundred dollar job" for me—a job I have often calculated the cost of, and relinquished as too expensive, but which I supposed could only be done by the patient labor of men and oxen. Had I known as much of freshet-power, and the way it works, as I now do, I could have pre-arranged the "job" which is thus done accidentally—could have set a trap, that is to say, for a cloud-team, that would draw more stone for me in a night (for nothing) than an ox-team would draw in six months at three dollars a-day.

While I am making these industrial statistics of the money-saving and stone-drawing uses of water, the *Tribune* (of August 31) comes to hand, containing an erroneous statement as to the result of a lesser employment, of the same element by me. Thus says the Washington correspondent of our leading daily paper :—

> "The President is fond of display, and is rather foppish in his tastes and style of dress. For instance, he has his hair oiled and curled after the fashion of N. P. Willis, and frequently receives visiters in the morning in an embroidered tunic, or semi-robe de-chambre, such as is worn by the flash and fancy men of New York, supposed and said to be kept by women. His taste for dress and equipage may be traced also to the company he keeps. Pierce Butler, the ex-husband of Fanny Kemble, is his most intimate friend and associate, and, next to Caleb Cushing and the ladies, occupies more of his time and attention than anything else."

Now, I may not only rescue the waters of Idlewild from the reproach of setting an example to the Chief Magistrate which is in any way artificial or effeminate, but it may also furnish Mr. Bancroft with an historical item as to the economy and simplicity of republican models, if I record three facts :—*First.* The humble head which his Excellency the President is thus authentically declared to have selected for his imitation, has hitherto known no external culture or embellishment beyond a daily souse in cold water—never, to my knowledge, having been touched by oil, pomatum, curling fluid, curling-tongs, or other onguent, art or emollient. *Second.* It has never known even the permitted luxury of hair-dresser or barber, having been cut from boyhood till now, whenever and wherever it was inconveniently long, by scissors in my own hands. *Third.* Its daily officiation as a model for the President (though I was wholly unaware, hitherto, of having ever been seen by his Excellency) is performed without crest, plume, or livery, it being known to friends and neighbors by the covering of a straw hat—which straw hat, I may add, is now near the close of its wear for a second summer, and was bought in the village of Newburgh for *eighteen* cents.

Dear friends of the *Tribune* (P. S.), I should like to be believed to grow old. Willing to serve my country in any way, I am honored to have the *outside* of my head chronicled as a copy for the President, though I would rather it were the *inside* that were a copy for the schoolboy. If you *will* strew my secluded path with mistaken *roses*, however, I must be excused for such drops of *otto*-biography as the truth compels me to distil.

But let me describe my experiences of freshet-power :—

The blemish in the beauty of Idlewild, when I first began to track it with a path, was a spot where the two precipitous walls of the ravine widened at a ford. It had come very nearly being the gem of the scenery for twenty miles around—a green terrace jutting out from the precipice on either side like two sites of cottages, *vis-à-vis*, a chasm between and darkly wooded cliffs rising behind—but in the far-down bottom, at low water, lay a shallow pool. With the spread of the channel, the brook here lost its swiftness, and the retarded ripple left an ooze which there was no time (between freshets) to grass—a frame of rock and foliage around a picture of mud.

How remedy this defect ?—for it was a daily fret to my eye. I sought my most trusted Egeria—shirt-sleeve advice. Dam-builders and wall-layers, pickers and pilers, took a look at it. The "prettiest thing," as they expressed themselves, would be to build out the lower terrace, so as to shove the stream up against the opposite wall—confining it so that its force would perpetually clean its channel, while, at the same time, the terrace would be extended to "quite a lot." And, with the deep-down softness of light upon this hidden lawn—a table with a cloth of green velvet at the bottom of a well—I longed for this perfecting of my Paradise. But the cost ! With the headway of descent with which the flood sometimes came to that opening, Windsor Castle would scarce be "rocks enough to stop it." Oxen alone could move the material that would be required, and "five-hundred loads upon a stone-boat wouldn't begin to be enough." And where to get the stone, and how to draw it over those crags and precipices !

No, we must do the best thing—build a little dam below, and cover the ooze with still water. It cost a trifle compared with the estimate for the other job—twenty dollars, perhaps. But a pond may be too small for poetry. The picturesque becomes puddle-esque (does it not, Kensett ?) when reduced to, say, less than an acre. In water's beauty, as in that of women, tranquillity is a grace for large surfaces—small bodies of either looking best in motion. I had only negatived a defect by putting the mud out of sight with my little pond, leaving the splendid capability of what it *might* be (with swift water around the rock edge of that hidden lawn) wholly undeveloped.

But nature was, meantime, contriving a lesson for us. Over my small dam, spanning the breadth of the ravine, the stream cascaded in an even and indolent sheet—no wise head having suggested to me, that, if it were opened in the middle, like the nose of a pitcher, the escaping water would leave the two sides bolder for a freshet-trap, thus stopping the rocks which might else tumble over. And with the first rush of the torrent (from the water-spout that broke recently with such unprecedented volume in our mountains), a gigantic tree came down end-wise, like a catapult, taking out the middle of my dam as if discharged at a target, and so forming it into the *unsuggested* assistance which the freshet required. It was a flood, indeed. I have elsewhere described it. The mischief it did to my paths and bridges, roads and meadows, was great. But *it brought down the five-hundred cart-loads of rocks that I wanted*, and (with a check from the dam-trap of which I have just spoken) piled them evenly and solidly over the area of the pond—enlarging my terrace with stone enough to build a cathedral, and walling up the scattered brook in a deep and rocky channel at the foot of the precipice. It needs but earthing and grassing now, to complete a picture which the artist's imagination could scarce have conjured. But we *liked not* to have it done—though, as I said before, I could have contrived it with the teaching from a similar lesson elsewhere ; and this mention of it should be read as a contribution to the cause of labor-saving. With the increasing cost and trouble of Paddy-power, such digging and carrying as a freshet will do (a freshet that does not bargain, either, for the extra of a horse or wagon on Sunday) is worth the study of at least one man in every valley with a millstream.

LETTER XXVI.

Wet Seasons Unfavorable to Hemlocks—The First Inland Mile on the Hudson—The American Malvern and Cheltenham—The Steamboat Landing a Fashionable Resort—The Highland Gap at Sunset, &c.

September 17, 1853.

WELL—even hemlocks are not allowed to be too happy ! One tree may not long out-bloom or be more admired than another—vegetable envy will, perhaps, be happy to hear. It was only a week ago that I was recording the unprecedented impulse given to the spread and beauty of the *hemlocks*, by the wetness of the season. With oaks paling from lack of sunshine, chestnuts thinning, and maples, hickories, and butternuts prematurely undressing for autumn, the evergreens did but brighten and wax glorious—particularly this one so hated by carpenters. Its destiny—to be idly beautiful, and have no other history on the page of lumber—was unequivocally smiled on by nature, the merely ornamental tree exultingly prospered above the exemplarily-usefuls. Idlewild ventured to be happy at this (with nature alone responsible), for we are little but a wilderness of fir-trees ; and, to our new cottage, in the midst of seventy acres of hemlock good-for-nothingness, it seemed a special dispensation. My thought-peg, especially—the pyramid of emerald fir-tassels, which lifts its beautiful idleness before the window where I scribble—was as light green, when September came in, as when called upon to play May-morning for the more respectable leaves belated.

But at the close of last week, a sprinkling of yellow was observable in these brilliant masses of fir-foliage. While the outer edges of the new shoots were still of an unseasonably soft green, twigs near the trunk were evidently dying. Seeing it, at first, only in the groves about the house, I attributed it to the artificializing of the wild soil by the removal of the underbrush and the manuring for grass and clover—evergreens (they say) dwindling, like the North American Indian, with the refinements of *haughty*-culture, and retaining their strength and beauty only by reproduction from their own elements ; from a soil left unenriched about them, or rather from such stuff for renewal as falls only with the stir of their own breeze-obeying branches. I was still musing on the apparent contradiction in the laws of nature—the Aztec priesthood and the Portuguese nobility dwarfing and dwindling by this same "marrying in and in" which seemed to be the only strength of the Indian and the fir-tree—when a drive back into the country, showed me that the blight was universal. The hemlocks in the wildest places were sprinkled with twigs of decaying yellow, like those in my own grounds. Excess of growth, and the continuance of tender bark and flowing sap—profitings by this particular tree, from the moisture of the season—have proved (it seems to me, after examining the dead stems) an attraction for a destructive insect. The twigs that have turned yellow, are hollow, like reeds, the sap, apparently, eaten out for the passage of the worm.

Since writing the above, I have found a record, in Downing's Horticulturist, of a similar blight upon spruce trees in England, in 1845—the cause the same, though the *agency* of the blight is not attributed to an insect. Downing quotes an account of it from Professor Lindley, the botanist, who communicated it to the "Gardener's Chronicle." The season had been "a very rainy one, and had caused an exceedingly gross and luxuriant growth." To this cause Dr. Lindley attributes the unusual signs of disease. He says, "We do not recognize in these symptoms anything incompatible with a watery condition of last year's wood ; arising not so much from excess of water, as from want of heat and light to carry it out of the system. Under these circumstances it may easily be conceived that the resinous secretions, necessary to the health of coniferous trees, were inadequately deposited ; and that, now, when growth recommences, the young leaves cannot find in their neighborhood their food, or organizable matter, in such a state that they can assimilate it. The result must necessarily be that the foliage will drop off, and, in such cases, the wood will die back, or prove permanently diseased."

At Blackheath, the whole of the foliage was falling off from the spruces and larches, and, though new branches were breaking out, they were so few that the trees would have to be removed. Dr. Lindley says, "An alarm has arisen as to these symptoms of unusual disease among plants, lest such general affections in the vegetable world should be forerunners of like plagues in the animal." (?)

* * * * * *

I am afraid we are destined to be fashionable, after all. The beaux and belles of our neighborhood have, during the present season, organized their times and places for display to a degree premonitory of a coming Saratoga. It was a destiny to have been foreseen, from the utilitarian reasons that always lie at the bottom of the attractions of fashionable resorts. The Mouth of the Moodna marks the *first Inland mile* on the Hudson. The nearest spot to New York for complete change of climate—the first village beyond the Highland gap of the mountains which wall off the Seaboard—the readiest refuge for the delicate of lungs (and an atmosphere, indeed, that has already become a regular prescription with physicians of the city), is this rural terrace above the Landing at Cornwall. The villages of Moodna and Canterbury are to be the Malvern and Cheltenham of America—health-resorts to which Fashion (with its need of an excuse) is sure to follow. We may as well make up our minds to it—though, to tell the truth, Idlewild had thought itself more in a corner than it is likely now to be. Not that I complain. The mineral springs, a mile or two back among the hills, are waiting for their Priesnitz ; and the bright spirits, that soonest wear out will come hither for health—a charming promise for our society. Painters will come here for landscapes—professional men for exercise and inspiriting intercourse with Nature—youth for schooling amid pure air and ennobling scenery—strangers from other lands, for repose from travel within reach of the city and its news. It will be *pleasantly* populous, this Highland Terrace. There will be something to rejoice at, besides money-making, in what is drawn together by its attractions.

But "first steps" are interesting to read of, and this year's indication of a fashionable resort may be usefully chronicled for reference in our history hereafter. The public want which is supplied by a Hyde Park in London, and by the Champs-Elysées at Paris—a resort for those who have vehicles and leisure—has expressed itself, and found time and place. On the Landing at Cornwall you may now see at the twilight hour, the "respectability" as well as the fashion and gaiety of our rural neighborhood. The swift steamer Alida, which leaves New York at four in the afternoon, arrives here between six and seven ; and on board are husbands and brothers, lovers, visitors and *parcels*. There is excuse enough for any vehicle to be there. It is, besides, just the hour when the light is "becoming" for unbonnetted beauty. The time for the boat's arrival varies a little with wind and tide, and, for a half hour previous, there is a gay pouring down of visitors to the little dock at Cornwall. Each boarding-house has its carry-all, and a brilliant load of young ladies with uncovered heads. Of private carriages there is a liberal sprinkling, and, of female equestrians, with their attendant cavaliers, not a few. The long tie-pole is first occupied with closely packed horses' heads, and then the later arrivals are distributed back over the open area of the wharf, making a crowd of carriages, that, with the gaily-dressed people and the interchange of visits, is as like a "*soirée* on wheels" as the Cascine at Florence. Not the least interesting feature of it, to me, however, is one not seen at the Cascine—a free mixture of the laboring classes of the neighborhood in this lively half-hour and its sights. Among the loads of pretty girls, the shirt-sleeves take their walk, with full liberty to admire. And in a country where industry and intelligence are the steps for equality and companionship with what is thus admired, the influence is salutary.

Gaiety and fashion aside, however, and looked at with a painter's eye only, the scene at the arrival of that steamer is well worth taking some trouble to see. No river and mountain scenery in the world has a spot which surpasses the gap through the Highlands, in the sunset light. It is wondrously beautiful, as seen from the thronged dock of Cornwall at that hour—the cloud-touching amphitheatre of mountains flooded with rosy light, and a broad mirror of bright water at its base ; and then the magnificent spectacle of the handsomest boat on the river, suddenly rounding the wooded point and dashing up to the wharf with her gay streamers and crowded decks ! It is a sight which makes an enlivening close, indeed, to a day in the country.

LETTER XXVII.

Highway Pigs—Giving the Old Woman a Ride—Her Favorite Jemmy—Pork and Poets—Common Folks' Knowledge of Neighbors—Letter from a Correspondent, &c., &c.

October 1, 1853.

I MENTALLY took back, to-day, some of my strong language on the subject of highway pigs. It was somewhat an unexpected retrocession, too ; for, coming out from my gate, on the river side, I had found some thrifty clover, which had been sown around the posts on the roadside, completely rooted up by snouts that should, at least, have had rings in them. With my home thus made slovenly and inelegant to the eye of the transient passer-by, I was making a large counter-charge of new happiness to which I had, by this new sorrow, become entitled, when I overtook an old woman loaded heavily with baskets and bundles. The look over her shoulder at the empty seat in my wagon would have been irresistible from the mere largeness of the favor—as she was doubtless bound to Newburgh like myself, and a "lift" would save her four miles of trudging in a hot sun, and the two tolls on the way ; but she was, to me a volume in a library I love to dip into—a history of a *life being lived*, of which I and the recording angel would thus read the chapter of to-day. A true book, thus opened for one when he has attention to spare, and walking on its own legs afterwards away, would be a favor to the reader, you would suppose—yet this old woman got into my wagon to be read for a half hour, and was grateful to *me !* How often the apparent givings of this complex life are thus secretly refunded with overpayings !

Under my recent irritation, there was but one subject upon which I was likely to converse, and, as a neighbor's dog crossed the road in chase of a pig, I remarked upon the different fates of the different classes to which the two animals belonged—dogs and donkeys valued only *before* death, pigs and poets valued principally *after*. Whether or not the old woman fully comprehended the analogy between pork and fame, she went immediately into the character of her pig "Jemmy," giving him such life-time praise as made him clearly an exception to my theory. His running loose upon the road, and fattening with no cost or trouble to her, his faithfulness to his *pen*, his endurance of the dogs, and his innocent ways with the children, were described lovingly enough to make a live poet envious. Unpopular as he must needs be abroad, "Jemmy" was, at home, an idol. She stuck to the theme. It was evident that the world, for her, might be divided into two equal parts—her pig and residue-dom. I regretted, I say, that I had been so general in my war upon the swine loose in my neighborhood. If "Jemmy" has chanced to be among them, it would not be amends enough that I should relish him hereafter as pork—pork, which had thus made an old woman happy, having been, it seemed to me, deserving of respect while in pig. (*Mem.* to advocate considerateness towards stigmatized classes, and especially to pre-pork the poets who are yet to be cut up and sold.)

* * * * * *

The road I frequent, between Idlewild and Newburgh, has no public conveyance ; and there is, of course, an understanding, along its four or five miles, that a foot-passenger is entitled to a "lift," in any vehicle going "his way" with a spare seat. In my plain wagon, with a pair of horses more useful than ornamental, I happily seem rather seeking company than bestowing any very great favor, in my daily pickings-up ; and, on that footing, men, women, and children are very communicative. If you could make the telegraph-wires drop down the secrets they are carrying, as you drive under them, it would scarce be more voluminous—certainly less interesting. Common people think something if they do not know something—about everybody within reach. In passing the villa of my magnificent neighbor "the Commodore," the other day, "who keeps a yacht, and never drives the same carriage twice," I was told (also), that he was "worth ten cents a minute." My own house was pointed out to me as the residence of a man that "publishes a paper in poetry." The different wages that are made, the different ways of employing odd time, the experience in cows, pigs, and poultry, and the characters of the "chaps and girls," are matters that let in many a side-light upon my trips to Newburgh. I find the common air very much peopled with all this, and even our beautiful scenery very much socialized and varied. The landscape is lovelier, I find, when, under every chimney-smoke which I see back of us on the mountain, I think it probable I thus have an acquaintance.

The new railroad which is to take us from Moodna to Newburgh in seven minutes, will, of course, displace the wagon-travel, and carry him, who is now a leisurely and chatty foot-passenger, in expeditious insignificance and silence. *I* shall be a loser by the "improvement." Whether or not I see more correctly, while thus looking daily through the eyes of other kinds of people, I certainly see afterwards much more freshly through my own. We have some flesh and blood, all of us, below books and telegraph-wires, which enjoys humble company best. It airs the ground-floor apartments of one's brain.

From seeing how my children are interested in the company thus picked up on the road, or how much more even friends at table enjoy the most common history of the day's drive than things of more wisdom and moment, I have mused over what we are doing-away-with, of the interest of life, by the generalizing operation of "progress." There was adventure and study of character in stage-coaches, which made travel more attractive before railroads were invented. As telegraphing becomes cheaper and more common, many a charming long letter will be economized down to a cold question or answer, written in a strange hand. Relief by schemes of benevolence will turn many of the little romances of private charity into large subscriptions. We are quickening and extending the scope of life by removing its details as hindrances—but are not those details, in themselves, valuable ? I shrink from being thus generalized away—my single pulses lumped into an apoplexy, for shortness. I shall go to Newburgh quicker and cheaper, it is true, when the enterprise of the country shall have completed the railroad—but I shall not go so pleasantly, perhaps, not so kindly or wisely, as in my wagon, with a spare seat for a stranger or neighbor.

* * * * * *

I have now and then a private letter which I grudge not giving to the public. Like the clerk at the "dead letter office," at Washington, who *first takes out the money*, I should like to subtract at least what is valuable, from much which I am expected to destroy. Responses to Idlewild influences—of which I am gratified to know there are many—would naturally come from minds of "out-door" naturalness and liberality ; and such will, even incidentally and carelessly, "scatter pearls. A letter has come in, at this moment, for instance, from a stranger who thus takes pen and ink to a thought-answer ; and he gives me a private-life sketch of the President (suggested by my recent allusion to him in one of these Idlewild pencillings), which, as not intended for publication, and undoubtedly truthful and uninterested, it were a pity to lose. I shall shock my viewless mind-acquaintance by copying nearly the whole of his letter ; for it contains a tribute to the *home* influence of the *Home Journal*, which I am proud to record ; and it contains also a corroboration of our counsel from a correspondent as to the transplanting of evergreens, which may be valuable ; and some memorials of Webster, which are well worth preserving. Thus writes my viewless friend :—

* * "Once in five or six years I *must* write you a letter—not that I wish to force myself upon your notice, hut to let you know we (my better half and myself) are still, and ever strongly interested in everything that pertains to yourself. Each Sabbath morning—or earlier, if the business of the week permits—I find the *Home Journal*, and first read your letter from 'Idlewild ;' but frequently 'Lydia' (that better half) has anticipated

the reading, by repeating to me what it is about ; she finds a 'world of interest' in your letters, 'Idlewild' to us, as doubtless to thousands of others, is as familiar in everything, except mere feet and rods, as our own native fields. We see through the medium (that you are) your untutored trees, cascades, glens, and the torrent, and its ravages, and yourself contemplating the scene from some invulnerable point, like Volney bending over his 'ruins,' or riding your pony along the winding paths, in pursuit of health and a glorious sunrise, or talking with a neighbor across the fence about the experiences of rural life. Indeed, your new habitation has a locality and a *definiteness* in our minds, like the remembrance of a city 'seen in a dream,' and if business should ever make it convenient for me to intrude myself there, and I should find the reality different from the image in my mind, it would occasion some sorrow.

"I followed the directions of your correspondent respecting the *transplanting of evergreens*, and had one set out in July—gave it but two waterings, and otherwise not the usual care, thinking the roots had been clipped so short that it would die at any rate, but it has never wilted, and is now growing. I have had four different evergreens set out in the same place, either in the spring or fall, with better roots, bountiful watering, and they all died. I think the hint worthy of notice.

"Frank Pierce's hair is most *obstinately curly*, and if there is much care bestowed upon it by himself or barber, it must be to *straighten*, not to curl it. The Washington correspondent of the *Tribune* is capable of writing some truth ; and it is a pity he thus strayed from it. The President is a man of much grace of person, as well as of mind (qualities which are found together more frequently than Nature has the credit for) ; and for the former, he has suffered some malicious criticisms. He is one of the *'best walking men'* in the world. His manners are very easy and entirely *natural*. I speak of him as a lawyer at the bar, and as such I know him well. Though he has been very much abused by his political opponents, he has never replied to any of their charges, except when some other person's character was compromised. I speak of him previous to his nomination for the Presidency. He has been charged with nearly every crime in the criminal calendar. But, though not one of the *formal moral* men, those who know him as I and thousands of others do in this State, know that he has one of the best of *hearts* that animates the bosom of man. You may think I overrate Pierce, because I have had no acquaintance with great men ; and, though there may be some truth in this position, it is not wholly true : for it has been either my good or bad luck to know something personally of many of the very first-class of statesmen in the country ; and while I do not claim for Pierce the Webster rank as a statesman, I do claim that he is a *frank and honest man*, and a gentleman in all his deportment.

"Is there not enough of interest in this vicinity to pay you for a visit here ? We are only a few hours' ride from the White Hills within seven miles of Kearsarg Mountain. Just below this—ten miles—is the island on which Mrs. Dunstin killed the Indians. This, too, is the native place of Daniel Webster, and here are some men who knew him in his childhood, and hundreds who have known him intimately through all the days of his fame. The farm—two miles and a half from our village, in Salisbury—where he was born, is still owned by the estate, he having purchased it two or three years since, and an exact copy of the immense elm which shades the well, adorns the diplomas of the State Agricultural Society. Two miles below, on the river-road to Concord, stands the old weather-beaten 'Tavern Stand,' which Mr. Webster's father occupied in Daniel's schoolboy days ; and nearly opposite is the old-fashioned, plain, two-story dwelling which was occupied by Mr. Webster's father in his latter years, and by Mr. Webster on his visits to this place, which were as often as twice a year—he spending from one to five or six weeks each time, just as his business would admit. There are fifteen or twenty dwellings here occupied mostly by the old neighbors (and their descendants) of Mr. W. Everything in and about the late residence of the great man was neat and plain, and regulated in accordance with his wish. In the house everything is just as he left it a year ago—tables, chairs, books, maps and manuscripts are unmoved, except to dust them. The old-fashioned rocking-chair in which he habitually sat, with its back running off with a long, continuous sweep, and in which he might as well be said to lie as to sit, stands in its particular corner. And who is there that can look at these things, *now*, with indifference ? And opposite, and a little below, is the little, old, time-worn law office in which Mr. Webster spent a few months, studying law with William Thompson ; and still further down, is the old and decaying 'white oak,' on which he '*hung his scythe.*' This is called the 'Elm Farm,' on account of the great number of large and beautiful elms that grow upon it.

"I have extended my notes farther than I should have done had I not known you to be an admirer of Mr. Webster.

"Is there nothing, I repeat, to pay you for a visit here ? I have a plate and a bed to spare, and an 'old John' (horse) and a buggy, which shall be all at your service. Excuse this careless writing, and be assured that there are warm hearts that beat for you in the Granite State.

"Yours, with the best wishes for health and happiness."

LETTER XXVIII.

Autumnal Privileges—Extent of Personal Orbit—Dignity of a Daily Diameter—Difference between Saddle and Carriage-Riding—Health in a Nobody-bath, &c., &c.

October 8, 1853.

THE autumnal coolness gives me back a certain spaciousness of personal dignity (if I may confess to, and analyze it), which the summer somewhat suspended or diminished. But, a word first upon the principle of Nature which I may hope to elucidate by the mention of it.

The extent of the earth's surface which each animal personally inhabits, must, to a certain degree, I think, be a measure of his feeling of personal consequence. The snail's to-and-fro is, perhaps, a foot of ground—the bee's a mile. Yet, though the snail has a separate house over his head, and the bee has but a chamber in a boarding-house, I should estimate their probable respective dignity by the difference between a foot and a mile. And this conscious orbit seems to be only the distance that one travels over *with the means of locomotion that are incorporated in his personal identity* ; not what one does with adventitious aid—the fly in a rail-car, we suppose, having no more respect for himself than a fly in a kitchen. A habit of riding in a carriage is thus a short-coming, as to its power to enlarge the conscious dignity.

But a horse may be added to a man. With daily habituation to the saddle, the animal becomes as naturally a function of the system, as the wings become part of the consciousness of the worm, on its changing into a butterfly. Henry Ward Beecher says, in one of his clever letters to the *Independent*, that "the horse is a gentleman"—and so he is ; for the art of a gentleman is, to blend his presence, insensibly and deferentially, into the presence of another. As you get used to his paces, and he to your wishes and motion, the horse's four legs and better wind grow into the consciousness of your own two legs and lungs. You take him into your general sense of existence and power, dismissing him from particular remembrance like a hand or a foot. There is a facile naturalness about this which seems either like a memory revived, or a prescient instinct. (*Have* we been quadrupeds ? Or *shall* we be centaurs ?)

By the summer's temperature and by its demands upon *social* locomotion, the use of the saddle is more or less displaced. With friends and children to see scenery and take the air, heat to avoid, and working-man wanted in the garden, one plays driver every day, doing what travel is agreeable on wheels. Although more extent is thus passed over, perhaps, it is as a passenger conveyed, not as a single creature moving by the exercise of its unconscious will and limbs. And this (the experience which I wish to record) is a lessening of the personal orbit, a reducing of the individual and prerogative occupancy of the earth's surface, to the extent of what one walks over on foot.

But the equinox—which takes the languor out of the air, and which drives friends and visitors to the city and makes children prefer exercise to a drive—gives back the five-mile diameter to my dignity. There is a horse power in my consciousness—for I daily move where I list, with a horse under me. And oh, the *proportion* there is in it ! Trees are too tall, mountains too far apart, streams too long in their courses, and winds too chilling and too wild in their wanderings—for man without a horse. We are amputated, without one, when abroad with nature. The instinct, among mountains and valleys, is that all around was measured for horse-reach—"upon thy belly shalt thou go," expressing the fatigue and effort that constituted the serpent's degradation from his first allotment, confining him to a small space by incapacitating him from the use of the saddle. Birds can walk after their wings are clipped, and men can live without horses in cities—but both are mutilated.

It will be understood that this enlarging of dignity as a human being, by a daily ride on horseback, is not an increase of conceit as to one's relative consequence among neighbors. On the contrary (unless a man is riding a thousand dollar horse, while mine, upon which I build this theory, cost fifty), one wholesomely gets away from his own fences and his undisputed dictatorship over pigs and chickens—wholesomely airs his other-peopleness—by going upon that which he *forgets as an advantage*. In a carriage, he takes with him his proclaimer of something from which others can be excluded. But, on a horse which habit has made a part of his identity, he feels abroad—the wayfarer that he looks to be—unstarched of privileges and open to chance companionship ; and this is a *nobody-bath*, of which those who live in great cities get more than is healthful or pleasant, and those who breathe only the atmosphere of their own estates get too little.

But I have spun philosophy with a pen mended to note the season and its bringings-about. October to-morrow, and not a leaf changed at Idlewild ! Yet, three weeks ago, refreshing my memory with a drive about the Eden-suburbs of Boston, I found every maple, between Roxbury and Milton, crimson with the red-letter chronicle of a frost. Have we so much more summer, on our Highland Terrace ? The Autumn haze and stillness are here, slumbering over the bright green woods, like the brief tranquillity of a first revolt from the world, thrown sometimes over the face of a beauty of sixteen. The brooks are oh, how brilliant, in their autumnal fulness ! Idlewild's cascades have strengthened to an anthem. The two inner door-posts of the State—the two mountains between which the Hudson passes out to the sea—are curtained with June's drapery of emerald. Yet this lingering Summer was brought us by an early Spring.

LETTER XXIX.

October's First Sunday—Silverbrook, and the Blacksmith's Story of its History—Storm-King and Black Peter—Effects of the Avalanche—Tribute to Children's Love, &c., &c.

October 15, 1853.

OCTOBER'S first Sunday seemed to be a celebration of High Mass out of doors. Our mountain-galleried temple with its ten-mile floor, was decorated by the first frost ; and the three glens which traverse it were like three aisles carpeted with rainbows. Stillness, brightness, purity and all, it seemed to me I had never seen a morning with more Sabbath in it. By common consent, the winds seemed excluded from these open-air services. It is only when they are hushed that nature seems devout. But the streams played their varying chant—Idlewild (perhaps because a new-born daughter of mine was cradled among its leaves) the loudest voluntary of all. The Moodna, descending more gradually to the Hudson, is the *basso* of this Highland choir ; and Silverbrook, on the other side of our own wildest and most precipitous torrent of all, is the slender-voiced and less constant *soprano*. I listened to each in turn, with slacked bridle, on Sunday morning. If there was any other sound in the wide world, it was no interruption to the hymning trio ; and the vibrations of their music, amid the light incense of the sunshine and leaves, seemed to have meaning without words—a worship of God inarticulate but eloquent.

My morning ride was to the knee of old Storm-King[.]* I had not yet seen the piling-up of rocks in his lap by the avalanche of a month or more ago—a neglected pilgrimage, considering the magnitude of the phenomenon to our quiet neighborhood. The stream I crossed (and the thickly cottaged-valley of which was the main scene of destruction by

* The tallest mountain, with its feet in the Hudson at the Highland Gap, is officially the Storm-King—being looked to, by the whole country around, as the most sure foreteller of a storm. When the white cloud-beard descends upon his breast in the morning (as if with a nod forward of his majestic head), there is sure to be a rain-storm before night. Standing aloft among the other mountains of the chain, this sign is peculiar to him. He seems the monarch, and this seems his stately ordering of a change in the weather. Should not STORM-KING, then, be his proper title?

the freshet so memorable) was long and patiently mined for silver by the first settlers—Silver-brook being thereby made its history and its name. I sat on the village anvil, the other day, while a loose shoe was fastened for my mare, and listened to a love-story which the blacksmith tells of those early days—the victim, a daughter of the chief who had given the white man shelter while he delved for ore. It was capitally told, and I would re-tell it if I could ; but it needs the click of the hammer for emphasis, and the look up from under the smooched hat for pathos, with here and there the parenthesis of a "whoa !" to my kicking mare. The Indian vengeance, by the way, was only calm scorn and a leading to the door of the wigwam with expressive pointing of the finger to the distance—the daughter retained and cherished, and the seducer driven forth with contempt. It was a traditionary lesson of pity and dignity, worthy of seal and vellum, though told by the historian over a leather apron and with a horse's leg in his lap.

The road along the Storm-King's lap—half-a-mile or thereabouts of Highland level—turns off from the turnpike between Canterbury and Cornwall, and is as lovely a walk or drive, views and background together, as the world has to show. As a mountain shelf, overhanging the broad bowl of the Highland Bay, it will be jotted with the villas of the lovers of scenery, as soon as the railroad on this side of the river shall bring us within suburban distance of New York ; but, at present, it is a secluded green lane, kept in fine travelling order by the liberal farmers who live upon it, and ending at the cottage of Black Peter, whom I found sitting at the door and coaxing his rheumatism in the sun. From my saddle I could see down upon the decks of the sloops becalmed in the Bay, and almost seemed near enough to count the passengers in the cars on the railroad opposite. Busy life was very near. Wild fastnesses of rock were very close behind. For villa-ground of combined picturesqueness and liveliness of surroundings, I know no spot of greater capability. As the birth-place and burial-place of our country's young hero, Duncan, it is a neighborhood enriched, besides, with a sentiment and a memory—a spot of earth with a soul.

But Black Peter, at whose cottage I had dismounted, is next neighbor to the avalanche, the cataract of rocks having descended a few rods beyond his chimney-smoke ; and, after prescribing for his lame leg, I walked on to take a closer look at the bared ribs of the Storm-King. I was surprised to see that the multitude of enormous rocks, which had come down with the burst of the water-spout upon the summit of the mountain, had nowhere accumulated with sufficient strength to check the headway of the flood. The vast fragments, many of them eight or ten feet square, were tossed out of its way to the sides of the torrent, leaving a hollow gulf cut quite through the terrace, or lap of the mountain, and forming what will be, hereafter, a rock-walled channel for the melting snows. It gave me quite a new idea of the power of the element that flows so gently in the brook. Those who, from ten miles around, see the scarred seam down the breast of the Storm-King, can hardly conceive the resistless ploughing up of ribs of rock by the cataract that did it. Geology might well illustrate a lesson there.

But next neighbor to the Storm-King with his avalanche—poor old Black Peter with his rheumatism—is quite as noteworthy ; and, indeed, after stopping to exchange another word with him on my return, I found more of my Sunday's sermon in the cripple—(the old man mused upon, and the mountain forgotten)—as I rode leisurely homeward. There is one thing said of Peter by everybody :—"*It is wonderful how the children always loved him.*" His time-worn face tells the reason of it—broad-featured, simple, kindly, and cheerful. He has passed his life as gardener and working-man for the different wealthy families hereabouts, and many a gentleman and lady, now moving gaily in city life, has been made happy by dandling on his knee ; but, for the last few years, quite disabled, he has lived, in the small hut up against the mountain, supported by the charity of neighbors, or hobbling down to the turnpike on his crutch, to "show his paper" to the passer-by. It is curious how singly and universally his character for *making children fond of him* is established. "Yes," said an old gentleman, to whom I spoke of him yesterday, "the boys and girls would leave the luxuries of the parlor table untouched, to go out and eat salt pork and bread with Peter, any time !" And he is made famous, at last, by this long life of child-love. Nobody speaks of him without naming it. Though not particularly cherished or petted by the neighborhood, he has a better specialty than most of us—a loveable specialty, which makes him an example, while it provides that he shall be remembered. He must always have been genial, truthful, self-sacrificing, and considerate—always both playful and judicious. His character is written in the tribute it brought—*better loved than anybody by the children*. Many a costly marble monument can say less of the man beneath it.

LETTER XXX.

Working for Neighbors—Answers of Inquiries as to the price of Land, Farms, &c.—"Harriet's" Letter—Apples Promiscuous on Barn-floor—Account of Society around us, &c., &c.

October 22, 1853.

MY neighbors, who ride past, look upon Idlewild as the napkin in which a talent is buried—a place where a man lives who never plants a potato. To the annual estimate of the produce of Orange County I do not add pig or pea. Yet I find myself doing a great deal of work of which my neighbors are not aware—and for which, of course, they can give me no credit, though it may quadruple exclusively their own pigs and peas. I do, at least, the work of one public secretary, in answering letters of inquiry about the desirableness of the neighborhood—the price of land, the nature of the soil, access to markets, communication with the city, churches, water, public spirit, roads, taxes, butchers, bakers, and Sunday schools. Of the fifty thousand readers of the *Home Journal*, to whom I have the privilege of mentioning Idlewild and its neighborhood once a week, many, of course, are on the point of yielding to the new movement—business in the city, home in the country—and, of the locality whose comfort and loveliness I thus indirectly advertise, they naturally feel a curiosity to know more. A private letter addressed to me is the simplest way of coming at it, though occasionally I have a visit from an inquirer in person. To these letters I have endeavored to perform the duty of a good citizen, truthfully furnishing what information I could pick up, and at the same time throwing an encouraging light on the interests of the vicinity. In here and there an instance, the writer has been of the wealthier class, in search of a villa-site rather than a farm ; and feeling that my daily explorings of the scenery had chanced to make me a good reference on this point, I have freely offered myself as guide to such secluded Tempe, or fine point of view, as the purchaser might describe to me for his ideal. To the ten or twelve lovely caprices of nature, which I have found hidden away for Paradises in these romantic Highlands, I trust, in a year or two, to have guided tasteful appreciators and possessors.

But, to some of these letters of inquiry I am called upon to reply in print—the writer not giving name or address—and occasionally I have done so, by alluding to the subject indirectly, and thereby, perhaps, supplying information to others who might be curious on the same point. One lies before me at this moment from a mechanic who has lost his health in the city, and who wishes to change his vocation to market-gardening ; the great rise in the price of fruits and vegetables promising him a better return for his labor, while the nature of the employment will be better for his health. To his three or four queries I will reply briefly here. The best possible land for fruits and vegetables may be *bought* hereabouts for, from eighty to a hundred dollars an acre. Freight-steamers leave the dock, near-by, every night, arriving at a city pier on the North River before morning, thus giving the produce of this neighborhood a cheaper and more convenient access to New-York than from gardens on Long Island, where wagons must be used for some distance, and where one hundred dollars *rent* is sometimes paid for the acre. Commission-agents, who take charge of the produce and dispose of it, go in each freight-boat. The sales from one market farm of twenty acres, which adjoins Idlewild, have exceeded two thousand dollars in the season just closing, and the proprietor works his own grounds with the assistance of one man. The soil is particularly favorable to the growth of grapes, now the most profitable produce of the country as well as the easiest of cultivation.

I have another letter, however, to which I find the answer more difficult. It is from the wife of one of our subscribers whose household gods are turning their faces this way—but, while *he* would probably have inquired into the soil and products, *she* (playing scribe) asks for particular information with regard to the *society* of the neighborhood. Perhaps I had better give her letter as it stands :—

"*New York*, ——.

"Dear Sir,—

"I read with pleasure of your pursuits and pleasures at Idlewild, and the glorious country round about you. How I long to get free from this dusty, suffocating city, and its money-loving inhabitants, to roam about among the sunny hills and shady valleys of the beautiful body-and-soul-reviving country.

"My dear William and I, how hard we have worked ! how frugally we have lived ! We have denied ourselves every luxury, that we might the sooner accumulate the means that will enable us to buy the much-coveted farm, and leave behind all the cares of this busy life, and spend the remainder of our days amid the beauties of some country home.

"But, sir, there is one thing that gives me much uneasiness, and I shall consider it a great favor if you will be kind enough to put me right. You frequently write about the city folks that visit your place, and speak as if *they* were all that ever enter your grounds ; and you mention that fine *old man* on the bridge (who in the nature of things must soon pass away). Now, sir, when the long-wished-for day shall come for us to gain our country home—humble it must, of a necessity be—what *society* must we look for ? Are the farmers, mechanics, and laboring men, mere boors ? Are they really and truly only the bone and muscle of the country ? Are there no men and women with hard hands, but soft and loving hearts, whom my children, from instinct, will climb upon, who will put their hard toil-worn hands upon their little heads, and press their sunburnt faces to their rosy cheeks, and say, 'God bless them ?' Are there no spirits there pregnant with celestial fire—hands that the rod of empires might have swayed, or woke to ecstasy the living lyre ? Are countrymen so dull, are their minds so narrow, that they take no interest in the glorious landscape, the glowing sunset, the bubbling brook, the roaring cataract, or the singing of the countless birds ? Are there none of these that dear William and I can take by the hand, and go out beneath the quiet stars and talk of the beauty of nature, and the goodness of Him who made this world so lovely ?

"My dear, sir, tell me the whole truth about this matter, that we may know what we must expect ; for you know we must have some one with whom we can hold sweet converse. We do not expect to meet educated poets or painters among the hard-working people of the country, but we want some who have the souls of such within them, whom we can call by the sacred name of friend.

"If such as these cannot be found—if such noble souls do not exist, apart from the polished circles of city life, tell me plainly and truly. If there are none such as I have pictured, then farewell, a sad farewell, to my long-cherished hopes of spending the remainder of my days in some quiet home, endeared to me by the love of such noble, generous hearts as I have here described.

"Dear sir, I remain your constant and admiring reader,

"HARRIET."

I am embarrassed with having only this *letter* to reply to, dear Mrs. "Harriet." Without seeing *you*, and knowing something of your stage of womanhood and your experience of life, I can scarcely choose with safety between describing our "society" as profoundly stupid, or most varied and agreeable. There are those to whom it might be either. I, myself, find it the latter—but then I have got through with my *crust*-experience of life, and like people neither more nor less for the house they live in or the clothes they wear. Charming women are everywhere—some smothered under their husbands' good dinners, or shelved away in bank-stock and splendid carriages, some unthought-of in dairies or forgotten behind wash-tubs and single blessedness. Nature's noblemen are everywhere—in town and out of town, gloved and rough-handed, rich and poor. Prejudice against a lord because he is a lord, is losing the *chance* of finding a good fellow, as much as prejudice against a ploughman because he is a ploughman. Are you ready, dear Mrs. "Harriet," to take a second look, after reading the outside label upon a man or a woman, and to confirm it, or not, according to God's mark, which will show itself somewhere ? If so, the society of Highland Terrace will be delightful to you. But let me illustrate it by something I found to eat, yesterday, in one of my rides.

Wiled along by the wilderness of unbent rainbows and the swoon of passionate stillness in the Autumn noon, I had got farther from home than my breakfast had provided for—seven or eight miles of lovely road, but my dinner at the other end of it. The trot of my high-stepping mare reminded me of my aching void—in fact, I felt, like Mrs. "Harriet," that "there must be some one with whom I could hold sweet converse," if they had anything in the world that I could eat. At this crisis I noticed a large barn, with the doors standing invitingly open, and the floor *covered with apples !* "Manna in the wilderness" was my first thought ; but, with the second, I remembered a stomach rather over-delicate with cosseting and nursing ; and then came a third thought (which I wish to recommend to Mrs. "Harriet's" notice), that, possibly, this might not be hog-feed *altogether*—possibly not *all* cider-apples and colic—better have a look, at least, before turning hungry away.

I dismounted, and tied my mare to the snake-fence. The barn was just over the bars. I introduced myself to the promiscuous society of the apples. But, thank God, what a mistake I had escaped making ! Here was every kind of apple that grows—the multitude of a most varied orchard mellowing unselected in the sun. There was Pearmain and Pippin, Greening and Lady Apple, oblong Spitzenburg and rosy Maiden's-blush—there was golden Russet and juicy Seek-no-further, sturdy Baldwin and handsome Tewksbury. Tumbled together on the rough floor they certainly were ; but, with a close look and a press of the thumb, you might find, in every dozen, one apple, at least, well worthy of slicing with a silver knife. The country's best stock and quality were there—*only they were not barrelled.* Why, the pippin I ate—a juicy satisfier, picked from a clump of cider-apples and tardy russets—might have been the tempter on a fruiterer's show-basket. Now, Mrs. "Harriet," would you have been capable of satisfying your hunger on this barn-floor ; or must you have waited till the apples were sorted, barrelled, and offered at a city price ? Because apples and society are very much alike.

Without exactly making out a census of the agreeable people in our neighborhood, I may, however, be a little more explicit in my reply to Mrs. "Harriet's" query. Within four or five miles of Idlewild, I believe there are most sorts of people. Fifteen or twenty "old families" still live very conservatively on their estates, within calling distance, and are as learned on game dinners and Madeiras as any "William" could desire. Of wealthy manufacturers, brick-makers and millers, we have a dozen or more—smarter men not to be found. Quaker farmers, in easy circumstances—plain but genial folks with well-educated families—are sprinkled thickly over this end of the country. Of clergymen, lawyers, and schoolmasters, we have, I am sure, an unusually superior befalling, for a country neighborhood. We have several unanimous belles, and several others who would be beautiful to Raphael's eye or Titian's, but whose unfulfilment of destiny, like a sun's dial in a grave, happily keeps them cold also. Then, this side of Snake Hill, we have a celebrated prose author (Headley), in a beautiful villa—a successful architect (Vaux), building charming houses—and a poet (Clarence Cooke), in his cottage of "The Roses." There is an anonymous authoress or so, to whom I must thus anonymously refer. And, after thus showing what might be "picked for barrelling" from our society orchard, I might name intimates of my own, among the working men and the children that come to Idlewild for chestnuts. But I will save this last enumeration till Mrs. "Harriet" comes herself. We will then take a look together at the barn-floor.

LETTER XXXI.

Autumn Splendors—Road Tax and amateur Road Making—Society for Volunteer Raking—Difference of Roads and Neighborhoods—North and South of Idlewild, &c., &c.

October 29, 1853.

SUNRISE—but what a scene out of my window ! Has our "fast world" overtaken a sunset ; or has a sunset overslept itself and been surprised among its blushing blankets by a frost-shod morning ? Really, what I see is almost unnaturally beautiful. Idlewild glen looks like a "rosy West," through which one may walk like a garden. To the sickening to-morrow-ishness of life-hopes but *a little* out of reach, birds that will *not quite* wait to have the salt put upon their tails, and glowing sunsets always *just over* an horizon, twenty or thirty miles farther on—there seems, at last, to be an exception. Here are the crimson and gold, the scarlet and purple of a sunset—close to—touchable—pluckable—and in no hurry to fade away—tree-clouds, of every color in the rainbow and of boundless prodigality of beauty, slumbering immovably around us. Who will come and be astonished ? We are *somebody's* horizon, of course, as somebody is ours. Storm-King mountain is the West, from *somewhere*, and Idlewild (on its other side) is just over the border-line betwixt land and sky—the elusive *beyond*, into which have dropped all the sunsets of a Summer. I think, if they (whose West we are) would but step this way, and look over the horizon, now, they would think we had contrived to detain a "dying day" or two ! Come, my dear General ! You, who, at Undercliff, are the other epaulette of West Point, and the two of you being my next neighbors East—come and see us with your military eyes ! The glen will look to you like an encampment of sunsets on a halt. And then take one look, as a poet, and sigh over such a heaped-up wilderness of to-days showing brightest when passing into to-morrows.

* * * * * *

Harvest in, and weather cool, our neighbors are working out their road-tax—most of them preferring to pay it in labor, though the wages of a working-man are now *ten* shillings a day, and the law makes the payment of *five* shillings a day an equivalent for the tax. It is a very fair exponent of what kind of a "day's-work" is usually given to that unpopular master, "The Public." If they would halve it once more, however, it would be a public advantage, I think—going over half as much ground, and not hauling half as many loose stones upon the track. A pick-axe, too, which would remove the stumbling-stones from the old road, and level the ruts, would do better service than the plough and drag, which only cover a bad *old* road with a worse *new* one—but then a pick-axe is the Paddy-tool, for which the brain, at the upper end of the Yankee's spine, seems to disturb, somehow, the equilibrium which keeps up the willingness of the elbow ; and, if the farmer brings team and plough, it reckons as a man-and-a-half extra. So there are more ploughs than pickaxes, and the roads are "mended" by ripping open and heaping up—the "charming drive" of the Summer being thus converted into a prolonged potato-patch.

Amateur road-making is a small-pox, of which the remedy (a vaccination-tax, to pay an engineer for much less labor judiciously applied) will, of course, make its way very slowly ; but, if it were not so unpopular to prescribe for any public epidemic, I should like to suggest an alleviative, meantime, and set the example by first applying it myself. *An hour or two of labor with an iron rake*, after the path-master has finished his job, would remove the loose stones from almost any half-mile of the soft dirt he leaves in heaps, and vastly facilitate, and better its packing and hardening. This, repeated once a month throughout the year, would be a gain to the country at large, if it were only in wheel-wear and stumble-damage ; but those who are pious and have land to sell along the river, should be reminded also of the greater tendency to profane language on stony roads, and of the air of discomfort which "rough going" gives to the neighborhood, in the eyes of visitors who might otherwise fancy the scenery and "buy lots." A modest citizen would not venture to be the founder of a Society, of course, without the urgency of some grand moral and utilitarian improvement ; but, with the two objects of piety and profit just named, I think I might safely propose to the inhabitants of Highland Terrace, the formation of a *Society for Voluntary Raking*—every member agreeing, in addition to his road-tax, to keep the highway clear of loose stones in front of his own walls and fences. My own road-tax (twenty-one days) I have preferred to settle by the pecuniary substitution, being handier at a pen than a pick-axe ; but the "voluntary raking" I will do, in my own proper person, commencing to-morrow morning, October ——. After that date, I promise my brother-farmers the example of a diligent rake along the fences of Idlewild, trusting to their prompt approval and co-operation.

The junction of the Moodna with the Hudson (close to the river-gate of Idlewild) divides two neighborhoods which are in very different stages of advancement, as to excellence of roads. From the *north* side of the Moodna to Newburgh, four miles, it is as smooth wheeling as in the

Hyde Park of London ; while, from the *south* side, in any direction, it is as rough as public spirit exercised upon amateur road-mending could well make it. The difference is owing partly to the longer settlement of the Newburgh side, and to its being the river-road, along the estates of wealthy proprietors ; but it is owing still more to the liberality and enterprise of an individual—the munificent "Commodore," so well known on the Hudson, having long held the office of "path-master." At the toll-bridge over the Moodna, the highway leaves the river, and enters upon a track of smaller farms and wilder scenery ; and worse roads, with this change, are both natural and excusable. Close as they are to each other, the two neighborhoods are probably half a century apart in their notions of "what will answer" for a road[.] An idea of the standard, on *our* side, may be gathered from a reply made to me, not long ago. I had engaged one of my neighbors to furnish me with eight or ten heavy sticks of timber, for the construction of a couple of bridges across Idlewild brook. They were to be "snaked down right away." Three or four weeks passed without my seeing anything of them, however, and I was about calling on my friend to enquire why, when a wood-chopper, with his axe on his shoulder, passed me on the road, just at sundown. "I have been cutting down your sticks," said he, as we exchanged a nod at meeting.

"Ah, then, I may look for them to-morrow ?" I replied, somewhat pleased at the prospect of soon having my bridges passable. "Why, no !" he said, feeling of his chin, with a thoughtful estimate of the difficulties ; "not so soon as that, quite. You see they are a mile or two back in the woods, and there's *a mile of road to cut,* before we can snake 'em out. But you'll have 'em next week, I guess." And the "mile of road" *was* cut, and the timbers duly made their appearance, five days afterwards.

LETTER XXXII.

Discovery of an Iron Mine in the Neighborhood—Lack of National Quickness at Beautifying Scenery—Poem on the Flood-ravages at Idlewild—Drawing and Landscape-Gardening, &c., &c.

November 5, 1853.

We have an addition to the moving scenery of our neighborhood, in processions of broad-wheeled, four-horse wagons, laden with iron ore, a recently discovered product of the valley of the Moodna. The newly opened mine is a remarkably rich one, about two miles back from the Hudson, and the enormous wagons with their fine horses, and other signs of the lavish enterprise with which it is worked, give quite a stir to the highway, usually so quiet after the departure of summer boarders. The scientific miners, whose divining-rod has made such a true dip, tell us that there is *coal* under the bed of our own romantic brook. I find its most picturesque gorge was once sold for a slate-quarry, too. And, between these alarms, and a bank or two of such clay as they make bricks of, and the expression of surprise, by now and then an engineering visiter, at the "beautiful water privileges" we throw away (in two hundred feet of descent of brook between our upper fence and the Hudson), I am in daily terror of finding our lovely uselessness grown valuable. The nymph of Idlewild, the Egeria of our secluded brook, might, of course, be too saleable to keep ; and I feel like the peasant mother of Italy—when her daughter is ripening into womanhood, too beautiful not to be a high-priced model for the sculptors and painters—in dread of the hour when home could no longer afford to keep her sacred.

But our lovely nymph, so in peril, is not likely to pass into a utility, unlamented or unsung. There are those who watch her with the inspired eye of tenderness and poetry. A poem is beside me—one I had no thought of publishing, till this chance turn of a thought made it so fitting as to be excusably given to the public—suggested by my record of the ravages of the beauty of our valley by the recent avalanche and freshet. It comes anonymously, but the hand is a lady's. I shall look to her for a monody over our beloved Egeria, should her sacred veil of privacy and beauty be rent from her by hard-fisted utility. But thus runs her sweet poem, written to be read at Idlewild only :—

THE FLOOD AT IDLEWILD.

A torrent swept on in its foaming wrath,
And destruction marked its stormy path ;
It deluged the valley, it washed the steep,
Then scaled its sides with a mighty leap ;
And we saw the tall trees sway and cower,
As it hurried on with remorseless power.

There lay in its path a spot so fair,
It seemed no evil should enter there :
For, to it, unnumbered hearts were bound,
And wingèd thoughts were hovering round,
And, at the touch of a poet, smiled
The woods and dells of Idlewild.

But what cared the flood, as it thundered on,
That a thousand nameless charms were gone,
Which the kindling eye of the bard had traced,
Evoked by his will from the trackless waste.
It did not pause in its mad career,
Nor spare the spot to so many dear.

But on through Idlewild it sped,
O'erflowing the quiet streamlet's bed,
And lingering not, though it bore away
The love and labor of many a day ;
And on it gazed, with mournful eyes,
The framer of this Paradise.

Would *we* could choose his lot for him ;
No cloud should ever his pathway dim,
But joy's clear sunshine his life illume,
Untouched or unshadowed by grief or gloom ;
And his beautiful Idlewild should be
From the touch of the spoiler ever free.

But he is afloat on life's stormy sea,
And chance and change must his portion be,
And the love that would gladly gild his way,
Can only look above and pray,
God shield him from trial ! God keep him from wo !
And henceforth but with bliss may his path o'erflow !

A HOME JOURNALIST.

Bristol, Pa., August 22, [1853].

I have thought it curious, by the way, that, among the many who have strolled with me through our wilderness of acclivities and wood-paths—coming upon all kinds of views and landscape surprises, and seëing every variety of surface, and every possible tangle of wood, rock and water—no one has ever yet suggested an embellishment, or pointed out a natural beauty that might be modified or taken advantage of. Yet the improvements that might be made, seem to me as obvious as they are almost numberless—charming paths that might be cut, precipices and water-falls that might terminate vistas, terraces that might be turned into glades and lawns, chasms that might be romantically bridged, and rapids that should be seen from eminences. Admiring the little that is done very kindly and warmly, as beautiful, the imagination of a visiter does not seem to busy itself to lend a thought as to what might be done to make it more beautiful still. Omni-creative as the American mind would seem to be, the creation of beauty seems not to be among our habitual and alert instincts, as a people. I have felt a lack of sympathy in this, sometimes—not atoned for by the many discoveries that are made of the salable values that lie hidden among our paths and woodlands. A highly educated gentleman, whose intelligence and good sense I very much admire—so handsome a man, too, that he is ungrateful to Nature for not being alive to what else she has done that is admirable—was walking with me in the glen, the other day, and I was showing him a kind of rocky parlor at the foot of the rapids, where the springs trickle in curtains down the walls, and the floor of stone lies half islanded between rapids and still water. Overhung by a crag on the eastern side, it is dark and cool from sunrise till nearly noon, and I looked at my friend, as his beautiful profile was relieved against the brown wet rock, and expected him to jump at once to my favourite idea—what a place to turn into a grotto for summer breakfasts ! His large hazel eyes fell on point after point of the loveliness around him. "Ah !" said he, "when they come to build that depot for the Syracuse and Hoboken Railroad, this stone will sell, I can tell you !" Yet a charming woman was listening, when this precipitate was thrown into the romance of the spot.

Downing's genius was our country's one solitary promise of a supply for this lack of common currency—this scarcity of beauty coin in our every-day pockets. He was the one person who could be sent for—by a gentleman who had purchased land for a country-seat, and who had not given up his attention to the development of natural beauty—to look at fields and woods, and tell what could be made out of them. It takes a *habit* of looking at such things—at Nature wild in contrast with Nature improved—to know how to lay out paths and clump woods, plant avenues and inlay brooks among greensward and foliage. It takes a poet, perhaps—or, certainly, it takes imagination mingled with taste and practical good sense—to follow it skilfully as a profession. I am glad to know that the poet who was a brother-in-law of Downing—Clarence Cooke—and who studied under him and was much with him, has made it the vocation of his life. He is employed at present on one or two estates in the neighborhood of Newburgh, and can be addressed, on such subjects, at his own cottage of "The Roses," at that place.

LETTER XXXIII.

Sudden Fall of Leaves—November Haze—Fame of Newspaper-wrappers—Naming of a Village—Legend of MOODNA, the Indian Chief—Importance of Immortalizing Men and Events by the Naming of Towns, &c., &c.

November 12, 1853.

NOVEMBER the first, and almost every leaf already fallen ! The trees seem subject to the same law as we. With the extraordinary vegetation of the wet and warm summer, they have lived a little too fast, and are paying for it by a more early decay. It is an apoplexy of Autumn. During a sudden shower which I watched from my window, about the middle of October, every large drop seemed to strike off a leaf of full vigor. One hickory tree, more particularly, was almost wholly stripped in an hour—the foliage, too, as it lay upon the ground, showing very little of the usual preparatory embrowning. It would be disrespectful, of course, to blame Nature (though she has cut up several remarkable shines, with her weather and water, this A.D. 1853 !) but I must venture to mourn over this loss of drapery for our Indian summer. And not only for the fullness and beauty of the trees (whose trusting and adhering foliage usually denies the winter to have come, till long after the blowing of the first bitter winds of November), but, for the actual shade, I mourn as well—here and there a noon of December itself being too warm for comfort in the sun. There is one curtaining of the landscape still left—our forlorn hope for the beauty of this year's Indian summer—*the November haze*. Even the splintered ribs of the old Storm-king look graceful, through that ; and those, by the way, who have not seen our Hudson Highlands in one of these English atmospheres, should vary their lounge at Williams-Stevens-and-Williams's window, by a railroad trip hither on the first of those dreamy-looking days. Painted landscapes are but "cold victuals" to such pictures as we then have, lying warm around us.

* * * * * *

The newspaper-wrapper is Fame's most enduring tablet. No word can die that is once scribbled on brown paper as a Post-office direction. And it was with a realizing sense of this responsible opportunity to eternize something or somebody, that I lately found the naming of our new-sprung village kindly deferred to me. Hidden away in a crook of the stream, the secluded nest of factories and cottages in the next valley to Idlewild, has thriven like a swarm of insects in the folds of a rose—the beauty of the overlapping hills, and sheltering woods, not at all blemished by their teeming industry—till at last they have outgrown even the town of whose town-*ship* they were but a distant and nameless part. Larger and far more prosperous than New Windsor (from which they were divided, also, by a stream and a toll-bridge, and a long and hilly road), their erroneous direction must still be "New Windsor," unless the Postmaster-General would graciously recognize the village as large and separate enough to have a name of its own. After a summer of discussion, the petition was drawn up and signed by the proprietors and residents, forwarded, replied to by a letter of minute inquiry, and finally granted some ten days ago. MOODNA, *Orange County*, is now a note in the Postmaster-General's anthem of ever-swelling repetition—a hero's name, familiar, hereafter, while the world lasts, to Fame and the clerks of the Post-office.

The choosing of the name brought up various embarrassing questions. If it had not been an important principle that the honor should be rigidly a posthumous one, there are two venerable septuagenarians among the present inhabitants—models, both, of private lives brought to a beautiful completeness—for either of whom it would have been acknowledged by the neighborhood to be a well-deserved memorial. More practically, still, it might record the enterprise and manufactures of the mills and factories of the place. I had an unacknowledged poetical hankering to call it Lotus-dale, from the profusion of water-lilies which open their fragrant cups among the ponds and sluices. Then Lafayette had once been quartered with his staff, in its prettiest house, and I did not see how my friend Lossing, the Historian, would excuse me for not commemorating that. But no ! There was an earlier claim than any of these. A savage, whose wigwam was here—one of those from whom our fathers took the soil, and to whose virtues at least we owe a memory—had, on this spot, set the Christian an unsurpassed example. Tradition still told the story, though it differed as to his name. Whether the stream was called after him, "MOODNA Creek," or whether, as some say, Murdner is the word, and the name of the English wife for whose life he gave his own,* the heroic deed, we thought, would be best commemorated by adopting the former supposition, and naming the village MOODNA. In that word, now brown-wrapper-ized till doomsday, is told the story of an Indian chief, who took the death-blow of the tomahawk when his silence only would have made the white woman the victim. Children will be better started, I think, who are born where such nobleness is remembered to have been native to the soil—cradled in the home of a great deed. The factory-bells ring

* For this story see page 37 *et seq.*

poetry, and iterate a sweet lesson perpetually, as Moodna bells. Idlewild, *near Moodna,* makes Idlewild worth more. It is a privilege to have that bright example writ with sweet repetition on the outside of every letter that comes to me—better, at least, than "Cornwall," as before, the name of an English haunt of begrimed over-toil and starvation. In a country where new towns are being named every day, it may not be trifling with public attention, perhaps, to ask for a little more care over the bestowal of this single-word immortality, this ever-strengthening brown-wrapper commemoration and familiar-ization.

LETTER XXXIV.

Mellow Middle in a November day—Ascent to Storm-King—Road from Newburg to West Point—Chances for Human Eyries—Difference of Climate between the two Mountain-sides—Home-like familiarity of a Brook, &c., &c.

November 19, 185[4].

THE scoop of the rich yellow centre from a slice of nutmeg melon, leaving a respectable depth of the colder-tinted unripeness at either end, is very like the cut of warm and fruity sunshine which lies mellow in the middle of a November day—say from ten o'clock till three—and by confining oneself to these delicious mouthfuls of noon, the summer feast of out-doors need scarce be perceptibly lessened. An artist might reasonably miss the long shadows of morning and evening, it is true. But the renewed overflowingness and sparkle of the water-courses, at this season, redeem any tameness of the landscape ; and, with exercise in such elastic sunshine, one looks, somehow, through different eyes. What would be glare in summer, is joyous illumination now.

We started after breakfast yesterday (Nov. 5th), to ascend to the cloud-piled shoulder of old Storm-King, and look over upon the parade-ground of West Point—the young "sodgers" being near neighbors of ours by straight line, though the mountain between is a mile or two thick through its un-tunnelled bottom, and divides us as effectually as the Appenines cut off Florence from Bologna. With the work made by the water-spout of a few weeks ago, it promised to be something like the cat's walk over the house-tops, for any smoothness of road. We should properly have been mounted on mules. Nothing ever happens to a lady on horseback, however ; and my neighbor's daughter, and my own daughter and niece, were young travellers enough to rather wish for an adventure, while my neighbor and I were old travellers enough to make the best of one. Besides, we were out for the idleness of an autumn day. We could let people in Broadway see a month's sight in a morning—we could let electricity travel its 300,000 miles a second—and be happy, ourselves, for that day, with neither the fashionable indigestion of event nor the popular distancing of thought and observation.

The principal road across the mountains, from Newburgh to West Point, is a fork or two farther west than the pass for which we pointed our horses' heads ; and, after leaving the Highland level upon which Idlewild stands, we had little to follow except the track of the woodsman and such gullies as had been ploughed by the floods. The ascent of this range is by no means the gradual acclivity that it looks to be, from below. It is a labyrinth of knolls and hollows, over which one travels like an ant through a basket of eggs, coming continually upon small mountain farms, islanded among irreclaimable rocks, and so hidden behind and among them as to seem contrived by hermits for inextricable privacy. Oh what eyries, for such human eagles as wish to live alone, and yet have the world within pouncing reach ! The bright springs make miniature meadows, just large enough for the rear window of a mountain hut to look out upon, and the crags and slopes are the models of walls for grasses. Sheep and cows are charmingly at home there—fences unnecessary—wood plenty—land eight to ten dollars the acre—West Point music gratis with every South wind—and society and other epidemics wholly unknown. These attractions prove sufficient for one very cultivated man, by the way. He tried city-life for a while, after leaving college, and then expended a small competency in a farm on this ridge. After getting his cottage built, he sought out a beautiful and poor girl, wholly uneducated, married her, and commenced cultivating a virgin mind and a virgin farm. Both succeeded to his entire contentment. His wife grew a lady of uncommon dignity and intelligence ; and, while they passed their evenings with books, their farm and dairy were models by daylight. The story was told me by one of my working neighbors who knew them well.

Somewhere about noon we came upon brooks running the other way, and began to smell (we thought) a little of the salt air of the seaboard—the ridge we had mounted being an effectual Panama between this and an inland air much more Pacific for the lungs. In the cannon of the military post at the foot of the descent on one side and the rolls of Orange County butter at the foot of the descent on the other, my chronic cough-memory found a very correct exponent of the two climates which the mountain divides. To my eminent friend Doctor Gray, who prescribed the velvet side of this Isthmus so near New York (instead of the Trip to the Tropics which I took in spite of him, and found so ineffectual), I owe what gratitude my present better health is worth ; and I mention it here for the benefit of the large public of consumptive given-over-dom of which I have now ceased to be one. To the pulmonary patients who abound in our harsh seaboard atmosphere, this Highland Terrace is a far better Malvern than the Antilles—the poor, at least, should know.

Descending through a silence-bound, tree-riven, wilderness (a place that feels, as you ride through it, like a chaos, with an eternity or two still on hand), we came suddenly to a breathless little mountain lake, sprinkled with rock islands, and lovely enough for a poem or a dream. Its outlet is a water-slide, overhung by a romantic crag, and, just now, a flood dashes brilliantly down the slanting precipice ; though, in summer, I believe, when most resorted to by riding parties from West Point and Cozzens's, the cascade is perversely dry. Hereabouts terminates the military road commenced by the Government as a Simplon between West Point and Newburgh ; and into the proposed route of this we now struck to return to Idlewild. Our neighbor, who with his fair daughter had accompanied us, has a family of yeomen sons—manly fellows at the perfection of the first American remove from English stock—and the stone house of one of them stands not far from the lake, in the centre of a mountain farm. The rosy wife soon spread an excellent dinner for us. General Washington, who often earned an appetite by the same ride (for, it was the only road between Fort Putnam and his head-quarters at Newburgh), would have felt his patriotism improved, many a time, I doubt not, by as good a dinner on the same spot.

Idlewild brook takes its rise hereabouts ; and, as the road down the mountain follows its course for three miles, till it brings us to our gate (the stream here leaving the highway, and plunging into a deep gorge of our own grounds, quite hidden from public view)—it was like being accompanied home by a member of the family accidentally found astray among the hills. How domesticated a brook gets to be, to be sure ! We praise its beauty—we blame its violence—we have a good-bye for it when we leave home, and a feeling of how-d'ye-do when we see it again—take pride in it when the stranger sees its loveliness, and confide to it (when we are alone together) many a thought elsewhere untold, many a wild dream, many a sadness. For moods which could not bear solitude, the running brook is often company enough. It was reasonable in the ancients to recognize them as nymphs. They grow to seem conscious and friendly, as the motionless rocks never could do. And we frequent them, open heart and mind to them, let their murmur dispel melancholy, and let them wile away discontent with their music without words—believing in them irresistibly, or with the same instinctive and vague credence with which we believe it forever to be the same brook, though the same water is never seen in it twice.

LETTER XXXV.

Instance of Stick-a-pin-there—Survey of Premises after a Freshet—History of a Dam—Specimen of Yankee Coax-ocracy, &c., &c.

November 26[,] 1853.

THE out-door improvements at Idlewild have here and there a marginal note, visible only to myself—a point of country knowledge I have learned in the doing of them, or a light they have chanced to throw upon the character of neighbors or working-men—and I am tempted to ink over one of these viewless memoranda, occasionally, for the reading of others besides myself, though it is rather ticklish literature on the spot where it is written. We are so in the habit of thinking books and newspapers to be altogether about distant places and other people, that individuals—country-folks particularly—are startled to find themselves punctured, even with the "stick-a-pin-there" of approval or admiration.

I went down yesterday, after the abundant freshet which has been flooding our brook for the last few days, with rather a nervous curiosity to see whether the dignity of American aristocracy was vindicated—whether the dam of my big pond, that is to say, which was built in defiance of it, and has stood through a year of unusual wear and tear, unhumbled and water-tight—was still curving its broad lip over the meadow. There it flowed, however, a silvery sheet of eighty unbroken feet across, and there swam the boat upon the saucy brimfulness of the rebellious pond above ; and how and why this continued proof that it was a "good job," is unpalatable to the predominant nationality of our neighborhood, I may show by a little history of the building of it.

There was one unsightly spot in the brook—the place where it left the rocky gorge, and first spread upon the level of the upper meadow, six or eight feet above the Hudson. Its descent, here, in the frequent freshets, was too violent for the grass to grow, and so, for the greater part of the year, we looked down upon an area of bare mud and gravel. With rocky precipices and wooded slopes forming an amphitheatre around its upper side, the opening outward was a hundred feet in width ; and a dam across this would turn our eyesore of mud into a beautiful little lake. It must be done—and, if the advice of all my neighbors was to be trusted, there was but one "team" that would be likely to make a "good job" of it. A. and

B. (we will call them for the present) had a yoke of oxen that they could handle like a knife and fork, and drive anywhere—snake any stone into any place—could lay a wall like a slice of plum-cake—outwit the frost-heave, drift-ice, and flood-wood, and build for the least money, the best kind of no-you-don't dam for a freshet. The two men took jobs together, but A. was rather the "boss," and with him I must make my bargain.

Acquainted as I am with most of the working-men hereabouts, I had not chanced to fall in with these particular wall-layers ; but I found them at work on a farm near the village, and, with some persuasion, engaged them to come and look at the ground, that afternoon. They came. A. understood at a glance what I had been six months studying up, as to handiness of material, risks of flood, time, labor, and cost. It would evidently have been a waste of words to try to tell him anything about it. And, as he sat on a rock and whittled, he was quite too smart looking a Yankee to have any chance with in a bargain. So I simply proposed that he should do it at the usual price of labor by the day—terms cash, commence on Monday morning, and finish as soon as convenient. To this entire trust of the matter to the working-man's own honesty and industry, there is, of course, no objection ; and, leaving A. whittling and B. stoning squirrels, I turned on my heel—enough said, as I supposed, but wondering, as I walked up the glen, why my own prompt readiness, as to terms, had not un-puckered the purse-tight lips and eyes of boss A. and his man B.

Monday came—and another Monday—and the dam-builders did not make their appearance. Everybody said, "Oh, you have got to go after *them*, two or three times, before *they'll* come !" but not understanding fully what this meant, I waited another week. Still, no beginning of the job—and it seemed strange that I did not, at least, get some message or excuse, as they knew my own men were on the ground to take hold and work under them, and there was a certain expense to me, of course, in the waiting and disappointment. Every day, on the way to the post-office, I passed my delinquents laying up stone in a neighbor's field ; but as I did not tie my horse and get over the fence to speak with them, I, of course, had neither renewed promise nor explanation. Contrary to the advice of all my practical friends, I gave them up, at last, and undertook the building of the dam myself—with the aid of my tenant that is to say, who is handy at anything, and the three or four Irishmen in my regular employ. We built it ; and the neighbors gave us a laugh in advance at the way the first freshet would walk through it. But the worst one remembered in fifty years has gone over it, and the usual half dozen more ; and there it stands, to-day, a year old, and apparently as good as ever.

Now, if the reader fancies that what I have told, thus far, is a very plain story of two men who didn't want a job, after looking at it, and merely broke their engagement as a bungling way of letting it alone, he is mistaken. They knew what they were about, and it was of some importance to them to get the job, and to perform it well ; for, with a newly undertaken property, walls to lay, embankments to raise, roads to grade, and woods to clear, I was the best customer for their particular work, within twenty miles. And they were not men who could afford to lose character, either for 'cuteness or honesty. They have houses, family, stock, and are known to be the smartest men, with tools and oxen, anywhere about. But there was the pinch ! *I* was to be made to understand and feel that superiority. They were not going to let *me*—a new-comer with city-fied notions—fancy *they* could be hired and paid off like Irish laborers. Oh no ! But how to enlighten me ? The price of labor and team, by the day, they could not very well alter. Of mere money, they could ask no more than the established usage. But they *could* insist on being COAXED to earn it. I could be made to know that there were some men who must be talked politely to, as well as paid. Did I suppose that American citizens, like them, were to be hired with two words, like Paddies, and paid off with that darned silence that no man ought to stand ?

I am defining, not condemning, the COAX-OCRACY, let me add. Having committed no manner of overt offence against boss A. and his man B., I am grieved that they should have stopped speaking to me (as they have) when we meet on the road, and that my Paddy-built dam is necessarily a disparagement to them, while it continues to hold water. Hang the money-only-dom, say I, though my dam keeps a stiff upper lip in glorification of it, for the present. I am willing to pay tribute, only let us give a look, now and then, to see whether the claim is exhorbitant. The working-class feels that it has the power, in this country, as the nobility has it in England. But there is proper deference, and there is *toadyism*, to England's ARISTOCRACY. Let us talk enough, and not *soft-sodder* too much, to America's COAX-OCRACY.

LETTER XXXVI.

Fine Specimen of a Boy—Young America—Mr. Roe's Boys' School—Surveying Class in the Paths of the Ravine, &c., &c.

December 3, 1853.

Coming home on a smart trot, yesterday, from a long ride in the rain, I was overtaken by one of my bowing acquaintances, a young gentleman of twelve years of age whom I frequently meet, mounted on his active little pony. As he galloped gallantly alongside, and commenced conversation with the politeness and self-possession of a gentleman of forty, I could not help admiring the exponent that he was, of the age that is coming after us. Cased in India-rubber myself, I was, of course, independent of the mud and rain ; but he, without overcoat, and with only his gray school-jacket buttoned tightly to his throat, was equally thoughtless of the dirty water from the horses' hoofs and the clean water from the clouds, and he entered into the discussion of the relative merits of our steeds, with a glow on his wet face, and a mind entirely at liberty. In the two or three miles that we rode together, he accommodated his horse's pace to mine, phrased his remarks with entire propriety as to our respective ages and the fact that we had never before exchanged a word, and gave me, altogether, as much pleasure as I could have received in the same time from any grown-up traveller on the road. Here was boyhood doing well, it seemed to me. In health, good manners, and proper confidence as to intercourse with those older—three important points—Young America is thus doing better than it used to do, caricature and ridicule on the subject, notwithstanding.

I have been indebted, also, to some fine boys, for a picturesque filling up of the foregrounds of my landscape, recently the handsome groups of a surveying class, from the school of my neighbor, Mr. Roe. Our precipitous and labyrinthine ravine of Idlewild is the best of fields for the practice of this out-door science ; and, with their tri-colored flags planted on the crags and terraces, and their busy movements and lively voices, these healthy and happy lads have added much to its charm, of late. Youth is beautiful. Its friendship is precious. The intercourse with it is a purifying release from the worn and stained harness of older life. I rejoice that Idlewild is a playground to which the lads of the neighborhood can be agreeably made welcome—a wilderness of wood-paths and waterfalls, squirrels and chestnuts, boundless shade in summer, and a mile or more of dry gravel-walks in winter—nothing nice enough for a "trespass," and nothing too cultivated to frolic over. But I must show, by the way, how the good-will of my young neighbors turns to account, after all. They have enriched me with a report of their survey—telling me (what I should have been long enough in finding out, with all the serpentine twistings of the roads and the wildness of the ravine of two hundred feet of depth lying between) the distance, by air-line, between my gate on the Hudson and the gate toward the mountains in the rear. Thus writes the able and indefatigable instructor of these practical surveyors of from ten to fifteen years of age :—

> * * "The distance from the centre of the one gateway, mid-way between the posts, to the centre ditto of the other, is 21,247 feet (128 rods, and a fraction), bearing N. 12°, 43", 36", E. Anything further that we can do, within the compass of chain and theodolite, that would promote your convenience or amusement, will afford me much pleasure, and my boys much valuable exercise and practice. If they can make their work close, and check lines balance, when taken across your ravines and among your trees (which I require that they carefully respect), they can do so anywhere else. With your permission I shall, through the winter, give them other exercises in the ravine.
>
> "Yours, with much respect,
>
> "ALFRED COX ROE."

I have copied my friend's private note and given his name in full, without his permission, but it is partly to answer letters frequently addressed to me for information. The descriptions of the climate and scenery of the neighborhood, and the occasional allusion to schools, have induced parents among the readers of the *Home Journal* to send inquiries which this name and our fullest recommendation of the discipline, instruction, and manners of the school, may here answer.

LETTER XXXVII.

Interesting to Invalids only—Letter from an Invalid Clergyman—Reply—Keeping Disease in the Minority—Climate of the Tropics—Importance of Attention to Trifles, in Convalescence, &c., &c.

December 10, 1853.

ARE you quite well, dear reader ? Are all those who are dear to you quite well ? If so, perhaps you will kindly pass on to another topic, allowing me, under the Idlewild caption, for this week, to answer a letter from an invalid—the information thus called for being interesting to invalids only, or to those with precious invalids—for whom they feel and care. In a world where mortals walk beside death with a face averted, the sick can talk safely of their sorrows only to the sick. I do not claim, therefore, the attention due to a general topic. Though, with pulmonary consumption for our country's most fatal liability, any experience, in eluding or defeating it, may be of interest to so many, as to be, at least, excusably tedious to the remainder. It comes appropriately from Idlewild. The Highlands around us, I fully believe, are the nearest spot to New York, where the acrid irritation of our eastern and seaboard climate is unfelt. Poke your fire, then, dear, delicate reader ! (for you are an invalid, by your following me thus far)—and settle yourself comfortably in your arm-chair, while I lay before you a sad and well-written letter from an invalid :—

*C******, *November* 21, 1853.

"MR. WILLIS.—*Dear Sir* :—You will perhaps think it presumption in me, an entire stranger, to address you as I now do ; but I shall be willing to abide your judgment after you have heard my story. I am a Presbyterian clergyman, in feeble health. After five years' preaching in one happy parish, my lungs gave out, and I was obliged to give up my calling. By the advice of physicians, here and in New York, I spent two winters at the South, roaming from place to place, but spending most of the time in Jacksonville and St. Augustine, Florida. I was there during the winter of your tour in that region, and on the same sad errand. And I may here say, that I have taken great pleasure in reading, weekly, your record of travel in those parts.

"But I got no essential benefit from the 'Sunny South'—nothing but some disgust for it, weariness of travel, and a warmer love for the North and for my home. Neglecting further medical advice, I bought, two years since, a pleasant site for a country residence in this, my native place, built a house, and devoted myself to tree-planting and gardening of all sorts. This has been my sole employment for two summers. In winter, I warm my whole house, moderately, not allowing the mercury to rise above sixty or sixty-two degrees, and connect with this a thorough ventilation. I remain within doors most of the time. Between romping with my two children, playing with grace-sticks, battledoor, etc., fighting imaginary foes with my cane, and the music of a piano, I manage to get regular, daily exercise and recreation. In favorable weather, I also take a brisk walk of half a mile.

"This mode of life makes me quite happy, and I enjoy a tolerable degree of health ; but *I don't get well.* I followed you to Idlewild with much interest, having a fellow-feeling on one point, at least, and watched to see whether you would get the mastery of disease. In your last letter, you say that you are no longer to be classed among the consumptives. Alas ! I can't say as much for myself, I fear. And on reading your lines, I resolved to write to you, as a once fellow-invalid, and ask, *What has cured you ?* The doctors advise me to go South and take cod-liver oil, but their prescriptions do me no good ; and I improve most when following my own judgment. I spade and hoe and rake quite lustily, and ride horseback, in summer ; I cough but little, and eat and sleep as well as ever—but cannot use my lungs. Now, may I trouble you to give me some plain advice—a little of your own daily regimen—if you are willing to do so, an account of what has helped you ?

"I consult you, not as a doctor, but a man of benevolence, knowing by experience the feelings of a young man arrested by disease, and laid aside from the activities of life.

"If you do not think proper, nor find it convenient, to address me personally, I beg leave to suggest that you give your friends, through the *Home Journal,* some of your views and your experience relating to the treatment of pulmonary affections. A large and eagerly attentive audience would listen to your words, I assure you.

"Pardon me, sir, if I have annoyed you by this letter ; and if you are willing to do so, please allow me to hear from you, and greatly oblige, yours, with true respect, A. D. G."

[To which straightforward and touching letter, the following was the bulk of my reply—not very satisfactory, I fear, though possibly there may be a point or so, in which it is either suggestive or corroborative :]—

* * The politicians teach us how to treat a disease, I think. They do not try to *convert* the opposing party. They are content if they can *keep it in the minority*—sure that it will tire, in time, of its want of power, change sides, or disappear. The patient who troubles himself least about his disease (or leaves it entirely to his doctor), but who perseveringly *outvotes it* by the high condition of the *other parts* of his system, is the likeliest to recover—and it is of this *high condition,* alone, that I have anything to say. Of twenty who may be sleepless with a cough and weakened with the raising of blood, no two, perhaps, are subjects for precisely the same medical treatment, or diseased in precisely the same

locality—though all are called "consumptives." Our friends, the physicians, are better geographers than we, as to where the healing is wanted—though they strangely confine themselves to the specific ailment, taking it for granted that the patient keeps the rest of his body in proper training for recovery. It is medical etiquette, I believe, to refrain from any very particular inquiry into this. But, few sick men are wise or firm-minded enough to be safely trusted with their own general condition ; and I, for one, came very near dying—not of my disease, but of what my doctors took for granted.

To leave generalities, however, and come to the personal experience which you ask for :

I went to the Tropics, as a last hope to cure a chronic cough and blood-raising, which had brought me to the borders of the grave. I found a climate in which it is hard to be unhappy about anything—charming to live at all—easy to die. (At least, those who were sure of dying, and did die—and in whose inseparable company I thought I was—were social and joyous to the last.) The atmosphere of that Eden-latitude, however, is but a pain-stilling opiate, while the equator might be called a kitchen-range for a Sardanapalus, and the Antilles are but tables loaded with luxuries. The Carribbean Sea is the Kingdom of the Present Moment. The Past and the Future are its Arctic and Antarctic—unthought of except by desperate explorers. Hither are sent invalids, with weakened resolution, to make a pilgrimage with prescription and prudence ! You may see by the book I have just published ("Health-Trip to the Tropics"), with what complete forgetfulness of care or caution I made one of an invalid company for months. Was anybody going to be shut up in a bedroom with such nights out of doors ? Was anybody going to be dull and abstinent with such merry people and a French breakfast or tempting dinner on the table ?

I reached home in July, thoroughly prostrated, and, in the opinion of one or two physicians, a hopeless case. Coughing almost the whole of every night, and raising blood as fast as my system could make it, I had no rest and no strength. I lingered through the summer, and, as the autumn came on, and the winter was to be faced, I sat down and took a fair look at the probabilities. With the details of this troubled council of war, I will not detain you ; but, after an unflinching self-examination, I came to the conclusion that I was myself the careless and indolent neutralizer of the medicines which had failed to cure me—that one wrong morsel of food or one day's partially neglected exercise might put back a week's healing—and that, by slight omissions of attention, occasional breaking of regimen, and much too effeminate habits, I was untrue to the trust which Gray, my friend and physician, had made the ground of his prescriptions. And, to a minutely persevering change in these comparative trifles, I owe, I believe, my restoration to health. There was not a day of the succeeding winter, however cold or wet, in which I did not ride eight or ten miles on horseback. With five or six men, I was, for most of the remaining hours of the day, out of doors, laboring at the roads and clearings of my present home. The cottage of Idlewild was then unbuilt, and the neighboring farmhouse, where we boarded, was, of course, indifferently warmed ; but, by suffering no state of the thermometer to interrupt the morning cold bath, and the previous friction with flesh-brushes, which makes the water as agreeable as in summer, I soon became comparatively independent of the temperature *in* doors, as my horse and axe made me independent of it when *out* of doors. With proper clothing to resist cold or wet, I found (to my surprise) that there was no such thing as disagreeable weather to be felt in the saddle ; and, when a drive in a wagon or carriage would have intolerably irritated my cough, I could be all day in the woods with an axe, my lungs as quiet as a child's.

With all this—and looking like the ruddiest specimen of health in the country around about—I am still (you will be comforted to hear) troubled occasionally with my sleep-robber of a cough ; and, in Boston, the other day, on breathing that essence of pepper and icicles which they call there "East Wind," I was seized with the old hemorrhage of the lungs and bled myself weak again. But I rallied immediately on returning to this Highland air, and am well once more—as well, that is to say, as is consistent with desirable nervous susceptibility. The kiss of the delicious South Wind of to-day (November 30), would be half lost upon the cheek of perfect health.

I fear I cannot sufficiently convey to you my sense of the importance of *a horse*, to an invalid. In my well-weighed opinion, ten miles a day in the saddle would cure more desperate cases (particularly of consumption), than all the changes of climate and all the medicines in the world. It is vigorous exercise without fatigue. The peculiar motion effectually prevents all irritation of cold air to the lungs, on the wintriest day. The torpid liver and other internal organs are more shaken up and vivified by the trot of a mile than by a week of feeble walking. The horse (and you should own and love him) is company enough, and not too much. Your spirits are irresistibly enlivened by the change of movement and the control of the animal. Your sense of strength and activity (in which lies half the self-confidence as to getting well, which the Doctors think so important) is plus one horse, with the difference from walking. As to pulling upon the forces of the spine and consequently upon the brain, it is recommended by the best English physicians as much the preferable exercise for men of intellectual pursuits. And, last (I think, not least), the lungs of both body and soul are expanded by the daily consciousness of inhabiting a large space—by having an eagle's range rather than a snail's—by living a life which occupies ten miles square of the earth's surface, rather than that "half mile" which you speak of as the extent of your daily walk. The cost is trifling. At this particular season, when horses are beginning, as they say at the livery stables, to "eat their heads off," you may buy the best you can want for fifty dollars, and his feed costs thirty cents a day. As the horse and the Doctor are seldom necessities of one and the same man, you may rather find it an economy—apothecary and all.

In that "majority" I have spoken of above, there are (as in all majorities), some voters of not much consequence individually, but still worth keeping an eye upon. Briefly to name one or two :—There are so few invalids who are invariably and conscienciously *untemptable* by those deadly domestic enemies, *sweetmeats, pastry* and *gravies*, that the usual civilities at a meal, are very like being politely assisted to the grave. The care and nurture of the *skin* is a matter worth some study ; for it is capable not only of being negatively healthy, but positively luxurious in its action and sensations—as every well-groomed horse knows better than most men. The American *liver* has a hard struggle against the greasy cookery of our happy country. The impoverished *blood* of the invalid sometimes requires that "glass of wine for the stomach's sake" recommended by the Apostle. Just *sleep* enough and just clothing enough, are important adjustments, requiring more thought and care than are usually given to them. For a little philosophy in your habitual *posture* as you sit in your chair, your *lungs* would be very much obliged to you. An analysis of the *air* we live and sleep in would be well worth looking into occasionally. And there are two things that turn sour in a man, without constant and sufficient occupation upon something besides the domestic circle—the *temper* and the *ambition.*

Thus much, of my reply to our clerical fellow-sufferer may interest you, dear invalid reader. Of the medicine of "Out doors at Idlewild"—the mingled salubrity of the climate of mountain and river around us—I should have said more to one un-anchored in a home and a parish. From one who writes so frankly and sensibly as he, we must hope to hear again, however, and with another opportunity, I may again ask for invalid indulgence, and return to the theme.

LETTER XXXVIII.

Summer in December—Flippertigibbet—Idleness—Annual Quarrelsomeness of Dogs—Pig-influence—Home without a Hog, &c., &c.

December 17, 1853.

How sweet is this unexpected smile from the Summer that we thought had forgotten us ! December, coming in, was more like August looking back over her shoulder. The pines (with their charming way of growing more fragrant, the more warmly they are loved by the sun) are as June-like in their breathings as in their looks. No ! Summer itself was not more out-doors-y than these first five days of winter. And we are so helped in the enjoyment of these delightful irregularities of Nature, by the evergreen woods which make the leaf-fall scarce noticeable at Idlewild. My children are playing under the hemlocks. Flat on the fir-tassels in the shed, lies their companion, Flippertigibbet, a smooth-haired terrier, who, on some days of September, looked for the sunniest corner of the portico ; the birds are about ; wasps and flies active and plenty ; my mare quite in a foam as she stands at the stable door, just unsaddled after an easy gallop home from the hills. One would not tire of such a day as this, to be alone with it from morning till night ; though there are few days, as there are few people, that one does not see too much of, without intervals of books or occupation. Blessed is idleness—for to-day !

* * * * * *

In my daily rides, of late, I had thought my neighbors' dogs rather more filibusterous than usual, and was wondering whether it was owing to the frost-sieve which I was allowing kind Dame Nature to spread protectingly over my upper lip, when a friend gave me the key to their excitability. This is the hog-killing season ; and it appears, that with the scent of blood in the air, the farmers' dogs become annually furious. They bark at all comers, even those with whom they are well acquainted, and, in their assaults upon the passers-by, they quite forget their usual polite distinction between beggars and gentlemen. Pig influence, even after death, is thus hostile to good manners. One cannot "kill his own pork," and have also a well-behaved dog. And I must own that I am pleased with discovering a new reproach to the animal—for it is one of the obstinacies about which I am most reasoned with, by my household advisers, that I cannot consent to keep a pig. "There's an unrighteous amount of swill wasted," as my man eloquently expresses himself—twenty dollars a year in good sweet pork that you know all about." But, satisfactory as it may be to eat pork with which one has been previously acquainted in the shape of swill, my abhorrence outweighs both the economy and the pleasure. If it were nothing else, the *voice* of the brute is doom enough for him. ("Oft in the stilly night," etc.) And as one must remember, daily, every creature of which one is bound, as the master of a home, to be mercifully mindful, I will have a home without a pig—if my own taste and my dog's better manners are arguments that continue to prevail.

LETTER XXXIX.

Visit to Seven Lakes and Natural Bridge—Torrey the Blacksmith—Sunday in Nature—My Companion's Hobby—Hollett the Quaker—Morning Sensations—Jonny Kronk's and its Cemetery—Mammoth Snapping-Turtle—Iron Mine, &c., &c.

December 12, 1853.

WITH my friend Torrey, the village blacksmith, I made, yesterday (December 11th), a mountain pilgrimage of twenty-five labyrinthian miles—first, to stand on one of the peaks of our tangled Alps, from which *seven lakes* are visible ; second, to visit a remarkable *natural bridge*, under which rushes the torrent which fills one of these Alpine lakes ; and, third, to pass the Sabbath (properly and reverently, I felt) in God's open temple, the sky-ceiling of which was supported around us by clusters of mountain-tops, while the floor and area were filled, for this day, with a glow of autumnal light so breathless, and so fragrantly, and warmly luminous, that it seemed like Nature's own higher worship—a service in the outer dome superseding, or uniting, around one grand altar, the devotional light and incense of the lesser chapels of man's building. If I do not record the more hallowed observance, amid the details of the day's history—where it was, that the heart knelt and the prayer arose, where was heard the anthem, and where shone the face of God—it is not that the day was unblest with these breaks in the passing of its hours. It would be hard to be wholly undevout among mountains that seem standing hushed in the presence of their Maker. Yet the cattle graze and the brooks run, and we count the herd, and see the sparkle of the water, with the awe at the heart uninterrupted.

The day's interest for my fellow-horseman and myself was not precisely the same, though he was, very likely, the greater enthusiast of the two. His mania, as he hammers away at his anvil in the village, is to discourse to his customers of the treasures of ore and minerals in the mountains near by ; but it was by one or two of his little *side-mentions* of what was to be seen in these same wild fastnesses, that my curiosity had become more especially enamored. It was a week ago that he was sharpening my mare's shoes for the coming frosts—his bright little smutty-nosed child, of three years of age, mounted on the ash-heap of the forge, and admiring the intermittent blast of her father's big bellows on the fire, and myself seated on the joist of his ox-frame, and admiring the equally mysterious blasts of his learned eloquence upon hematites and pyrites—when I proposed to him that he should mount my other bay mare, if the next Sunday should chance to be pleasant, and go and show me the great iron mine he talked of, where General Washington got the ore for the chain of the chevaux-de-frise across the Hudson. Not that I cared much to see the red earth and the holes in the ground, though the mine is still worked ; but, in the circuit to reach this locality (called the Forest of Dean), we should follow a pass through a cluster of mountain-tops, where the ponds were like milk-pans on different shelves—a score of lifted-up lakes one above another, two to five miles in circumference, and scarce a mile of distance between them, full of fish, and fed by unfailing springs of bright clear water, though at an elevation of two or three thousand feet above the Hudson. These thunder-shower tanks, so beautifully shelved among the clouds, I wanted to see. Torrey's friend, Hollett, a Quaker woodsman, whose oxen he sometimes shod, lived under one of the mountains, from the top of which you could see seven of them. And Hollett was an intelligent man, who had quite a collection of the minerals he had gathered round about, nicely arranged in his farm-house entry. And just below his house was the wonderful natural bridge, through the dark cavern of which passed the foaming outlet creek, which led the water into Popolo Pond from the pond above. It would be the full of the moon, and, by starting at sunrise, if the weather should be fine, we might visit the mines and all the rest of it, and get back somewhere in the early hours of the moonlight. I quite felt the sparks fly from my own anticipations, when my friend's hammer came down on the red-hot shoe, with his promise to go.

Probably even the city reader remembers with what almost summer softness and loveliness this Sunday came. The weather chronicle of the *Tribune* (December 12th), says of it :—"Yesterday was one of the most delightful winter Sundays New-York has ever enjoyed, the day without a cloud, and the sun in all the glory of June." As I opened my door with eagerly expanding lungs in the early morning, I could not help rejoicing in the procession which I seemed to be letting in—first, my friend Torrey, with his long surtout and his broad-rimmed hat ; behind him the magnificent hemlock and cedar which shade my threshold ; straight behind these, the lofty brow of the towering Storm-King ; and the radiated head of the god of day goldenly and gloriously bringing up the rear—each seen over the other's shoulder, and the blacksmith, with his fine intellect and immortal spirit, the fitting leader of the Five. And, by the way, I shall not fairly have introduced my friend to the reader, without mentioning that his tall spare frame is surmounted with a head that would be a sculptor's ideal of a Cicero—features classically correct, and the bald front Senatorially ample in its lift and development. Even through the red shirt and the soot of the shop, any observing traveller, chancing in, to have a shoe set to his horse, would feel the dignity of mind un-pedestalled. So have small neighborhoods their private Cicero sometimes !—and, to do our village justice, I think we value ours at the forge, as much as Rome hers at the Forum.

We had reached the brow of the mountain-range immediately overhanging our village, when the sun was a little more than an hour high ; and, after a few minutes' halt to breathe our horses and take a parting look at the glorious Highland vase of the Hudson (to which Newburg and Fishkill looked like the glittering handles), we turned towards our State's great warehouse of mountains to spare, the twenty-mile wilderness of peaks between the Hudson and the Ramapo. Our first descent along the Southern ribs of the Storm-King (after thus climbing over his majesty's spine), follows, for a little way, the stream which ends in the picturesque water-slide below Cozzens's, so familiar to the summer travellers on the river ; but, curving short to the right at "Johnny Kronk's," we turned our backs upon West Point, and pursued the loveliest of valleys along the western shore of Long Pond—water and woods entrancingly asleep, and the sunshine full of Sabbath balminess and beauty. How lovely this "weather" for everybody may be ! It is all "weather"—as it is all "words from the dictionary"—yet some words and some weather are in poems.

But (to retrace a step) I did not pass "Johnny Kronk's," without preaching a little sermon at the promiscuousness of a cow-yard and grave-yard all in one—a score of marble tombstones standing in the enclosure of the back of the house, and the cows and pigs rubbing their itching skins against the unresisting epitaphs ! Kronk is dead, and buried here, himself ; but, in his lifetime his house, now occupied by a tenant, was the mountain centre of neighborhood as a tavern, and its back-yard (oddly enough, where there is so much spare room) is the mountain cemetery. His children may throw slops from the kitchen window upon the old man's breast ; and his friends lie around him,—as comfortable, perhaps, under potato-peelings and broken crockery, for the present, as other people under the sod ; but, they are to "rise from the dead," and should lie, at least, in a clean place. Amen.

Long Pond meadow, which we followed, after turning at Johnny Kronk's, is a kind of *entresol*—a half-story valley, between the lower story of the West Point level and the upper stories of the mountains beyond. It is famous (the Pond) for one remarkable entresol lodger, the only one of his kind in the country about, and an object of terror to the swimmers and fishermen—a *mammoth snapping-turtle*, whose head, by the general consent of all who have seen him, is "as large as your double-fist." He gives somebody a start, about twice or three times a year ; but, as the pond is two miles long, and its abundance of perch and pickerel may be caught off any rock or log, he is not fallen in with, for the rest of the time, and probably gains, in mystery and dignity, by the unfamiliar seclusion. How he came here, no one knows. Weir the artist, who lives only five or six miles off, should come up and paint his portrait, if only for the probability that it is the metempsychose of some political party out of power. "The snapping-turtle" (says Natural History) "is very tenacious of life, and will move, weeks after being deprived of the head ; and this last will continue to bite, long after it is severed from the body." Come, Weir ! Should not the portrait of this typical patriarch of the "Outs" and the way they act, be painted and hung up at Washington ?

Our route along the Pond, lay between two ranges of hills ; and, as all American mountains range from North to South, while all European mountains range from East to West, we duly felt the republican groove that we were following in the southerly course of the valley. The earth soon began to be reddish in spots, and my enthusiastic friend grew eloquent in pointing out the dips of the strata of rock, and the mineral indications of the iron mines we were approaching. Somewhere about eleven o'clock we tied our horses to the cedar-trees of the unfenced wild, and I followed the scientific blacksmith into the caves, and around among the pick-axes and windlasses, blasting-tools and Irishmen, all idle with Sunday and sunshine. I was interested in the spot historically. The sloops that anchor off Idlewild bring up occasionally a link of the big chain of the chevaux-de-frise thrown across the Hudson in revolutionary times, for which this mine furnished the ore ; though, if Washington and Putnam had been as sharp geologists as my friend, they would have found the ore close by the forge on the Moodna, where it was worked, in a mine now yielding plentifully—saving thus the long track of horseback-transportation over the mountains. So we travel far, sometimes, for the ore of happiness that we might have found nearer home—a moral, I think, we may venture upon, with less risk of irrelevancy, in the story of Sabbath day.

LETTER XL.

Many-Lake Alps and their Woodsmen—Highland Life—Contrast between it and New York, only three Hours' Distance—The Difficulty—Natural Bridge—Driven on the Rocks—Hollett's House, and our Ascent to the Peak—Seven Lakes—Quaker and Panther Meeting in the Woods, &c., &c.

December 31, 1853.

[DESCRIPTION CONTINUED FROM LAST LETTER.]

THE inhabitants of these Many-Lake Alps are principally woodsmen. They farm but little, even where they have strips of meadow on the water-courses which traverse their land. With the state of their mountain-roads, they prefer crops to which customers help themselves, or which can both grow and find legs to walk to market—cattle to graze, sheep to browse, and colts to board (at pasture), for a dollar a month. It is not uncommon to let horses run wild through the winter, and they thrive very well upon the mosses of the rocks and the bark of the sapling elms. The sapling hickories, from being so saleable as hoop-poles, are jocularly called "the mountain-wheat." Perhaps the stranger is most astonished at the tracks over which these people drive their teams, with a cord of wood at a load. A rock of the size of a nail-keg or a flour-barrel is no obstruction to a wheel. The wagons are so put together as to work pliably like timber baskets—though, how their horses' legs and shoulders stand the jerking and the violent and perpetual twisting, I could less easily understand. At five dollars an acre, the average freehold price of the land in this region, and, with the four dollars which they promptly get for the cord of wood, which it is an easy day's work to draw to West Point or Fort Montgomery (their two nearest villages), a mountain farm is soon paid for, even without stock-grazing. The larger wood renews itself every twenty years, and it is very much bettered, meantime, by the constant thinnings of the prolific and profitable hoop-saplings. There are various incidentals by which the children can turn a penny ; such as cranberries, hickory nuts, chestnuts, black-walnuts, and wild-cherries ; and, as we seemed to start up partridges everywhere in riding along, and wild rabbits are "as plenty as blackberries," there can be no lack of good feeding here abouts—to say nothing of the lakes full of perch and pickerel within sound of every man's dinner-horn.

And, now (to digress a moment), will the reader please take the above statistically true picture of a land of easy livelihood and romantic beauty, and place it alongside of the harrowing descriptions of hunger and lack of employment among the emigrants and laborers, given us daily by the newspapers of a city distant but three hours by steamboat or railroad ? The difficulty is not in an impassable gulf of "no money to make a beginning." All through this region, throughout the year, it is next to impossible to get "hands" enough (for the iron mines, clearing, and other labor) at a dollar a day—an easy opening for an industrious man to lay up money ; while, once known enough to be trusted, he could readily get trusted for the necessary land and implements to make a beginning. But no—there are two other difficulties. It is too lonely for the Irishman. And neither the Irishman nor the German can be his own wheelwright, carpenter, blacksmith, doctor, cobbler, tailor and schoolmaster—as the Yankee can, and is. The *lack of society* in the mountains, and the *lack of American omni-'cute-ness* in the settler, are the two difficulties. With the welcome given to my companion (at whose forge, of course, every man for twenty miles around had looked in), I saw something of the home of one of the Yankee mountain-farmers, on our route. Just inside the barn-yard, through which we entered, stood the ox-frame where he shoes his own oxen. A new wood-wagon stood near by, just finished by his boys—one specimen of the many kinds of "jobs" that they can do. The entry was ornamented with a set of narrow shelves, upon which were arranged specimens of all the minerals of the mountains round about. A most plentiful dinner, to which we were cordially invited, smoked on the table. In conversation, dress, kind and intelligent politeness, and personal health and bearing, this farmer's grown-up family—products of this spot of his own earning—were fine specimens of the human race. I asked the hale and vigorous father, whether he ever found it lonely. "Oh," he said, "we don't care to be any more crowded with neighbors."

But, I have a little anticipated the story of our route.

We reached the natural bridge a little before noon ; and here my voracious hunger (with four hours on horseback) got the upper hand of my romantic curiosity. There stood the bridge, it was true—but short of it, lay a mossy rock shaped like a luxurious sofa, upon which might be spread, between the blacksmith's reclining figure and my own, the various sandwiches, etc., which had been prepared in case of meeting with an appetite hereabouts—and I proposed to let the bridge stand, till we could get something under our collapsing enthusiasm. Torrey objected. The natural bridge is one of the neglectednesses of the neighborhood about which he habitually discourses, and his bottled up eloquence was just ready to pop cork—and, besides (as I discovered afterwards), he expected a better dinner half way up the mountain beyond. But I carried my point, being his visiting guest for the day ; and, with the sunshine of a genial noon of mid-December for a table-cloth, we spread our repast. It seemed to me I had never in my life before eaten with such an appetite. The picturesque scenery and hallowed stillness around us feasted the eyes and heart at the same time. My "grace after meat" was a devout recognition of the exceeding beauty of that winter afternoon, as well as vivid thanks to God for a full use of the senses given to enjoy it.

The natural bridge is a massive porch, covering the last stair of a staircase by which a cascading stream descends into a mountain lake. Three lovely things so close together, as that leaping cascade, that singular archway, and the lake below, could hardly be found, even in the composition of a landscape painter. The long sheet of water narrows to this point, like a receding aisle ending at a glittering altar-step, and far down is a little fairy island standing out from the shore—the garden of wild-flowers, perhaps, to which the descending stream has its errand. What Naiad, of name as yet by poet unuttered, comes down those bright steps through the hemlock grove, and, laying off her foaming mantle under the rocky porch, glides silently along the smooth floor of the lake ? Here is a poem in the mountains—wanting only its echo inked over.

Torrey once sent a friend to see this bridge, and he rode across it without suspecting it was under him, though he might seat his country congregation (our friend was a clergyman) under shelter of the rock. It is part of the common horse-path around the head of the lake. There is no daylight to be seen under it, however. The stream, on the upper side, dashes into a dark cave and is lost to sight ; and it comes out of another dark cave on the lower side, the two caves being separated by a partition of solid rock, under the deep-down foundations of which the water finds its invisible way. The well, across which this partition rock extends, is open on the side next the lake, and has been plummeted to the depth of sixty feet. It is always kept full by springs, even when the cascade dries up with summer-heats—a reservoir of cool and pure water, ready made for the happy scenery-lover who will one day make his home upon this prettiest cottage-site in the world. I hope to stand upon the bridge and look down the lake to that fair island, in June, when the lake itself is islanded in leaves.

My friend moused about the dark corners of the cave, and pulled out various minerals which would wear most scientific holes in a horseman's pocket. I spent more time in praying that the woodman's axe might spare the tall hemlocks on the stream above. After strolling around till I had got the bridge well learned among my lessons by heart, we remounted and pursued our way up the mountain, arriving soon at the hospitable house of Friend Hollett, the Quaker woodsman-farmer already spoken of. Here all looked like plenty, vigor, self-reliance, and independence of all ordinary usages that were not convenient. A dinner (for which we had just spoiled our appetite) smoked on the table ; but Torrey sat down, while our horses were being fed in the stable, to have a chat with his friends in the house. The shelves of minerals interested me. They showed the self-cultivated intelligence of the hard-working old man. He settled down there between thirty and forty years ago, when first married, taking the land on credit and owning little besides his axe, and here he is, as healthy and active now as he was then, a grown-up family of well-educated sons and daughters around him, and the three hundred wild acres, of which he has gradually become the independent master, converted by his industry into a fine mountain farm, covered with stock, and amply sufficing for the employment and the wants of his tall and strong children. Amore cheerful, bright, healthy, and hearty home could not be found in the world. Such are our country's best of citizens, and happiest of men, I think.

Of the hardest part of our day's doings—the ascent the two mountain-peaks on foot—I have not left myself room to say much. It was the part of the day's exercise that tried my new lease of health most severely ; for I have scarce taken a long walk for a year, without a horse under me to do the walking, and it seems a short allowance to have only two legs and those my own. But I panted along, after the better wind of tough Farmer Hollett and the blacksmith, and we accomplished our second ascent, to the highest peak, somewhere about an hour before sundown. It was a table summit of platform rock, covered with crisp moss which the Indians boil and can subsist upon in winter, and partly shaded with dwarf hemlocks and hickories. The rifts in the rock, and the square-angle shape of the huge fragments, look as if designed to accommodate hermits ; for there were scores of cottages with three solid sides ready built around a floor of stone—carpeted with moss—nothing wanting but a roof and a door.

With the autumnal haze in the atmosphere, we could only see *five* of the "Seven Lakes" usually visible from the summit. But the *difference of level*, between these beautiful sheets of water laying around us, was startlingly novel as an effect in so wild a landscape. There were two, particularly, into either of which it looked as if we might almost toss a pebble—one, *fifty* feet below us on the *right* hand of the peak where we stood, and another, *three or four hundred* feet below us on the *left*—like two silver balance-scales, of which one had sunk into the valley and the other had mounted to the sky. These lofty cloud tanks are from two to four miles in circumference, and each one seems formed into a cup by four mountains—vases with scalloped rims—and their edges and steep sides looked to be of unbroken foliage and wildness. What stops for summer haunts ! To think, that for the price of a small house in a brick block in New York—say for the ten thousand dollars which a man pays for a barely respectable number in a street—he might here build a cottage and own a mountain and a lake for its belongings !

We had left our horses tied in the woods, and it was important to get to something like a "critter-path," at least, before dusk ; so we hurried our descent, Farmer Hollett accompanying us, with his active feet, as far as the ridge from which water would run down hill towards the Hudson. On the way he showed us a spot where he once met a panther and went at him with a hickory stick—all the weapon he had—the "painter" (as he called him) frightened out of the encounter by the halloo and the fury of his first onslaught. These dangerous animals are no more found in this region, however.

Parting from the vigorous and bright-spirited old mountaineer with real regret, we started for home in the gathering twilight—eight or nine miles of hill and valley stretching away before us. In the glow of the full moon which was soon flooding our way with silver light, it was a beautiful ride, even with the scenery of leafless winter. The road soon grew smooth, our horses were fast, and my friend was most instructively eloquent upon local history as we passed along. I left him at his shop-door, somewhere about eight o'clock, and, hitching his bridle over my arm, I trotted home with my led horse—three good appetites, at least, entering my own moonlit gate together.

LETTER XLI.

Degrees of Horseback Acquaintance with a Road—Slaughter-House "Round by Headley's"—Geese and their Envy—Goose-Descent upon Unexpected Ice, &c., &c.

January 7, 1854.

I FIND there are three degrees of horseback acquaintance with a road. First, you are charmed with its novelty, and see only its beauties. Second, the novelty wears off, and you see its unsightly spots, and tire of it. Third, you become habituated to it, as the place for exhilarating exercise or for indulgent reverie with slacked bridle, and then it is a friend—the spare friend of undiscussed confidences that one needs—listening always, blaming never. Considering how much the roads are talked of, both as to preference and comfort, by all kinds of people living in the country—how much more than the brooks and rivers—it is a little strange that it has never been thought poetical to *name them*. I could be very tenderly fanciful about one or two that I know—infallible dis-irksome-izers, within a gallop of Idlewild—but that the world, growing less romantic, might prefer to know them by the mile-posts.

But the world is, at least, ready for a fact ; and I may tell, statistically, how one of my road-nymphs is lately desecrated beyond all hope of poetical naming. "Round by Headley's" we commonly call it—an upper road, along the bank of the Hudson, on which our friend the hero-grapher built his beautiful house, and the most charming of carriage-drives, avenued with cedars and country seats for miles. As the finest rural outlet from the handsomest streets of Newburgh, we drove over it often, particularly with friends and strangers, whom we wished to impress agreeably with the scenery between Idlewild and there. The house, consecrated by having once been the house of Durand, the artist, is at the Quassaic bend of the road. But Newburgh has a new prosperity. With the trick of milder winters that the world has got into, it has been found necessary that the Ohio pork should die nearer to market. To the Newburgh end of the railroad, therefore, it comes with legs down instead of up, and the hundreds of thousands of postponed Ohio deaths take place at this point of embarkation for the city. While the pig's *post mortem* road (down the throats of New Yorkers) is thus made sweeter, no doubt ; the road I speak of, on the heights above the Hudson, is made almost impassable, at one point, by a different stage of the same sweetener in progress. Just out of reach of the suburbs, on an ascent cresting a romantic curve, winding away towards the hills, where I oftenest drew rein to show the stranger a landscape unsurpassed—close to the road and as inevitable as a toll-gate has arisen one of the fruition-halls where the pig-deferred passes into the dignity of pork, a slaughter-house as long as Westminister Abbey, and filled with a wilderness of busy butchers. Oh, the obituary notice of these deaths, which one gets, first and last, on the publishing winds ! It has stopped off that upper road, for me. And, indeed, for the other end of the pig-Styx there launched upon—the resurrection as a roasted chine, glorified in gravy—I must confess a prejudice not lessened by the knowledge of these last moments.

Dryden speaks of the copyright a man has in his own nose ; and there seems an invasion of such copyright, certainly, in a slaughter-house, which waylays and takes, uninvited, possession of the traveller's sense of smell for a mile. Should there not be some more definite legislation on this subject ? A law prescribing a distance, for this class of buildings, from any public highway, would be grateful, at least, to the nostrils of Newburgh, with its increasing business in Ohio disembowellings. It might be advocated, indeed, as a protection to life, from the terror which often seizes a horse in approaching the vitiated atmosphere. My own team requires some persuasion of whip and voice to go past the golgotha I speak of.

This law seems a necessity for the *nose*. But I suppose one may venture to name a law that would be a luxury to the *ear*—in the way of promoting agreeableness in the road one daily rides over. A statute providing that *every adult goose should be muzzled*, when turned loose on the public highway, would remove, for me, a very considerable nuisance. There are few farmers who have not their flock of geese. It is an animal tolerant enough of mediocrity—a slow pace, as you pass along, provoking no very hostile notice. But the high stepping and fast trotting of my blood mare is distasteful, as far as my experience goes, to all geese, far and near ; and, from every pond and puddle that I pass, comes out their chorus of hostility. With music from almost everything else—cow-bells, horse-neighings, snow-bird twitterings, hoof-patterings, mill-streams, ice-crackings, flails, wind-sighings, and telegraph-wires—the discord, the only one discord in the wayfarer's anthem, as I hear it on the road, is from the screeching throttle of the goose. As it is not only unmusical but unmeaning—a silly rage provoked by nothing—we might reasonably muzzle geese, by a law requiring some show of sense or reason in any utterance thrust upon the public.

But I had a laugh at a goose, yesterday—with a lesson in it too. Coming home, towards evening, with my wagon-full of children, the air over our head was suddenly darkened by the wings of a very big bird—my neighbor's fattest waddler, who, chased by a dog, had concluded to up feathers, fly over the barn, and take refuge in the ever-reliable and long-tried bosom of the river. But it was the day after the first sharp frost, and the stream, though as clear as crystal, was of icy smoothness, and as impenetrable as a rock. Down came the goose, with full faith in it for long-tried water—and the way she slid over, and brought up at the frozen bank opposite, after that heavy bump upon her astonished egg-basket, was boundlessly delightful to the children. Besides the instruction in it, as to a winter-trial of summer friends, it was a comfort, with a pleasant spite in it, to have one good laugh at a goose that waddles and screams after me every time I trot past my neighbor's barn-yard.

LETTER XLII.

Pool of Bethesda above the Highlands—Climate of Highland Terrace—Late Snows—Christmas, and Dressing of Church—Poem on Farmers' Christmas Preparations—Black Peter—Snake Love of Solitude, &c., &c.

January 14, 185[4].

SAMUEL B. RUGGLES, our State's torch-bearer and pre-historian of Internal Improvement, has mapped down the majestic river-pass through the Highlands as the Gate from the Western Lakes to New York and the Atlantic. To our American Palestine, New York is the Jerusalem ; and, outside this its gate, physicians have now located a "pool of Bethesda" (the Bay above the Highlands), such as blessed the outside of the gate to Jerusalem of old. With the healing that is found upon the beautiful shores of this spread of the river, it might be called BETHESDA BAY, with Scriptural propriety ; though the angel that goes down and troubles the healing pool is the morning and evening breeze ; and the "first stepping in," after the "moving of the water," is a correspondingly enlarged cure for many instead of one.

Writing from this Bethesda, I feel bound to chronicle for invalids its allotments of climate ; and, by comparison with the reports of the weather in Boston and New York, there seems to be a protection to our Highland Terrace in the arm of mountain-range that encircles us. There was sleighing in Boston at Christmas-time, and a snow-storm in New York ; and yet, here, the temperate and bright autumnal weather (without a flake of snow) lasted till the evening of December the 28th—the river navigable till then, and our roads as hard and dusty as in summer. For the invalid who wishes to ride, and clings to the liberty of open air, this is a blessed belating of the coming of imprisoning winter. Of the twenty human souls who form the homestead census of Idlewild, none but the two lately born (one in my tenant's cottage and one in my own) would have found it cold idling out of doors, any noon till the third after Christmas.

But, with what bridal apparelling winter came ! The sleigh-bells have rung merrily from the first evening of snow (it is January 3, as I write) ; and, with neither thaw nor high wind, the eider-down cloaks of the evergreen trees in the procession, are scarce disturbed—a six days' wear of white favors, unusual even for Winter's evergreen bridemaids, while the icicle groomsmen of the New Year hang round the church with splendor quite as undiminished.

And the beautiful church within a mile of Idlewild—a most English-rural and tasteful Gothic chapel of stone—was charmingly arrayed in the evergreens of our neighborhood, home as it is of hemlocks and cedars, laurels and ivy. How like the glow of a smile from within the altar—a Redeemer's smile—seems this time-honored brightening of the church at Christmas ! *Esto perpetua !* It is a custom that should be followed by all churches, of all denominations. A simple and admirable poem on the subject, came to me yesterday, and I will insert it here, suggestively and commemoratively as well as admiringly :

THE FARMER'S PREPARATIONS FOR DRESSING A COUNTRY CHURCH WITH EVERGREENS AT CHRISTMAS.

EMANUEL. GOD WITH US.

To work ! to work ! ere rise of moon ;
Lo ! Christmas-tide is coming soon ;
The church needs many a fresh festoon.

'Midst heaps of glossy evergreen,
The farmer's daughter now is seen
With busy hands and dimpled mien.

Here are no palms in victor pride,
But mountain-laurel branching wide,
And dwarfish pine from bleak hillside.

We do not feel of palms the loss :
Come, let us weave a green-leaved Cross,
And write GOD'S name in wild wood-moss.

Come ! write the word "Emanuel,"
And add, "God with us," lettered well,
And arch-wise let it eastward swell.

Wreaths, for the lecturn of the priest,
On each side-wall three rings at least ;
A green star for the rosy East !

Above the panes the Star must shine,
Above the consecrated wine,
And lift all hearts to hopes divine.

Thus shall the farmer's quiet home
A greenhouse of the Lord become,
A fore-court to a heaven-high dome.

The gentleman who sends me this simple and beautiful common-life poem, says only that it was a favorite of one now cold in death, who, last Christmas, assisted in dressing their village church—but, though it reads like verse by George Herbert, I suppose it to be now first published.

The oldest Idlewild-ian passed New-Years' day with us—black Peter, who, years ago, had charge of the farm of which our seventy-acre glen was the wilderness portion, valued only for its wood. The old man has been three times bought and sold as a slave, and I have mentioned him before as famous for the way he was always loved by the children. He is decrepid now, and goes on crutches, and lives alone in his hut under the mountain ; but his memory is good, and he tells me where stood the monarch pines and primeval cedars we would give so much to replace—touching stories, to me, of beauty and stateliness that have here lived their half century and passed away. We muse on the coming round of our turn, when such a wheel of oblivion is brought to view ! A chance thread, like this poor black cripple's admiring remembrance, the only bridge back from the world's easy forgetfulness !

But, while the children spread out their Christmas toys before old Peter on the parlor floor, I stumbled on a scrap of knowledge in his rag-bag of experience. Wondering, that, in my two years' acquaintance with so wild a place as the glen, I had seen but two snakes : he said, snakes were slow to come back after they were once driven away. And sheep drove these away. Not that the sheep were the enemy of the snake, for they never took any notice of one, that he knew of. But a snake must be where he can sleep uninterrupted ; and, put a flock where you please, they will walk over all the ground they can get at—good feed in one corner of the lot making no sort of difference. It's seeing a sheep everywhere, that the snakes don't like.

My servants being colored people, and my daughter's nurse, who has had the care of all her bright eleven years, having been also a slave, Peter was a symposiarch among his social-hearted race for the day. They made much of him. At night they loaded themselves into the double sleigh, to take him home to his hut with company and merry bells—a visit of the sunshine of love to a spot, where (from its being under the north knee of the Storm-King), there are six winter weeks that the sun does not look in at his door. I wish there were more like old Peter. The mixture of unembarrassed self-possession, simplicity, and respectful courtesy, which mark his manners, belong to a class that is fast passing away uncopied.

LETTER XLIII.

Trip of the Family Wagon to Newburgh—The Fashionable Resort—Chapman's Bakery—Aristocracy "setled down"—Newburgh as a Neighbor.

January 22, 185[4].

THE daily trip of the family wagon to Newburgh is the lump of sugar which it requires to make winter seclusion (palatable to *me*, "cold without") palatable to the less whirlsated tastes of children and servants. Ah, the event that it is !—its arrangements and discussions—the spare seats, and who are to have them—time of starting and list of commissions—probabilities of weather and proper cloakings and bonnetings—room for bundles and baskets, and plans for calls by the way ! And, with errands varying in importance, from a skein of silk to a friend expected by the railroad, the charmingly unfailing possibility of a package by Express ! I had never before realized how much there is, if not of necessity, at least of inspiriting variety, in daily *change of scene* for the inmates of a home in the country. City servants, particularly, are kept contented by having a possibility of it, at will. Children's spirits fairly effervesce with it. Parlor and kitchen are furnished by it with mortar for the bricks of daily duties and conversation. It seems unequal allotment for a household, to have all prisoners within home and around it, except the master ; and the master's sparkle of life is very much increased by the *expansion of home-talk for all*—the incidents on the road and the shoppings and sight-seeings, the meetings with friends, and the variations of light and shade upon hill and river. Of course I am not myself the Jehu, on these errand trips. It takes all the memory and management of Bell (my Yankee tenant and lesser-anxiety-man), to discharge the divers responsibilities of such a load of treasures on a pilgrimage of trifles. Even if I had the necessary un-fret-ability and hour-glass recoverableness from exhausting innumerablenesses, however, my lungs cannot stand the inactive exposure of a drive. I am off on horseback, meantime, resting my powers of attention while another animal exercises me. But I get the news of the wagon-trip at the tea-table, and it is all the livelier that we have separate excursions of which to tell the adventures.

Newburgh, our country-town, has twelve thousand inhabitants, and a long thoroughfare of shops, perpetually thronged with the custom of a rural population for twenty miles around. The farmers' wagons fill the street, and the farmers' wives and daughters crowd the sidewalks and counters. Each store has most things that are possible, to sell, and there are three equivalents given for goods—talk, produce and money. The expect-to-be-beat-down-age, in the first charge for an article, is about twenty-five per cent., though, for a regular customer, who spends without this skirmish of 'cuteness, allowance is soon made. Few encounters of sharpness are fought out with more skill and pertinacity, probably, than the purchase of a calico dress to be paid for in eggs or butter. It would interest the inquiring observer to have a bargain for a pocket-comb pending alongside.

But, the most interesting shop of Newburgh would never be found out by the stranger. It is, indeed, curiously contradictory in its looks and its "run of custom." You would go in and out of it, and describe it as a cheap bakery—one of those old-fashioned dingy half-shops, with a long single counter, on the street end of which is a glass-case for tarts and cake, while the remaining extension is covered with fresh loaves, scales and weights, brown paper and gingerbread. It is partly a grocery, too ; and behind you, against the wall, as you stand at the counter, are boxes of herrings, drums of figs, coffee-bags, pea-nuts, starch, soap, lemons, candles and brooms. At the far end, where the bags and barrels are set back to give a foot or two more of space, there stands a cheap old stove, with a rusty funnel running up to the ceiling, and one or two old wooden chairs around it. In all Newburgh there is scarce so shabby an old shop. Yet, in all Orange County there is not an apartment which receives daily such an amount of aristocratic society. With the first settlement of the town, Chapman's Bakery was the stopping-place of the vehicles of the wealthy families of the country around about ; and spite of a modern and spacious confectioner's shop, a little farther on, and larger and more comfortable "stores" of every kind, near by, the descendants of the old-family aristocracy have continued to make the narrow baker's shop their place of gossip and gathering. Towards noon of every pleasant day, winter and summer, the handsomest equipages of the neighborhood begin to assemble along that part of the sidewalk of Newburgh. The gentlemen hand the ladies into the shop, and there, for two or three hours, is the place of rendezvous after the different errands of each, the place to be found by their friends from a distance, and the place to exchange news and gossip away the morning. There are no better horses, more well-appointed turn-outs, or neater coachmen, on any public promenade in the country than are daily to be seen here. The gentlemen who group about the flag-stone step or inside the little glass door, are of high consideration in the city, for their fortunes and family names. The ladies, who lay their costly handkerchiefs down upon the flour-barrels, and sit around the stove in the old whittled chairs, and eat ginger-nuts at the counter, are very fashionable persons, in full promenade toilette. And so crowded is the long shop, between eleven and two, that the boy, who has looked in at the bow-window, and come in for his cent's worth of gingerbread, fairly elbows his way into the "best society" to get at it.

But the curious part of Chapman's Bakery is, that it *suffices for the social want* of a large and wealthy neighborhood. There is no other society. Nothing like a "party" is ever given by any of the rich frequenters of the bakery. Dinner parties (in the common acceptation of the word among people of the same fortune) are unknown. Even calls on each other, at their own houses, are rare. And this is from no intended economy of time or money. They lead lives of ample leisure, and are as liberal and cordial-hearted a set of people as any in the world. But the restless liquid, society, has here been permitted to stand still, and this (the social chemist will be interested to know) is the natural precipitate. The Ducal Cascine at Florence—that centre of the public drive, where all the equipages of the fashionable meet and stand still at a certain hour—is the Chapman's Bakery of the Tuscan court and nobility (only that they differ from the Newburgh aristocracy in wanting balls and suppers besides.) The English exclusives need a Hyde Park for a comparison of equipages, *matinées* for comparison of out-door toilettes, and dinner parties and routs for exchange of ideas and bettering of acquaintances—but all these "first principles" are met and their wants supplied by Chapman's Bakery, at Newburgh. Whether the bubbling champagne of fashionable life all over the world, would, if left long enough to itself, settle down into the same small modicum of fulness of the social glass, is—open to discussion.

One thing should be taken into consideration, perhaps, in all estimates of either the public enterprise or sociality at Newburgh. The town is, in fact, at the end of a long street of New York. Though fifty miles from the city, the railroad runs to and fro constantly, like an omnibus, and a large proportion of the well-off class transact business and have their circle of acquaintance in the city, though their families reside here, for better air, and for fine houses and gardens at less cost. There is *less concentration*, therefore, than is common in towns of the same size—less pride in the public improvements, and less dependence on the society of the place. The core of what would be the society, under ordinary circumstances—the Chapman's bakery of wealthy and well descended families—is without the usual tributary and emulous outer circles. In the handsome streets of comfortable houses and tasteful villas, on the upper side of the town, the residents scarce know each other, and feel no interest in the large estates of the gentlemen of fortune in the neighborhood. The farmers who bring their families in, to trade and shop, are again another public, and the migratory thousands from the city, who throng the Powelton and other boarding-houses in the summer, are still another ; and thus Newburgh has scarcely an identity of its own—the Faubourg St. Germain of Chapman's Bakery excepted.

But all this varied population makes very good shops and a very good sidewalk. To go to Newburgh is, in fact, a digestible meal of daily food for curiosity, compared with the glut and satiety of Broadway. It is four miles from Idlewild, a most convenient distance for just such a variation of solitude in the country—the family wagon which bridges between, being (to the children and servants) our golden link with a world else revolving without us. In my own circuits round, by the mountain-roads, I am apt to come home by the way of Newburgh—my sweating mare cooling her legs with a walk through the streets, two or three times a week, at least—and I confess to its pleasant airing of my gregariousness, at the same time. No, I should not like to have Newburgh farther off, nor nearer—though I pitched my tent without the thought of its propinquity as a neighbor. Like the moon and the stars, it is a much-used addition to our "extent of property," though not charged among the taxes.

LETTER XLIV.

Personal Experience interesting to Invalids—Difficulty as to Horseback Exercise—Advice as to Winter-riding—Economies in Horse-owning—New Idea as to Exposure—Philosophy of Exercise to Scholars, &c., &c.

January 28, 1854.

I HESITATED much before committing recently to print what might be thought but the button-holding story of an invalid—knowing well that the Public cannot properly be troubled with one's personal experience, unless it adds to knowledge upon points of common interest—but, by the extensive copying and comments of the Press, I find that my record of the results of *horseback-exercise in all weathers* was thought noteworthy ; and upon this I can, perhaps, throw a little additional light, by such minuter details of experience as may be valuable for invalid guidance. First, let me give a corroborative letter from one of the readers of this paper :—

> "In the *Home Journal* of 10th instant, I find a letter from 'An Invalid,' with your answer. I am induced to tell my story. I have been on the invalid list for twenty-five years. In October, 1834, by the advice of my physician, I prepared to remove to St. Augustine, Florida. All things were ready—my strength was not sufficient to leave for a few days, A friend had just been elected Sheriff of this county, who offered me a situation where I could spend as much time as I chose on horseback. I accepted the offer. The first six months were spent in great agony ; but I found my strength improving. It is now nineteen years since I commenced the *Horseback* remedy for tubercular consumption. In that time I have travelled on horseback many thousands of miles. I have now my business so arranged that I am compelled to ride sixteen miles each day. I allow no state of the weather to interfere with the ride, as I am always prepared with proper clothing to resist cold or wet. My health is now good ; perhaps no man enjoys better health. My disease was and is tubercular consumption. I have no reason to think that the tubercles in my lungs *will ever be dispersed*, but I *do* know that they can be *kept in a quiescent* state by proper exercise in the open air. With this in view, I shall continue the use of the saddle, in the open air, whilst I have strength to do it."

This is a stronger case than my own, somewhat, but it is the more confirmatory of my impression that the *unceasing jolt* of exercise in the saddle is preventive of any chill to the lungs, from cold or wet, while they profit by the change of air—the spirits at the same time enlivened by rapid motion and the perspiration started and kept up *without effort or fatigue.* That a fast trot of ten or twelve miles will soothe and refresh the lungs, when the ascent up a flight of stairs will irritate and set them to bleeding is a certain fact, which makes the *unfatiguing* nature of saddle-exercise a point of some importance.

But a gentleman, who writes to me from Maryland, mentions a difficulty. He says :

> "I am aware how completely your time must be occupied by writing and reading ; but should you be able to catch a moment of leisure, I shall be obliged to you to let me know what you think the warmest and most protective costume for a horseman in winter. I have a fine Morgan mare which I rarely back on account of *cold toes and shivering legs.* I usually prefer pedestrianizing, though there are seasons of the year when my horse and myself almost form a Centaur."

The old farmer's remedy for "cold toes" on horseback is to hang the feet out of the stirrups for a few minutes—the removal of the pressure, from the sole, letting the blood flow into the extremities more freely. But, as perspiration might be checked, especially when going against the wind, by the slower pace at which one would ride without stirrups, a safer remedy for the invalid would be larger boots and an extra pair of stockings. There should be no scrupulous nicety, in fact, in the "horseman's costume" for a cold day. *Clothes enough,* is the simple prescription. The woollen leggins, such as are worn by the English drover, would be recommendable if they could be bought in this country ; but your heaviest pair of pantaloons, enlarged two inches on each leg by strips let into the two outside seams, and drawn on over those of the usual wear, answers as good, or better purpose. A shoe-stirrup can be bought of Bull the saddler in New York, which shelters the feet from the wind. And there is a short cloak called a "Talma," which you can buy, at present, at the ready-made-clothing stores in New York (a most classical and beautiful garment which cheap Fashion for the Many has chanced to stumble upon), which is exactly suited to the wants of the horseman. The half-sleeve gives the arm play, while it protects it, and the ample but short folds just come to the saddle.

Cold, however, was never a trouble of mine on horseback, even with the thermometer at winter's lowest. The sharp air may have a chance at the lungs, perhaps, in getting mounted and started ; but Dr. Hall's excellent hint to delicate persons going from a hot concert-room into the night-air—"keep the mouth shut, and breathe only through the nostrils"—is an effectual guard for these two or three minutes. After that, the motion gives warmth enough—only there should be no slow riding, and it should not be a horse with a rocking-chair canter or a shambling rack. A fast and even *trot*—of the jolt of which, by rising in the stirrup, you take as much or as little as you please—is the best pace for keeping the whole body warm ; while (an anatomical double-action which the doctors may explain in learned words) it both wakes up the lazy liver and lulls to rest the cough-weary lungs. Oh the blessed let-up—the soothing intermission—the merciful stop-at-last of a fast trot, after a long night with a cough unappeasable ! A triple blessing, indeed—for the rested and braced invalid comes home with a well man's appetite.

There is one other *horse* view of the subject, upon which I may say an instructive word. Pulmonary patients are apt to be poor men—clergymen, students, authors, schoolmasters, bookkeepers—and a daily ride is an expensive prescription. As a friend said to me, "you speak, in your letter to invalids, of a fifty dollar horse fed for thirty cents a day, but no tolerable horse can be bought in the city for less than three times the money, and the 'keep' is five dollars a week."

With city expensiveness in luxuries one cannot very well argue, it is true. The invalid with slender means should, for that and other reasons, go to the country. But there is a burthensome superfluity next door to this burthensome want, in cities, and it seems a pity that the two should not be brought together. The stables of the wealthy are full of horses fretting in the stall for want of exercise. Even those which go out every afternoon for a short drive, would be in better condition and more manageable, if ridden eight or ten miles in the morning. Now, why should not America have its republican liberalization of the courtesies between wealth and intellect ? The clergyman or the poor scholar in Europe feels no scruple of delicacy at borrowing a *book* from the rich man's library. Might we not enlarge the limits of independent reciprocity so that the American clergyman or poor scholar may feel no scruple of delicacy at borrowing a *horse* from the rich man's stable ? There are few intellectual consumptives who have not some friend with this superfluity of cure for consumption. It might easily become an incumbent courtesy, for the owners of fine horses, to inquire whether their clergyman, or the instructor of their children, or some favorite author of their acquaintance, would not be kindly benefited by the spare use of these costly belongings.

My friend's disparagement of my *price* of an invalid's horse ("fifty dollars") prompts me to turn over my experience, and I think I may, perhaps, give a hint or two upon this point, that will be useful to the country-resident portion at least of the un-practical class, at whose needs my remarks are aiming.

As a luxury, ownership in a horse varies with a man's means. At a cost above what he can afford to lose, it becomes a care and an anxiety—the intellectual invalid, of course, having those already overtasked powers of attention, to which any additional trifle to be nervous about is a double evil. With the liability of these domestic favorites to disease and accident, it is, at best, but skittish property. To be only a comfort, it should be a horse that is old and sagacious enough to know what is good for him—a horse not too valuable to lend—a horse that can work in the farmer's team, when, from illness, or absence, or interruption, you cannot exercise him yourself. It need not be a poor horse, with all this. It may be the *remainder of a good horse.* And there is a large number of this class of animals always for sale at low prices—just enough left in them for an invalid's using. With good feed, slight and regular work, and kind care, the overworked creature soon recovers spirit and looks, and though severe usage again would immediately break him down (as the farmer or jockey knows who sells him to you), he will be as lively and handsome in your keeping for years, as one of four times the value, and much less liable than a younger horse to disease or accident. Give one of your shrewd Yankee neighbors the "fifty dollars," tell him exactly how much of a horse you want, and ask him to make the purchase for you.

My own winter-riding has lately been valuably varied by the encouragement to an important freedom as to its *time,* suggested by a chance remark in a medical essay. The day, at its summer length, being much too short for my daylight avocations at Idlewild, and not half long enough in winter, I had found the passing of two or three of its best hours in the saddle (for exercise only, and with such inexorable punctuality in all weathers) a considerable tax. My eyes, which were long ago unfitted for lamp-light work, were, besides, blinded sometimes by the brilliancy of the sunshine on the snow. Winter nights being also less windy than winter days, and the roads frozen harder and drier, I had often wished that night-air were not so emphatically tabooed by the Doctors—this taboo preventing my day from being three hours longer and my ride from being cleaner and less of a battle with gusty winds and dazzling snow. Thus, ready for wisdom, if it should fall in my way, I stumbled upon the following remarks by a medical man, upon air and exercise :

> "Avoiding out-door air for the hour about sunrise or sunset, *there is no danger even to invalids, in exercising in the* NIGHTAIR, *if the exercise be sufficiently vigorous to keep off a feeling of chilliness.* This should be the rule in all forms of out-door exercise, and is an infallible preventive, as far as my experience extends, against taking cold in any and all weathers, provided it be not continued to over-exhaustion or decided fatigue. Such exercise can never give a cold, whether in rain, or sleet, or snow, unless there be some rare peculiarity in the constitution. It is the conduct after exercise which gives the cold—the getting cool too quickly—by standing or sitting still in a draft of air, or at an open window, or in a cold room. The only precaution needed is to *end the exercise in a warm room,* and there remain until rested and no moisture remains on the skin. * * * With the above precaution you need not be afraid of out-door air, NIGHT OR DAY, as long as you are in motion suf-

> ficient to keep off a feeling of chilliness. * * * Confinement to the regulated temperature of a room, in any latitude, is certain death, if persevered in. * * * The great object is, useful, agreeable, profitable employment, in the open air, for several hours every day, *rain or shine, hot or cold* ; and whoever has the determination and energy sufficient to accomplish this, will seldom fail to delight himself and his friends with speedy and permanent results. * * * If working or walking cause actual fatigue, then horseback exercise is the best for both sexes."

The prisoners to the desk, to the study, to the school-room—too busy all *day* to exercise, and afraid of *night*-air upon the lungs—will see a ray of bright comfort in this extract, I am very sure. It is a channel between their Scylla and Charybdis. And there is an incidental advantage and luxury in "air and exercise" the *last thing before sleeping*—it stretches the limbs, and quiets the nerves, and cools the brain, and so performs that *invisible and inward undressing for sleep*, of which the outward undressing is often such a weary incompleteness. There are those, too, who are fatigued through the day with the sight of people, and who need *utter solitude* with their exercise—no lookers-on except the uncatechizing, un-greeting, un-scrutinizing stars. To others, the poetry of this pulse quickened and heart-glowing companionship with beautiful Night—earth and its wintry unsightliness made indistinct, and heaven in its unblemished breadth all brightened—will be balm to the soul, taken in with health for the body. It will be understood, I suppose, that I speak of this only as a *variety* in exercise, to be used with care and discretion. I have supposed an invalid who could saddle his own horse, at starting in an unseasonable hour, and stall and blanket him on his return. And I have supposed a short, quick ride, upon a road familiar to the horse and his rider. To those who *walk*, only, however, for exercise, there are fewer difficulties ; and to such it will be even more a relief to know that there is medicine in night as well as in day.

LETTER XLV.

Snow and its Uses—Winter View of Grounds, as to Improvements—Old Women's Weather-Prophecy—Finding of an Indian God in the Glen—Idlewild a Sanctuary of Deities of the Weather—Name of Moodna, &c., &c.

February 4, 1854.

A LIGHT fall of snow is a wonderful *generalizer*. It does for scenery what the shroud does for the memory of a friend—not only concealing defects, but showing capabilities scarce dreamed of when every trifle was in sight—revealing, to our surprise, sometimes, how near perfection it was, after all, when we were despairing over its little blemishes and irregularities. Those who have "grounds" to improve, should not lose the winter opportunity of seeing them covered with an *uncut snow-sward*. The rough field, the bare rock, the accidental or irregular path does not then prevent the eye from taking in, at a glance, the natural expression of the spot ; while the lawn of unbroken whiteness throws into strong relief every clump of shrubs and every grove and tree—the slopes and curves also showing of what combinations they are capable, and so suggesting improvements necessary for the desired *one-ness of effect*. To "buy a place," midwinter, after a light snow, is a better time than midsummer. The leafless trees reveal to you, then, what views may be cut through. You see what the foliage happily hides, and where it hides too much. And then—(like the more comfortable confidence after seeing a sweetheart in dishabille)—the sight of your landscape-passion in winter makes you feel that you know what you are loving, in the after-pride and glory of summer.

"The winter weather," say the old women, "will be mostly woven according to the threads of the first three days." And thus far it has proved true. The first of December was fair and mild—so was the general weather of December, winter's first month. The second was mild and changeable—so has been January, the second month, thus far. The third was bitterly cold—and so will be February, the third month, if the oracle hold good. We have had but three or four days of sleighing, up to the present one day's blanketing of the fields (January 22), and, for six or eight days near the middle of this wintriest month, the hills and meadows have slept quite bare in autumnal sunshine. I scarce know whether to wish for more snow or less. It perceptibly enlivens the spirits of country-people—partly from the exhilarating atmosphere it brings, and partly from the variety that it makes, in vehicles and occupations—but they rejoice as much when it goes as when it comes. The air of our climate, complained of as too dry, is agreeably moistened by it, the snow air being commonly said to be pleasant to the skin. The worst inconvenience of snow, to me, is the ball that it makes in the horse's foot, and the consequent irregularity and uncertainty of his gait under the saddle. "Grease the frog," say the farmers, but that lasts only a mile or two. With fast riding it soon sponges out, and then, with a ball in the foot and a man's weight on the back, the most active horse runs great risk of a sprained ankle. Without the refuge of blue spectacles, the dazzling glare of the sunshine on snow would make prisoners of the weak-eyed classes in sleighing-time, though Nature has perhaps provided against this evil by making it short of stay, or changeable in color where it is perpetual. It grows red in the Alps. "*Ipsa nix vetustate rubescit.*"*

We were fortunate enough to identify, yesterday, a mysterious inmate of Idlewild who has been the subject of a great deal of discussion. In taking advantage of a drought to clear away the loose rocks and enlarge the small lake in the depths of the glen, summer before last, the ox-drag turned up something which immediately attracted the curiosity of the men. One of them lifted it up to me, as I stood on the bank—to all appearance, a spirited bust, carved in gray rock. Whatever it was, I had seen many worse likenesses of mankind, and there had evidently been great pains in the cutting of it. The crown of the head was broken off, but the lower part of the face remained, and the neck and shoulders, and the fold of the drapery across the breast, were still complete. The design was that of a head turned aside with a look of aroused attention ; and to me it seemed exceedingly expressive and well conceived. It has since been our principal investment of Barnum, but among those who were called upon to wonder at it, of course there were unbelievers. Some said it was cut for a fishing anchor to a canoe—some that it was a two-handed pestle to grind corn. A stone tomahawk and other Indian relics had been found in the glen, however, and, with these, it was carefully preserved as an aboriginal antiquity. Placed on the mantel-piece in the library, between Petrarch and Tasso, it was treated with respect, at least, till our friends and neighbors had all given an opinion upon it. Latterly, I grieve to say, it has been used to crown the upper shelf of the hat-stand in the hall ; and, being a little smaller than the heads of most of our visiters, the spirited chin has daily been the dropping limit of hat-rims—apparently a disrespectful likeness of a gentleman with his tile smashed over his nose and eyes.

* Saussure observed red snow on the Bevern in 1760, and on St. Bernard in 1788. Ramond met with it in the Pyrenees, Captain Ross in Baffin's Bay ; Parry, Franklin and Scoresby collected it in still higher northern latitudes.

But, yesterday, our friend Copway, the Ojibbeway chief, took us in his way on a lecturing excursion through the neighborhood ; and, in passing through the hall, he stopped, surprised, before the nameless bust on the hat-stand. "What !" he said, "you have an Indian god, there !" He looked at it a little closer, as I told him how we had found it. "It is the god of The Winds and the Birds"—he continued—"Mesa-ba-wa-sin." He then explained to us that there were five Indian deities :—the gods of War, of Hunting, of Medicine, of Fishes, and of Winds and Birds. They had their particular shapes ; and their images carved in stone, were usually hidden away in the most secluded places where offerings could be carried to them and securely left ; and it was easy to understand, be thought, why one should have been found in so wild a fastness as our almost inaccessible glen. And so was solved the mystery of Idlewild ! It was the sanctuary of the god of the Winds and the Birds—the nearest mountain (which I had instinctively named the Storm King) being his Vicegerent upon the cloud-compelling throne, and the multitude of birds, for which our ravine is famous being his winged priesthood—whom (happily) I have chanced vigilantly to protect, with a love for their beauty and their singing. Of late, by the way, the *miserere* of the night-owl has been unusually frequent and prolonged in the precipitous hemlock grove under my window ; and the iron crosses have been blown, in a whirlwind, from the Gothic points of the roof of our Highland Chapel. I gave a vague look at Mesa-ba-wa-sin, as I remembered these precedents of his recognition. He shall be duly honored with a fitting place and a pedestal ; and his storm-ushers, his priesthood of birds, shall be reverently looked upon—those as they pass in their robes of cloud, and these as they sing on their swift service with their bright colors and shapes of beauty.

But our neighborhood deserves the smile of Mesa-ba-wa-sin. We have just commemorated an act of Indian heroism by naming a village and a post-office after Moodna—the chief who gave his life to save the white woman from the tomahawk. There is no monument, after all, like a word that will be often repeated. The old sachem, as he rose from his seat in the council and stepped forward to receive the blow for her, who was meeting death to be grateful and true to him, lit a fame-star on the spot where he stood. It should burn, and the spot be known by its light and by his name, while the world stands ; and so it will be, now—his noble deed better commemorated by this baptism of perpetual repetition than it could have been by the costliest column of marble.

We have a busy neighbor in this little village of Moodna. Hidden away as it is, in a deep-down crook of the swift tributary to the Hudson—out of sight from the main thoroughfare of travel and from the eminences of the country around—it is nobly watered for its mills, and kept under a thriving headway of prosperity by industry and enterprise. The cotton factory of the Leonards, a large machine-forge, and the spacious paper-mill of Carson and Ide, employ a stirring population of two or three hundred operatives—their bells at morning and noon, their flickering lights by night, their playing children and familiar faces on the road, all combining to make a spot of lively variation, in a part of the country otherwise Secludedly and only agricultural. It is a covert picture of life, if you like to go to it. And, for those who are interested in the maze of ingenuity and industry which turns rags into those beautiful fabrics that receive our thoughts, the Moodna paper-mill would be a resort of no little interest and curiosity. We are pleased to know, that, from the next glen above us, are always going loads of the fairest of every variety of note and letter paper, (sixteen hundred pounds a day, the makers tell me), and, as they are about to add to their extensive works, with the increasing demand for it, we shall soon find our letters to be but return-birds—Moodna paper coming home to roost, with the messages it has picked up in its flight.

In the rural village of Canterbury, a mile or more on the other side of Idlewild, we have lately had a beginning of more life. Copway lectured successfully to an audience of a couple of hundred, exciting great interest for the remnants of his people. And Clarence Cook comes to-morrow, to give the same audience a lecture on his passion-theme of "Gardens." We hope yet, as a neighborhood, to be a regular customer for the thought-market of the Lecturer. It is a delightful novelty—this coming of a load of thought upon one subject, to be given to a whole community at once, exacting a sympathy in knowledge, and socially promoting its spread and value, as single and different books, read by individuals at home, never could.

LETTER XLVI.

Hudson Frozen Solid—Boats on Runners—Water-lilies—Indian Legend, and Poem on it by a Friend—Philosophy of naming Streams hereabouts—Angola and its Epidemic—Story of Smart Boy, &c., &c.

February 11, 1854.

THE Hudson is frozen solid, from the Storm-King's foot to Danskimmer, but the ice seems rather to accelerate than hinder *navigation*. A sail-boat upon three runners—the hinder one rigged upon a piviot, and operating as a most effectual rudder—has been flying over the ice to-day with a velocity quite marvellous, and tacking and rounding-to so gracefully and instantaneously that it is a pity it can only be done when the swallows are at the South—their preeminence at a short turn being a nose out of joint, just now, for this neighborhood. From the distance of the shore, the runners are invisible, and the flying craft looks like an ordinary boat ; while its unnatural speed and the tangle of horses and sleighs through which it zigzags, in the thoroughfare between Fishkill and Newburgh, makes a strange confusion of sails and trotting horses, to an unaccustomed eye. With locomotives passing continually on both sides of the river, and the multitudes of skaters in every direction, velocity of all kinds seems easy enough.

The first of February is the spoke of the Year's wheel of Seasons that leans towards Spring ; and, in the country, we are already contriving for the softer months we shall now drop upon in succession. Among the things to be done, we have not forgotten the water-lilies to be anchored in Idlewild brook—the seeds of which were kindly sent us by one of our fair parishioners at the South. They shall have their safe corner out of the freshet path. And our nameless friend, by the way, will not be sorry to know that we have a new poetry for the lotus. When Copway, our Ojibbeway friend was here, a day or two ago, he told the children an Indian legend of the water-lily—how it came to earth—heavenly flower that it is. One of our fair neighbors, who chanced to be a listener, thus rendered the beautiful story into verse.

A star looked down from its glowing throne,
In the azure-vaulted sky,
And said, "I am weary here all alone,
Doing nought but throb and sigh.

"Far down in the valleys of earth, I see
The red-men's children at play—
The innocent sound of their careless glee
Rises faint on the air all day.

"I will speak to the braves at their council fire,
And ask them to let me dwell
Where earthly love may warm my heart,
With its human, holy spell."

So they told the star she might come at night,
When the wood and the wigwam were still,
And sit on the mountain, and throw her light
Through the vale and along the hill.

She came, all trembling, but, when the morn
Woke the birds and the children again,
The star sat grieving and all forlorn,
For she knew that her hope was vain.

"Not near enough yet ! I can hear and see
The red-men's children at play,
But they waste neither wish nor thought on me,
From morn till the close of day !"

Then they bade her alight on the tree-top old,
That lulled them to sleep with its song ;
And she rocked and wailed, and shivered with cold,
Impatient the whole night long.

At length the children awoke once more,
And they heard the pine-tree sigh,
But took no heed of the watching star
Between them and the sky.

She saw them skimming, in light canoe,
O'er the lovely lake below ;
But the longing that hourly tenderer grew,
How could she make them know ?

She pondered another night away,
  And at length when morning brake,
She dropped from her height, with a hopeless plunge,
  And sank in the silver lake.

The star was shivered ! But every ray
  Was caught by a faithful wave !
Each scintillant beam grew a snowy flower,
  Where she thought to find a grave !

And when the red maiden, in birch canoe,
  Seeks lilies for bosom and brow,
The star is content, for she softly says,
"I have conquered ! They love me now !"

The hostility, in this part of the country, to names of long descent, makes rather uncertain wedlock for the lilies. The streams to which these Southern nymphs come to be wedded, are scarce known by the same name, for any two consecutive miles. Our large "creek" (larger than the Avon), for instance, is known as the Moodna, for a mile or more from its junction with the Hudson. It then begins to take the names of the different farmers through whose lands it successively passes. The main branch comes down for eight or ten miles through what is called "The Clove"—(the main valley-pass, in our amphitheatre of mountains, toward the South)—and, all along this beautiful valley, it has as many names as there are dwellers on its banks. It is "Smith's Creek," "Townsend's Creek," "Sawyer's Creek," "Cox's Creek," etc., etc.— *ending* only with the name of the brave old chief Moodna ; although it is to be hoped that his heroic memory will, in time, send that name *up* stream, as great deeds usually do, imprinting it on all that flows from the same sources.

"The Clove" has a curious local celebrity. Its main township, Angola, is famous for the number of inhabitants who have hanged themselves. As the population is strictly agricultural—a class certainly not addicted to excess of imagination—and the cases have been invariably of mediocre persons, "doing pretty well," and with no special unhappiness on hand, the suicides have been difficult to account for. It is only the English who hang "from weariness of buttoning and un-buttoning." My friend the blacksmith, by the way, showed me a graveyard on the hill-side, in our trip through the Clove, the other day, and told me a story which would show that imagination may grow wild, hereabouts. They were burying a man, during the revolutionary war, and were just sliding the coffin into the grave, when one of the mourners gave the alarm of a "red-coat" concealed among the bushes. Down went the dead man, and was left standing on end while the "funeral" took to its heels—returning no more to the grave-yard for that afternoon. But, the next morning, there was some careful reconnoitering by the relatives, and, after some trouble, and a narrow escape of a new alarm, the red-coat turned out to be a sassafras-bush—the scarlet berries having loomed up rather bright, with the sun's breaking out, just then.

Dull-witted, the people of this region certainly are not, if one may judge by their children. A little way back among the hills, we had ridden up to a very secluded farm-house ; and, while my friend was making some inquiry, I opened conversation with a little puny-looking chap, of eight or ten years of age, who sat astride a log, disembowelling a grey squirrel. A younger sister sat also astride the log, facing him, and a still younger one looked on from a little distance. As he took no notice of our approach, but went on, spreading the skin out, to nail it to the log, I was compelled to force myself upon his polite attention.

"Where did you get that squirrel, my boy ?"

"Shot him," he said without looking up.

"Yourself ?"

"Myself."

"And what are you going to do with the skin ?"

"Nothing."

"But," said I, "why not make a fur glove of it ? There are four legs for your four fingers, and then you can run your thumb out at the mouth and use those little teeth to scratch your head with."

The boy quietly puckered up his little mouth, and cocked his eyes sharply up to me, as I sat over his head on horseback.

"Suppose," said he, "that you just come and scratch *your* head with it first !"

By the hearty laugh of my friend the blacksmith, I saw that I was not as triumphantly facetious as I had expected.

But it is only where hickory-trees grow, that a boy of eight or nine years of age, who does not see a stranger once a year, would think of measuring wit with any stray horseman who might try to crack a joke upon him.

LETTER XLVII.

Boy-Teamster—Our Republic's worst-treated Citizen—Boy Condition in the Country—Our Neighborhood suited to Boy-Education in Farming—Vicinity of New York Market—Boy-Labor and Boy-Slavery—City Parents and their Disposal of Boys—Gardening Profits, &c., &c.

March 4, 1854.

HAVING bespoken some chestnut post-logs, a while ago, from a farmer in the mountains, I found them duly delivered on the different spots as directed ; but it was not till the last of the eight or ten loads, that I chanced to see the teamster. He was throwing off the heavy sticks and laying them in a neat pile, as I came up, and I stopped to take a second look at the dexterity and ease with which it was done. He was a slight-made and handsome little fellow, not quite fifteen years of age ; and, with that double team and as heavy loads as could well be laid upon a wagon, he had made the trips alone—the four mile distance being mainly a descent down the mountain-side, and by as precipitous and rough a road as could well be called passable. Twice back and forward, between sunrise and night, he did what would be called a very fair day's work for a hired man at a dollar a day.

Constantly applied to, as editors naturally are, for information as to "places" for boys in the city—and the rage throughout the country seeming to be to plunge all "boys that mean to be anything" into the seething caldron of city life—I have felt my curiosity, for the year past, turned to such casual observation as I could make of *boy-condition* in the country. The above-mentioned instance is one of many that I have noted, as illustrative of the value of boy-labor. With my farming neighbors, and with working men, I have gossiped considerably about the proportion of farm work that requires the main strength of a man, the treatment of boys generally, the cost of their clothing and schooling, and the opportunities given them for reading or for relaxation. I have come to the conclusion that *the worst-treated citizen of our "great and glorious Republic" is the boy on a farm.* It seems also very evident to me that there is no occupation, at which, while learning the art of it, a boy can so well earn his livelihood and reserve some daily leisure for himself. And it seems to me, too, that, considering the healthiness of it, the out-door variety of its work, and the neighborhood of rural liberty and amusements, the ease and simplicity of its acquirements as a pursuit, and the certainty and readiness with which its knowledge can be early practised for himself, it *might* be of all apprenticeships, the most attractive to a boy.

I wish to write down a few suggestions on this subject, but with no aim at a direct and present reform in country-boy condition. The present race of short-sighted and tyrannical farmers, who take boys from the work-houses, and "get all they can out of 'em," must first die off. Public opinion must be so changed, and boys' rights so well understood, as to over-rule farm tyranny ; and this is a work of time. The *pauper* boy will not be decently treated, probably, till the next generation. But, meantime, the rush of "all the intelligence" to the cities needs to be checked ; farming needs to be rescued from its present stigma of being "only work for the stupid ones who can do nothing else ;" education and science need to be added to the farmer's business necessities ; and (last and perhaps not least) *pride* in it, as a profession for a manly boy to prefer, is to be carefully contrived for and sustained. With our American shop-keeping getting to be more and more overdone, and our American farming yearly complained of, as meeting less and less the wants of the country, it is clear that *the standard of respectability, for this class of our population needs raising.* Farm Colleges and Farm Schools are excellent seed-sowers for this. They are principally endowed and started as Public Institutions, however, and as such are cumbrous and slow to get into popular operation—besides the political bias and sectarianism that are among their difficulties. While grafts and seedlings from these nurseries may doubtless be transferred to any soil or distance, and do well, it is safer, we may say, to have the plant *first take root where it is to grow.* My object, at least, is to show how boys might be made farmers in *this neighborhood,* and commence the acquirement, *here,* of a farmer's independence of means. I may treat the subject somewhat locally, perhaps ; but the material that I find around me at Idlewild, may be suggestive, to others, of more to be found elsewhere, and so give incidental impulse to an inquiry by which every neighborhood may profit.

I find the farmers generally willing to admit that a boy's work for *four hours a day,* would fairly pay for his *board.* In pushing inquiry as to the different kinds of farm work, I find, too, that there is but a small portion of it which is beyond the strength of a well-grown lad of fifteen. For ditch-digging, hay-pitching, cradling of grain, wall-laying and heavy ploughing, they would depend, of course, on the main strength of a regular "hand ;" but for sowing, light-ploughing, hoeing, weeding, carting and scattering manure, reaping, thrashing, and all the lesser industries of stock-tending and barn work, a smart boy is often as capable as a man. This applies to grain farms, or to those mainly devoted to hay and stock. Where the produce is only fruit, or vegetables for the city market, the work is easier, and perhaps the whole of it could be done by boys.

The people of this neighborhood have discovered, within a year or two, that they have exactly the right soil, distance, and facilities, for supplying the New York market with fruit and vegetables. The freight-steamers which leave our Cornwall dock at eight or nine in the evening, reach the North River wharves at three in the morning. Everything put on board is taken charge of, on commission, and sold to the market-men in the city ; and the cash (minus the per-centage) returned with the baskets and barrels. The only trouble the gardener or farmer has, is to deliver his produce on board. He does this, of course, easier than he could cart it to the market from within five miles of the city, and with less care and cost, and better preservation from accident and jolting. At present, the produce passes through two or three hands before it is sold to the city consumer ; but by a combination of two or three to establish stalls supplied directly from their own farms and gardens, these several profits would be reserved (as they rightly should be) to the original growers. And, with the high city prices, they would thus be most profitably paid.

It has been found that the rocky and cheap lands at the bases and on the sides of our Hudson River mountains, are particularly favorable to the growth of the Isabella grape. Several of our neighbors have gone into this culture very largely. When it is remembered that the pioneer of this particular growth (Underhill of Croton Point) estimates the year's product of one acre of his grape vines at a thousand dollars, and that the land about here, which is thought to be even better soil for the purpose, may be *bought* for from fifty to a hundred dollars the acre, the opening for enterprise (in connection with the market facilities) seems ample. For fruit-trees of most kinds, this same mountain-terrace soil is very favorable. It is an old custom in this part of the country that the farmers' wives and daughters should have the profits of the farm fruit for their *pin-money* ; and, from the intelligent commission-captains of the freight-boats, I easily procured a little statistic on this subject. The pin-money paid at Cornwall dock—or the proceeds of fruit from a neighborhood, say four miles back from the river and two miles broad—amounted, last season, to between eighteen and nineteen thousand dollars.

The table-land behind us, walled in by our circle of mountains, has been treated like a rough and out-of-the-way corner of the world, poorly farmed, and bought and sold at very low prices. Farms that would be every way suitable and convenient to supply the New York market with fruit and vegetables (as stated above), may be bought for from fifty to a hundred dollars an acre—the fancy-mile within view of the river, and the fields of old and rich culture, of course excepted. Almost anywhere, from two to six miles back, an enterprising and skilful gardener might establish himself with small capital, and commence in the second year to realize a large profit on his investment. And it is the labor on this kind of farm that could be done almost exclusively by *boys*—better done by them, indeed, for it is mainly an exercise of *intelligent attention*, for which the Irish laborer is vexatiously incompetent.

But boy-labor, to be reliable for the master, must not be boy-slavery. It must be enlivened and steadied by an understood footing of reciprocities between boy and master—both having an interest in its being faithfully done. And this is a state of things that could not be entered upon to-morrow, with the present general idea of how boys may be used. Information is sadly wanted on this subject. The most valuable addition that could be made, just now, to "literature for the people," would be a manual of boy-employment and treatment—defining his rights like those of a hired man, giving the terms of an agreement for his labor, specifying his privileges of spare time and agricultural instruction, describing the care of him by the mother of the family, and plainly stating the ways to make him think for himself and respect himself, and so be thought of and respected by those around him. With this kind of understanding, every intelligent farmer could profitably take half a dozen boys to work with his one or two hired men, and teach them farming while allowing them to play enough and read enough as well as earn enough—a Utopian idea for the present, perhaps, or, one, at least by which the *poor* boy is not likely to profit for a while.

There is a class of boys, however, for whom I think a beginning might be made immediately practicable—the sons of parents who could clothe them, provide them with books, and see to their schooling and incidental wants for the first year. [The *clothes*, by the way, are the sore spot in *boy wrongs* in the country, and the extinguisher to that *boy pride*, without which his character becomes the fruitful soil for rustic meannesses. Among the old farmer's "dodges," the excuse for all his overworkings of the boy is "the money it costs to clothe and school him"—while the poor lad's habiliments are the remainders of the old man's worn-out coats and trousers, fitted and patched with such skill and taste as Heaven may have vouchsafed to the old woman's needle. The consciousness (No. 1) with which the "young farmer" walks about in a pair of patched and big-breeched pantaloons, "fitted by only cutting the legs off at the knee,["] and the consciousness (No. 2) with which he hears himself glorified by a political orator, a few years after, as the country's "independent bulwark," "bone and sinew," "Nature's gentleman" and "best citizen," are two points between which, to say the least, there is a — chasm.]

City parents, who know what city "prospects" for a son are likeliest to end in—and who, unable to give him a college education, wish him to enter upon the pursuit that will soonest support him and be least liable to reverses—are those who oftenest wish to make farmers of their boys. These can commonly afford to clothe the lad, and provide him with books, for the year or two years that he is a beginner and earning only his board ; besides taking him home for two or three months in the winter and providing him with the means of going to and fro. It is from this class that I think the boy-labor of vegetable and fruit farms, in this neighborhood, would be eagerly supplied. There would need to be, first, probably, an example. And this would, perhaps, be something of the character of a farm-school—except that the labor of the boy would pay for his board and his tuition in farming. He would be an independent laboring boy rather than a scholar. But the employer should be one who would take proper care of his health and conduct ; and the farm should be a large one, worked by a sufficient number of boys to make the enterprise worth a superior man's while. It would be very easy to arrange a system by which each boy should have his corner of a garden to be worked in spare hours of his own—or it might be possible that the rent of the land, the cost of seed and labor and the profits of the crop should be shared by them as a community of gardeners under a superintendent employer. There are many shapes which the unquestionable *utility* of boy-labor might afterwards take, to be turned to profit. But the *beginning* I hope for, and think easy in this neighborhood, is for some one intelligent farm-gardener to let it be known that he will give boys board for their work. With the scarcity and uncertainty of Irish "hands" at the critical season when labor is most wanted, boy-labor would *supply a demand ;* and, the demand once begun to be supplied from the wilderness of unemployed "Young America" in the cities, our wasting race of farmers would soon be re-stocked. We know of one or two capable men, among our neighbors, who, with the aid of capital to enlarge their conveniences and add to their stock, tools, etc., would at once enter upon this system.

There are progressive steps of agricultural life under this phase, of course, which would follow in due succession. A literature for the boy-class of farmers is wanted—beginning with a simplification of so much of the science of soil and products as the youthful mind could readily understand. Other and correlative knowledge might be selected and combined into a series expressly designated The Young Farmer's Library. A newspaper for them would soon flower upon this stem ; and it is not difficult to imagine that the pride and enthusiasm of boys throughout the country might thus be gradually interested in the pursuit.

One word as to an important point—the subsequent setting up of the young farmer for himself. It would be but a "middling sort of chap," in this part of the country, who should have lived and worked in a neighborhood, for years, and not have character and credit enough to get "trusted" for land to live upon. Almost every one of our oldest and now independent farmers took his land originally on that tenure. But, while a much smaller quantity of land is wanted for the skilful and well practised gardener, the profits are far beyond those of ordinary farming. The soil increases in value, too, under the hand of the cultivator. By purchasing forty acres, he could so improve, while taking off crops, that twenty would sell, after four or five years, for more than the cost of the forty. This has occurred so often, hereabouts, as to be calculated on, among regular prospects and resources. And it is for this facility of a first start on arriving at manhood—a start upon character without capital—that I should advocate the education by boy-labor upon single farms, in preference to education in Farmer's Colleges. Ever so well instructed, in a large institution, the youth is adrift, when he leaves it. To have a farm (as a stranger wishing to settle anywhere), he must buy and stock it, with "money down." And, not only has the laboring boy the advantage of having supported himself, and extended his roots of character and credit where he means to grow and flourish, but the practice of his agricultural education has been *upon the soil, and in the climate, and among the associations, where his future industry is to be applied.* He is already at home when he begins—already familiarized with the obstacles and resources which so vary with different locality.

Hoping soon to see our Highland Terrace, of ten miles square, the vegetable and fruit garden of New York, and cultivated mainly by boy-labor, I shall keep an eye on facilities as they open among us, and return to the subject.

LETTER XLVIII.

Living in the Country all the Year round—Trips to the City—Hindrances by Snow on the Track—Chat in the hindered Cars—Mr. Irving—Bad Ventilation—Late Arrival, &c., &c.

March 11, 1854.

LIVING in the country all the year round, has its occasional misgivings of worth while. There are "spells of weather," as the country people call them, which, for a day or two at a time, in this northern climate, make all out-doors intolerable. The "sloshy going" is discouraging enough—when the snow is just so much melted with a raw east wind as to hold water six or eight inches deep on a side hill—but this, though it makes an island of the house, imprisons only those vintager snails,* the women and children. There is a worse stage of winter which imprisons also man and horse—the cold after a thaw, when the roads are an impassable slough of false mud, and the animal that you ride plants one foot safely on the surface, but can scarcely extricate the other from the stiffening mud in which he "slumps" to the knee. There is no exercise to be got by riding, and walking is out of the question. The lungs pine for expansion. Blood runs slow. Sidewalks and omnibuses begin to loom up with a forgotten glory.

In watching the railway trains from my library window, I find I have no feeling of *being-left-behind*, except in the un-get-about-able weather. Happily at rest while others are wearily urged onward—or tiresomely on a shelf while others have liberty to change the scene—are two impressions receivable from the same smoke of a flying locomotive in the distance. I should often start for a week in the city, with the latter feeling, if it were not for the horse in the stable, and the chance of out-doors freedom to-morrow ; but, last week, the winter's "protracted agony" got the upper

* Nature seems to have distinctly endowed some of her creatures with the instinct and faculty of doing without open air for long periods. Of the peculiar snail that lives upon the grape, Berneaud says :—"On the approach of winter, the vintager snails, several together, retire into holes in the earth, shutting the openings of their shells with a *calcareous operculum*, and not making their appearance again till the following spring.["] Our ladies certainly have this "calcareous operculum," or some other compound of in-door resignation, unknown to the ruder sex.

hand, and, with my "7,000,000 pores" voting for a change of air, I gave in. And, of some of my experiences in getting to the city, I may as well make a passing chronicle—adding, as it will, to an understanding of that *life hereabouts* which it is the object of these sketches to illustrate.

We usually speak of the city as about two hours distant ; and, though a snow-storm came on in the night, after my preparations to go, I thought it would be such a ploughing as I had frequently seen to offer little or no impediment to the trains during the winter, and started from home at daylight to meet the cars, in full faith of a noon in the city. As I did not reach my hotel till the following midnight, and did not get my baggage for still eighteen hours more, the reader will see what slovenly service it is, after all, spoken of so grandly by the philosopher :—"Man is a world, and hath another world to attend on him." A pocket full of crackers may be a very comfortable addition to such a couple of worlds.

Missing the Newburgh-and-Erie train, which goes down upon our side of the Hudson, and then driving four miles in an open wagon against a snow-storm of powdered needles, and crossing the river to Fishkill by a ferry made doubtful by the ice, I got seated in the cars somewhere between nine and ten o'clock, thinking, that, for this trip of pleasure, the Compensation Office must have taken the payment in advance. We started well enough out of the village. The rails had been cleared by the brakemen. A little farther on, among the rocks, however, the drifts began to look formidable, and I soon saw that we had been reached, in the Highlands, by only a thin skirt of the storm of the night before. The drifts grew deeper and deeper—our headway slower and slower—and finally, in a rocky gorge, just opposite Cozzen's Summer Hotel, we came to a stand still for the day—a tall snow-bank on each side (neither of them "a bank whereon the *wile-time* grows") our only prospect from the windows. We found afterwards that the stop was partly from a dread of meeting an up-train and running the noses of the two locomotives together under the snow ; and that the delay of the up-train was owing to the break down of an engine—but our several halts chanced to be in spots where the demand for "pies and coffee" had not been anticipated, and the cause of the delay was less thought of than the famishing consequences. At one place, I believe, a passenger or two waded back a long distance to a country grocery of which they had got a glimmer in passing, and found biscuits and gingerbread ; but the remaining stomachs of our own train, and those which kept accumulating behind us from the West, "bore on" with unassisted resignation till midnight.

We Americans are a patient and merry people under difficulties. I do not think travellers have sufficiently given us credit for this national quality of *jolly indomitableness.* The successive additions to our long line of trains stretched to very near a mile, by sundown, and a mile of more gay and cheerful people—hungry as they all were—could not be found on a French holiday. A footpath was soon tracked through the snow, along one side of the cars, at each stopping-place, and merriment resounded under all the windows—everybody apparently acquainted with everybody, and no sign of the fretful grumbler that would have abounded in such a disappointed multitude in Europe. Yet most of those five hundred jokers were business men, to whom the delay was a serious inconvenience.

One of our long halts was under "Sunny Side," Irving's residence. It was long after dark, and the car was double-filled the passengers had been condensed into the forward trains, to detach as many cars as possible, and so save weight. As many persons were standing up as sitting down. Conversation was general, and whoever "had the floor" was heard by all. One man announced that we were but a stone's-throw from Washington Irving's. "Well," said a rough-looking fellow from the corner, "I would rather lay eyes on *that man* than any man in the world." "I've seen him," said another ; "he looks like a gentleman, I tell you !" And then they went into a discussion of his various works—two "strong-minded" ladies who were on the front seat taking a lively and very audible part in it. [Chancing to meet Mr. Irving, two days after, at the Astor Library, and finding he was at home at the time, I inquired whether his ears had burned, about eight o'clock on a certain evening ; but, as he said "no," there is less magnetism in a car-full of compliments than would be set down, for that quantity of electric influence, probably, by the Misses Fox.]

The only ill temper that I discovered, during the fourteen hours of unfed delay, was between those who cared for fresh air, and those who preferred the allowance of about the ventilation they would get in a coffin. With the standing and sitting passengers, and the cars motionless, the atmospheric vitality within was exhaustible in five minutes at furthest ; and, strangely enough, most of those sitting at the windows after dark refused to open them. I suffered painfully myself from the foulness of the atmosphere, all day. Then the stove was kept almost red-hot, and with the snow brought in by the feet of the passers to and fro, the bottom of the car was a pool of water. Like others, probably, who had not foreseen this, I was not provided with India rubbers, and of course sat with damp feet all the way—a dangerous addition to an empty stomach and a pestilent atmosphere. Ah, Messrs. Presidents and Directors of railways, is it not possible to have the ventilation of cars independent of those who do not know the meaning of fresh air.

We arrived at Thirty-first street in the neighborhood of eleven o'clock ; but, as no announcement was made of that happy fact, we sat fifteen or twenty minutes in the cars, wasting our resignation on a supposed snow-bank. With the discovery that the snow in the streets would prevent the cars from going farther, and that the baggage had so accumulated with the numerous trains that it could not be delivered till morning, the next query was how to travel the three miles to our various homes and hotels in the city. There was one four-horse sleigh in waiting, and probably between five and eight hundred passengers. Not sorry, myself, to stir my blood with a walk for that distance before taking my lungs to bed, I gave my check to an Express agent (who brought my trunk to me at seven the next evening), and, with hundreds of men, women and children, started down-town-wards. With a long stumble over the unshovelled sidewalks of slumbering and ill-lighted suburbs, I found myself, towards midnight, in the neighborhood of Union Square, and, over a venison steak which I found smoking on the supper-table at the Clarendon, vowed never again to make even a two-hours' pilgrimage in a rail-car without provision against accident—say a cracker or two and some shape of fluid consolation.

LETTER XLIX.

Frst Signs of Spring—A Public of Invalids—An Invalid Chronicle—Letter from a Lady—Our Friend S.—Beauty of Old Age, &c., &c.

March, 18, 1854.

THE Hudson has thrown off his overcoat of ice, and offers the welcome of a bare breast to the winds of Spring—and Spring it *has been*, for this first week of March, sunny and soft, and (wherever the mud could be forgotten) beautiful. The Storm King's shoulders, it is true, still show the chinchili edge of his mantle of *firs* and snow, and there is a swan's-down tippet, here and there, on the lap of a North-looking hill ; but, in corners, where you can get away from the Winds, and be alone with the caressing Sun, it is as sweet a courtship of Summer as any reasonable anticipation could desire. I have a seat in a niche of rock, between two precipices which come together as if to shut in the "due South ;" and here I could have sat, with the most shrinkingly delicate of my many "invalid" correspondents, and gossiped away any noon since the opening of March, with our respective coughs fast asleep in their cradles. The winds are doubly excluded by the tall hemlocks overhanging the cliffs above ; and the rushing cascade, which plunges a hundred feet in its two or three leaps below, makes a lullaby that would drown a cough if it did not help to still it ; so, come to Idlewild, dear co-Pulmonaries, and, in the sunny seat under the rock, chat or muse—the evergreen woods shutting you in with foliage like the curtains of Summer, and Winter's forgiven Out-doors taken kindly to your bosom.

That the Invalids, in our climate, amount to a "Public"—a Public on which "a paper might be started," to use a very definite phrase—I have a daily increasing conviction. There is a pulse of popular feeling which every editor has, in his correspondence ; and mine, on this subject, beats more and more strongly. Of medical books there is no end, it is true ; and you would suppose, at a first glance, that they must be all that an invalid could require ; but no—it is the patient, not the doctor, they want to talk with. Under every "Public" must run a nerve of common sympathy. And (besides its not having fellow-feeling enough for a large edition) every medical book is but a single theory, if not an old and disputed one. The experiences of yesterday, with the narrator's own life interested in the question, and no 'pathy-bigotry, are what is thirsted for. Every sufferer's case is, in some respects, peculiar ; and more is learned by comparison of symptoms and treatment, than by classified medical reports—each patient capable of becoming, by the exercise of good judgment and careful observation, a better judge of his own condition than most doctors. In the lack of "hubs" for the social wheels of a city, I wonder no one has ever thought of starting an invalid *conversazione.*

But, one of my anonymous correspondents suggests an additional element of popularity in a chronicle for invalids—no less than the pleasure taken by the gentler sex in reading of that condition in which man is dependent on their care. Thus writes a lady, in reply to a paragraph in the *Home Journal*, as to the objections to such articles :—

> "I am sure, I cannot see why any one objects to your holding a weekly chat with your invalid friends. I will not flatter you by saying how you make them look in print ; but, to me, sick folks are always interesting, in reality ; especially you 'lords of creation.' To see you stripped of all the might and majesty that make the *glorious* difference, and compelled to acknowledge you are very poor creatures without our aid ! What can be more elating than the sight of an indifferent one, who has been looking *down* on us so long, being made to elevate his eyebrows, and sue humbly for a little toast and tea ? But, really, *every one is more loveable sick than well.* If I were a novel-writer, I should certainly make all my characters sick once, at least, in the work. Some few authors do seem to understand this weakness in our sex[.] The very anxiety one feels for a poor fellow, endears him to us, no matter how slight his hold on our affections, when glorying in his strength. Talk on, then, with your sick, and let those object who never were, and are sure they never will be. I shall not, for fear I should be laid on the shelf some time myself. I write this because your valued hints to consumptives have been blessed to one I love, and I could not refrain from thanking you for them. M."

Well,—it shall be a side aim, in these "Out-door" chronicles (if you please, ladies !), to show what there is interesting hereabouts, to Invalid readers more particularly. The Highlands are a Hygeian home—the lap of the goddess herself—and, of a health-seeking life, here, the details may be valued as information for the sufferer, whether amusing to the general reader or no. To robust-dom we will minister, in turn.

Spring's most dignified and beautiful return, at Idlewild, has been with us, to-day—our venerable neighbor, of eighty years of age, whose white locks, and face with the benignity of a Summer's evening, came back with the first softening of the season. He goes to the city—this beloved neighbor of ours—when the roads become impassable for his tremulous feet ; but he gains health (as he was saying with his usual truthful wisdom to-day), not alone from the sidewalks and other opportunities of exercise. In the *mental "change of air"* he finds, an invigorating tonic—(one, by the way, which I am glad of this bright example to assist in recommending to the dispirited invalid, for there is more medicine in it than would be believed, without trial) and he inhales it in the larger field that he finds for the instructive benevolence which forms his occupation in the country. He passes his time in the city in visiting schools, hospitals, prisons—every place where human love and wisdom would look in together. He speaks fluently. His voice is singularly sweet and winning ; and with his genial and beautiful expression of countenance, his fine features, and the venerable dignity of his bent form in its Quaker garb, he is listened to with exceeding interest. Children, particularly, delight to hang on his words. One great charm, perhaps, is his singular retention of creativeness of mind—though so old, still continuing to talk as he newly *thinks*, not as he only *remembers*. The circumstances of the moment therefore suffice for a theme, or for the attractive woof on which to broider instruction ; and he does it with a mingling playfulness and earnestness which form a most attractive as well as valuable lesson. Can any price be put on such an old man, as the belonging of a neighborhood ? Can landscape gardening invent anything more beautiful than such a form daily seen coming through an avenue of trees, his white locks waving in the wind, and the children running out to meet him with delight ? Friend S—— strolls to Idlewild, on any sunny day, and joins us at any meal, or lies down to sleep or rest on a sofa in the library and, can painting or statuary give us any semblance, more hallowing to the look and character of a home, more cheering and dignifying to its atmosphere and society ? Among the Arts—among the refinements of taste—in the culture of Beauty, in America—let us give Old Age its preeminence ! The best arm-chair by the fireside, the privileged room with its warmest curtains and freshest flowers, the preference and first place in all groups and scenes in which Age can mingle—such is the proper frame and setting for this priceless picture in a home. With less slavery to business, and better knowledge and care of health, we shall have more Old Age in our country—in other words, for our homes there will be more of the most crowning beauty.

LETTER L.

Breaking up of the River-ice—Dates of previous Resumings of Navigation—Companionship in the distant Views of Travel—Nature's Illnesses—Hillsides, &c., &c.

March 25, 1854.

THE most stirring bit of news, probably, in the whole year, for this neighborhood, is the breaking up of the ice at the mountain-lock, at West Point, and the passing of the first steamer through. "A boat up yesterday" (March 9) is this morning's announcement of suspended life re-begun. Our dock is once more noisy and lively, like returning voice and color to the Highland lip ; and the wagons begin to come and go on the branching roads, like blood that has again found circulation in the veins. The trance is over. We shake hands with the city again, and resume our suburban interchanges and daily commerce, to and fro.

But, from a solid valley to a flowing river, the change is large. The rippled surface of the Hudson flows, *now*, where I was watching a trotting race of eight or ten sleighs but *a few days ago*. The manly boys of my neighbor Roe's school-family skated to Newburgh, it hardly seems further off than yesterday, and, to-day, the sloop-prows are ploughing on the track of their skate-irons. We could take a walk where now we must take a boat. The hills opposite were apparently across a two-mile *meadow*—they are now across a two-mile *river*. For the familiar landscape seen from the window of one's home, this is a startling variation.

The river has been closed this year for sixty-two days. It may be interesting to record the length of a few previous shuttings-up, as given in a little table by the Albany *Argus*—the dates of the closing of the river and the number of days navigation was suspended :

1842,	November	29	. . .	closed	136	days.
1843,	December	9	. . .	do.	95	do.
1844,	do.	11	. . .	do.	74	do.
1845,	do.	4	. . .	do.	100	do.
1846,	do.	15	. . .	do.	112	do.
1847,	do.	24	. . .	do.	89	do.
1848,	do.	27	. . .	do.	82	do.
1849,	do.	25	. . .	do.	73	do.
1850,	do.	17	. . .	do.	70	do.
1851,	do.	11	. . .	do.	105	do.

It is curious how the *mere visibleness of event and multitude*—the distant view of perpetually passing fleets of sails and steamers with which one has no communication—breaks up the solitude of the country. It makes the difference (duly priced in the acre) between living on the river and away from it. The *beauty* of the view is of less value than the *companionship* there is in it. I find the eye can take in the needed food for this social craving. At my window, on this terrace of the Highlands, I sometimes look off, from a tired pen, upon the fleets of sails, crowded steamers and lines of tow-boats and barges, and feel, after a minute or two, as if I had been where people are. It does not need question and reply to exchange magnetism with others, nor does it need nearer neighborhood, I fancy, than the distance to which the eye can ever so indistinctly, follow the imagination. Many a traveller up the Hudson has helped to break the solitude of Idlewild, by what he gave to my thought—the thought that went to him as he passed, and came back from him to me.

But I must not undervalue the human voice—startled as I was this morning by the first Spring addition of my children's voices to the brook-music of the glen. With the ice on the hanging paths of our precipitous rocks, those little feet were not to be trusted with full liberty till the sides of the ravine should be bare ground, at least ; but yesterday's west wind, after the soft coming in of March, took off the embargo. Never was change of season more joyously welcomed. Leave to trace up the bright windings of Funnychild brook, for play, and climb along the sides of the wild torrent of Idlewild, for wonder—the two streams, from their two separate glens, meeting in the meadow with a hemlock-sheltered lawn between such as fairies would choose to dance upon—was liberty indeed. More varied play-ground could scarcely be contrived, yet all shut in with crags and woods full of echoes. And the change this makes, in the music that is never still for us with these swollen torrents—words and laughter added to the voiceless voluntary, which, in every room of our cottage above, is, day and night, audible ! It is a long-played accompaniment that has at last started into a song.

With an invalid's eye, one *symptom-izes* beauty, more or less, even in Nature. In our poetic days of youth and health, we fall in love with a consumptive cheek, without a thought of its needing health to be more beautiful. Idle-wild brook *now*, swollen to a resistless cataract in the glen, seems to be glorious, most of all, for its defying health—so fearless of winter, so unimprisonable by ice, so louder and brighter for snow and rain. It triumphs in strength while the trees and flowers waste and fade—though one envies it less by remembering, that, in its turn, it will "sing small" while trees and flowers bloom and brighten. There is comfort in the thought that it is not in Nature to be always strong. She has her "ups and downs," without sins of diet or irregularity. And I am not sure that the *soul's* flood does not strengthen, like this brook in winter, while the *body's* summer gives place to weakness and decay. It may be

Nature's alternating law—the mind-freshets, which are part of it, being well-needed to sweep away the cloggings-up and incumbrances of health's careless season.

* * * * * *

Many a strange thing may pass by a man's windows ; and we should not too readily take an impression that the world has come to an end. One of our neighbors, last Saturday noon, however, might reasonably have relinquished for a moment his moral appetite for the dinner cooking before him—no less a passenger than a *neighboring hill* crossing the road, as he stood in his kitchen ; and, after a leisurely glide, along what was almost a level of three hundred feet, stopping and standing like any other hill, on the bank of the river ! His house was a new one, of two stories ; and if its foundations had been laid but a few feet farther north, it would have been swept under, with all his women and children, like a crushed band-box. It will be understood of course, that this was a slide of a clay-bank, occasioned by the excavations for brick-making ; but, even in the history of "slides" (one or two remarkable and fatal ones having occurred at Troy, some years since, it will be remembered), this will probably rank as the most remarkable. A train of cars would hardly make the same descent of three hundred feet by their own weight on a rail-road. From the base of the old digging to the present site of the removed hill, it not only looks to be a long level, but the public road, from Newburgh to Cornwall, offered a barrier of perhaps eighteen inches of elevation. At present, the tail of the slide lies across this turnpike, to the height of about twelve feet, and the interrupted travel is sent around by a back road.

My first inquiry, naturally, as a humane neighbor, was of the peril to life ; for it had been a scene of busy industry, with teams and workmen so close under the base, that twenty men and their horses might easily have been swallowed up. But it was, providentially, a rainy day, of suspended work ; and not even a passing traveller (who would also have run a very great risk) was on the road at the moment. The coachman of one of our neighbors had the only narrow escape, having just passed, and being only astounded at the noise of the crashing of the tall trees torn from the fields above. But my next feeling, I confess, was rather a rejoicing in the righteous judgment of the supposed damage—for these brick-yard diggings had been the disfiguring of one of the most lovely spots on the shore of the Hudson. It was a cresent bay, with a smooth beach of sand ; and the mountainous shore, following its shape, was a half-vase of natural lawn, shaded with noble cedars—a river frontage for a villa, such as a man could not get shaped and shaded in a life-time. To see these un-restorable and beautiful trees hewn ruthlessly down, and the green slopes torn open for clay-pits, had been a discord in the music of my daily ride along the river. I say I rather rejoiced in the calamity's happening to Mr. *Underhill*, the brick-maker—(willing only to be humanely pleased that his *name* did not express his bodily share in it). But I was a little too fast. Nature, with Christian "turning of the other cheek also," was helping rather than punishing her defacers. The job to fill up the new dock, *into the centre of which slid the hill,* was to be done by men and carts, under contract, for a thousand dollars. The teams and pickaxes had made a beginning ; but (like the squirrel who begged the Kentucky rifleman not to waste his powder, for he knew his skill, and would come down), the obliging hill walked across the road and "dumped" itself, just where it was wanted. Never was a greater saving of cartage—the Spirit of Beauty unavenged notwithstanding.

"Three inches of declivity to a mile" (they say of river courses) "gives a velocity of three miles in the hour to the stream ;["] and the great river Magdalena, in South America, runs a thousand miles, with a fall of only live hundred feet in all that distance. But, I suppose that a high hill, resting on a bed of blue clay, moistened by springs, would descend with quite as facile a celerity—obstacles once removed. The pickaxes of those Irish laborers had probably taken away the sand and gravel that alone blocked up the hill which stood on this slippery plane ; and, with a throe of the heaving frost (which farmers know to be so repulsive), it took its start. From its *look* of durability, however, almost any lover of a fine view might have built his cottage on the summit ; and he would thus have found his home suddenly changed into a projectile, in a way to entitle him to some astonishment. We should look to see what bases we build upon.

LETTER LI.

Weather-wise Squirrels—Effect of Spring Winds on Roads—Dodge of Turnpike Companies—Anecdote of a Teamster's Revenge—The Kings in Republics—Road from Newburgh to West Point, &c., &c.

April 1, 1854.

THE chipping-squirrels were right about it. They never appear till the last "cold snap" is over ; and notwithstanding seventeen days of most insinuating summer weather (since the first of March), they have let the more sanguine blue-birds have it all to themselves. On the sixteenth, the oppressive sultriness of the weather brought out myriads of musquitoes in our meadows ; but, to-day—the eighteenth—a cold and sharp northern gale is lashing the trees about, like whips, and the sagacious squirrels are well off in their holes, with last year's nuts on hand, and their little ones *not* started in too much of a hurry to seek their fortunes.

This furious wind, blowing under a brilliant sun, will help to dry up our roads, however—to the undeserved profit of the Turnpike Company, I am sorry to say, who, with roads thus made passable by a wind that costs nothing, will be entitled once more to close gates and take toll. Oh, the nice little chartered "dodge" there is in that "liberal arrangement" of taking no toll when the roads are very bad ! Of course there is *no responsibility when no toll is taken.* No complaint can be made ; no Inspector can be called out, at the expense of five dollars to the Company ; and (there being no Inspector's report for a compulsion), of course, there need be no mending of the roads till the sun and wind take the job off their hands. How full our free Republic is of kings in small pieces ! What a regiment of Czars could be mustered out of the collected fragments of tyrants, snugly hidden under Companies and Public Offices, all over our land of liberty !

But, now and then, a splinter of the American monarch's divided sceptre pricks a republican finger, and is enough rebelled against to require to be shaved down a little. I can illustrate it, perhaps, by a very small and common country circumstance—a subject of village gossip hereabouts not long ago.

One of our back-woods farmers, who comes down from the mountains with lumber and fire-wood when the farm-work is suspended (just when the roads are at the worst, unfortunately), had been in the habit of fretting somewhat over the payment of a toll—the most of the distance he had to travel being upon the district roads, and this one toll-gate covering a very small portion of his route, as well as its heaviest and worst wheeling. It was paying a tax for a worse road than there would be if there were no turnpike at all ; and, with his reluctant pennies, Farmer A. paid out usually some expression of his sentiments. This bred a cool state of feeling, very naturally, between him and toll-keeper B. So, seeing him come down the mountain with a heavy load, one day, when the gate had been open from the bad condition of the road, B. ran out and closed his gate, determined to vex his neighbor by exercising his discretionary power of demanding a toll. A. came along ; and, at first, refused to pay, and made a demonstration of opening the gate by force. But the quiet reminder by B, that the fine of that luxury was twenty-five dollars, made him think better of it, and he paid the toll and drove on.

The Christian resignation of farmer A. was not promoted by his experience of the turnpike privilege for which he had just paid. The sloughs and mire-pits were deep and desperate ; and, in one of them, his struggling and plunging team fairly stuck, and he was obliged to call help, and pry out with rails, after unloading. This raised his temper to the peg above caring for cost ; and, on his arrival at the village, late and tired, he made straight for a lawyer. To his furiously-told story, of the state of the turnpike, the lawyer listened, but shook his head discouragingly—knowing the slender chance of the individual against incorporated companies—till A. chanced to mention, last and incidentally, that the gate had taken toll from him on that day. Here was a ray of hope. The Company's usual dodge had been incautiously forgotten by toll-keeper B. The toll having been taken, the turnpike was responsible for the state of the road at that particular time. A complaint *could* be forwarded—the Inspector *could* be called out—the tyrannical Company *could* be made to pay, at least five dollars, besides mending the road at one particular slough. So A. had his one-vote-sized revenge—the getting a chance to crow, once, over the Turnpike Company, as an offset to paying forty years of toll.

The lurking vanity of *power over neighbors* is the only secret of the continuance of this nuisance. The stockholders do not make a cent by it, but they are still "stockholders"—and, to see a toll paid to *their* gate is to be able to imagine themselves the rulers of the country round about. But turnpikes are incorporated only to keep thoroughfares open till the inhabitants can afford to do it by gratuitous labor ; and the free "district roads" (which are all the other highways) are, at present, so much better kept than our turnpike, that the latter is simply a nuisance for which we have to pay. The stockholders *should* throw up their profitless charter, and let us district the route, and keep "decent going" for the traveller, and without charge. But, no !—they would not then be "stockholders." And so (as my lesser-anxiety man expresses himself) we must "connive and worry along," till public opinion compel our disguised monarch to abandon this for some other shape of power.

Along the river—with the land highly-priced for ornamental residences—the state of road-civilization is, of course, an epoch in advance of the back-country turnpike. From Idlewild to Newburgh it is one of the smoothest, as well as most romantically beautiful, of drives, for the greater part of the year—thanks to our wealthy and liberal neighbor, path-master Miller, for the best kept portion of it. And this is to be a thronged and fashionable avenue, by the improvement now busily canvassed. Idlewild is soon to be the half-way mark in an eight-mile drive along the river from Newburgh to West Point. Oh, the tempting trip it will be—a trot through the Highland gorge of the Hudson, when the hills throw the afternoon shade upon the road, to see the parades of the Cadets and hear the military bands—the crowds of summer visitors, at the thronged hotels at both ends of the drive, thus meeting for a sunset promenade, on a spot where, of all the world, the sunset seems most lovely. But, though Fashion and Gaiety are to use the road, Utility will build it. West Point wants access to the Newburgh market. That thriving town, with its twelve thousand inhabitants and its streets of city-like shops and provision-stalls, is quite too provokingly near the military village and its hotels, not to have a thoroughfare between. The Storm-King's granite-wall blocks up the way, at present—his mountain precipice rising bare from the deep water of the Hudson—but this can be soon shelved around with money and powder, and the remaining part of the distance is but easy shaping of the shore[.] The spot where, as Drake says,

"The moon looks down on old Cro'nest,
And mellows the shades on his shaggy breast,"

and all the fairy scenes of the Culprit Fay's romance of love and its trials, will be two miles down the river from Idlewild.

LETTER LII.

Deceptive Grass-Patch—Why Northerners love Home—Tragedy and Turkeycock—Suspicion of Neighborhood and Vindication—Don Quixote, the Newfoundland Dog—Flippertigibbet, the Terrier—My Mare and her Illness, &c.

April 8, 1854.

THE donkey persuasion, which I saw practised in the streets of Havana, has been very like my own out-door experience for the week past. The poor animal, harnessed to an over-loaded dray, was tempted onwards perpetually, with a tuft of green cornstalks kept just ahead of him by a negro-boy on a trot—constant disappointment, apparently, never lessening the charm of the illusory promise. With cough and hemorrhage getting quite ahead of me, of late, I have looked across the wintry valley, from my window, and rested a feverish eye on a half acre of bright green grass, the perennial verdure of which is kept up by a living spring on the hill-side above. March's last two weeks have been downright January, with the addition of unmoderating winds ; but—that tempting grass-patch vowing it was April out of doors—I have every day taken its word for it, and every day galloped off to the hills in a disappointed search after Spring. Here we are, with the month for violets close upon us ; and, across some new ice, on a mill-pond, yesterday, I saw a man safely walk with a load of rails upon his shoulder ! One's lungs and one's hope for Summer need the faith of a Cuban donkey, in such a season.*

With an inclement world *beyond* the fence, the interest upon the lesser world within is brought to a focus—and hence the reason, perhaps, why *home* thrives at the chilling North, but is a blessing unknown in climes of tropical luxuriousness. The thoughts, driven in from a forbidding horizon, nestle around threshold and hearth. In our out-doors family at Idlewild, the events, of late, have thus been magnified in importance ; though, of one small tragedy, involving the character of the neighborhood, I think

* A paper of the 18th of March, says :

"SMILES AND TEARS.—At New Haven, on Thursday and Friday last, the crocuses were in bloom. On the Sunday following, early in the morning, the mercury stood at only sixteen degrees above zero."

I should have made historical mention even with a milder Spring—a removal of unjust suspicion being properly a matter above dependence on the weather.

For some months, this winter, we have had our pomp and glory performed for us by the largest turkey-cock that could be found in North Carolina—a present from that distant region to show us what could come of unrestricted hominy and polygamy. Two of his wives (widows at present) accompanied the Sultan ; and, really, as he stalked through the pine-grove in the rear of the house, spreading his neck-ruff and his enormous halo of a tail, with his own and a new-added Fatima's around him, it was the *poultry* (if not the *poetry*) of the Arabian Nights. He neither walked like other turkeys, nor would he lodge as they ; but, retiring to the outermost of our largest hemlocks, overlooking the torrent of the glen, he nightly veiled his majesty in the impervious darkness of the branches—by this haughty separation from barn-door-fowl-dom (as it afterwards befell) sealing his melancholy fate.

He disappeared.

Now, the Sultan had been an object of much surrounding curiosity. Living with open grounds—inviting our humblest neighbors to make free with our wood-paths and gravel-walks—we have largely promulged his plumptitude and glory, even catching and weighing him, to ascertain the extent of the avoirdupois portion of his greatness, and telling all comers of his one-and-twenty mortal pounds, superfluities included. At his sudden disappearance, suspicion, with its usual injustice, made some random surmises. The winter resources of the poor were getting low, particularly with the wholly suspended labor of the brick-yards. Turkey had tempted a Czar. Human forbearance, with such a morsel within its reach, had its limits. I attributed the theft myself, however, to some of the straggling beggars who "squat" in the mountains occasionally and change their neighborhood as they find it necessary. Of the honesty and good will of the poor around us, I was made too sure by the friendly greetings on the road—to say nothing of the better assurance, that, for years, no theft had been heard of in the neighborhood.

But now a quadruped member of our out-door family becomes an actor in the romance.

One of my neighbors of whom I see the most—an uneducated and working-man, but a great reader and a very original and energetic thinker—is, in the way of his business, a good deal about in the country ; and he keeps me "booked up" in much that I wish to know, as to the haunts of scenery, the progress of improvements, the culture of fruits, crops, etc., etc. But my friend Chatfield lately returned from an excursion, with an account of a great beauty that he had seen in the way of a dog—a dog which, in his kind partiality for us, he thought quite too beautiful for any home but Idlewild. Enough said. The farmer in the backwoods readily parted with a "critter that ate as much as a man," and down he came—a Newfoundland pup, of glossy and raven blackness, joyous and buoyant as a bird, and almost as big as a pony. So excessively handsome was he, that there was a general acclamation to call him Count D'Orsay—but, as, in passing the mill of our neighbor Clark, he had burst open the door, dashed in, and made a furious onslaught upon the water-wheel, to the imminent peril of his life, I thought there was another celebrity he was more like ; and he now goes by the name of Don Quixote—"Don" for shortness.

To introduce the new Idlewildian to his water privileges—the large pond in the glen with the cascades above and below it—was the politic first thing, of course, in the way of endearing the new home to his Newfoundlandness. And prompt was his appreciation of it ; for, with the cold almost at zero, he bounded in and out of the torrent, and swam through the openings of the ice, as comfortable, on coming out, apparently, with the crystals instantly forming on every hair of his shaggy coat, as a gentleman in a vapor-bath with the dew on his beard. Through pools and rapids, and around over every crag and precipice, he bounded, swam and scrambled, to the infinite delight and admiration of the children ; till—of a sudden—there was a new wonder with a *tale* to it. The Don had come upon *a skeleton*, well picked of every particle of meat, but with the extremities perfect in their places—the well-known head and legs of the missing Sultan ! It was quite clear. Human digestion was not to answer for him. The same *fox* that had carried off our two white rabbits—the traditional pest of the glen—had found courage to climb to the hemlock perch of the solitary turkey, and slay and drag him to his fastness among the rocks—picking his plump carcass with a completeness unattainable by human tooth and nail. THE NEIGHBORHOOD STOOD FREE OF REPROACH. We felt once more encircled by the precious atmosphere of love and protection—thanks to the vindicatory discovery of Don Quixote.

I shall not make the *Home Journal* of this week acceptable in our play-room, however, without a tribute to *another dog*, added to this glorification of the Don—a long-loved play-fellow, banished with many tears on the day of the new arrival. Flippertigibbet had an incurable fault. He was a smooth terrier, of a choice breed, imported by our friend of Wodenethe, across the river—but though this is said to be the most intelligent kind of dog in the world, Flip could not be broken of a trick of seizing a strange horse by the fetlock. Delightfully good-tempered with the children, gentle to the kittens and rabbits, and patient of letting bipeds have their wilful way in everything, he still was most dangerous to the horses of visitors. Go, he must. Our friends of the paper-mill at Moodna had often begged him. Idlewild was for *his* idling no more. And the children must walk to the place of banishment with their long-loved playmate, and see him tied up, and leave him. Ah, it was bitter work—chokings and sobbings—and the new dog, splendid as he was, almost hated for taking his place. And the daily tease, ever since, is for permission to go over to Moodna and see Flip. They will never love another dog as well—my boy says he means never to—never ! So begin partings and sorrows ! Will the heart ache more, for more poetic ones, by and by ?

But there is another sympathy awake, in our out-doors interests just now—mentionable from its incidental bearing on the kind of horseback exercise which I have ventured to declare preferable to invalids. My favorite mare, during my recent visit to the city (from grief at her master's absence, I should like to say, but, probably from interrupted habits of work) was seized with what the veterinary surgeon calls a *colic*. This, in a horse, the reader may be aware, is not a trifling matter, within paregoric reach, but a fit of dangerous sickness ; and Lady Jane's stomach-ache was near ending in inflammation and death—reducing her, as it was, to a very invalid condition, and a cough almost as obstinate as her master's. With my partial recovery, which I have found altogether on her back, and daily hours of companionship with her for almost two years (as spirited and fine-strung a creature, besides, as ever was a part of a man's being) I have vibrated, to this cough under my saddle, with more regret than to my own cough above it, unable, at present, to do more than give her a daily airing in the sunshine. Her pace—the truest and most elastic of *trots*—was necessary to my convenience, however—the more showy, but far too easy gallop of Archy, my wife's palfrey, bringing me home from a long ride as *unchurned* as milk sent to market in a spring-wagon. I shall be better for the flaxseed and bran mash Lady Jane is taking, no doubt—but that cough of hers must be softened before my lungs are easy. I should not live long with a *canter* among my complaints—I here record, as a conviction of my experience which may, perhaps, usefully guide an invalid in the purchase of a horse.

LETTER LIII.

Cedar-Trees and their Secrets—Bird-Presence about Home—Our Night-Owl—A Bird's Claim on Hospitality—Difference between City and Country Influences—Death in a Neighbor's House, &c., &c.

April 15, 1854.

We are in a dilemma which Professor Mapes might instructively give us a word upon in his journal. What seems to be an eccentricity in the production of the cedar-tree from seed, stands in the way of a little of my Spring work. Our Highland Terrace, as every one will remember who has threaded the winding roads of its beautiful ten miles square, is studded thickly with noble cedars wherever they are permitted to grow—but, along the stone walls, particularly at the sides of the road, they form avenues of evergreen luxuriousness which strike the stranger as the careful design of arboriculture, rather than any accident of growth. With our long stretches of new walls built under the sides of the precipitous glen roads of Idlewild, and sustaining our terraces and slopes, I could not afford the *transplanted* cedar hedge which the soil would easiest nourish for wall support, and which good taste would dictate for their concealment and embellishment ; but, with time and patience, I thought we could produce the thrifty evergreens from the seed, and decided to sow them in the present April.

Of my friends, the road-side boys, with whom I sedulously cultivate an intercourse by the purchase of their various game, plunder and commodities—(gold-fish and slippery-elm, wild ducks, rabbits, and sassafras, and such other matters as employ the unschooled urchin's industry of idleness)—of these my ragged acquaintances on the highway I had bespoken the cedar-berries, early in March. They must be early taken from the tree. The birds eat them off in a very few days after their Spring arrival from the South. So, between the seed's coming to maturity, and the birds snatching it away, my little harvesters were to beat the trees with long poles (and one of their mothers' coverlets spread beneath), and bring me the gatherings—a shilling a quart—for the shade trees of the next generation.

Rejoicing over two large urns full of the berries, I was waiting for the first April rain to lay them in their trenches, when our venerable neighbor S. came in, with the damper which I have to submit to the kind consideration of Professor Mapes. He tells me that *the cedar berry must pass through the body of a bird*—exemplified by the lines of cedars that spring up along the walls and under the rocks and trees where the birds perch themselves. The seed thus auto-guano-fies for fructification ; or, rather, it is entrusted by un-laborious Nature, to be picked from the tree, manured, and sown at a distance, by a troop of her apparent idlers. That cedars are thus scattered and propagated, there is no doubt. But is the bird an indispensable medium ? Or, could we dispense with him by substituting a little boiling water for the animal heat, and a little guano (which is bird-manure) for the digestive fertilizing ? This is a more important question from the difficulty of transplanting the cedar. It is the most unlikely of trees to live after being disturbed. If we can neither transplant nor plant cedars, therefore, but must trust altogether to bird-sowing, it is time we were catching orioles and blue jays and teaching them habits of regularity. We like to choose where we will have their amiable bestowings of shade-trees.

I am sometimes a little superstitious about birds, notwithstanding this matter-of-fact view of their transmigratory uses. Now and then a bird has a *presence* of which I cannot but feel conscious—like the presence of another human being. We have had, for a year past, in the grove of hemlocks just under the library window, a night-owl, of most musical, but, at the same time, most melancholy note, and the members of our family know his song as well as one of the household voices. He is still, during the day, and his haunt of evergreen trees being on the side of the precipice over which the cottage is built, he is inaccessible and generally invisible. I have seen him but once—one winter twilight when he happened to have perched on a leafless tree—fearless, motionless, and solemn enough ! My man Bell, whom I called to look at him, was eager to seize the opportunity to shoot him. But there is mournfulness without boding of ill-will, in his music, to my ear, and, though it sometimes startles me when it breaks in upon a waking dream at night, I have grown to find company in it—a change from the other and more joyous music of the day. I would not have him killed. He may have an errand to sadden down thought to things that were, else, less often remembered.

Last night, however, we had a bird-visit which has furnished quite a day of poetry for the children. Writing in my own room at a late hour, I was interrupted by a sudden flutter of wings against the window, which, at first, I thought an accident of some bird startled from her nest and bewildered by the light. I looked out but could see nothing. The night was dark and stormy ; and wishing the flutterer safe from all perils of foxes and tree-toads, I resumed my pen. In a few minutes the attempt to enter was made again, and repeated upon the larger window of the adjoining room, in which slept my infant in her cradle. The nurse raised the lattice, and in came the stranger—circling around and around the cradle, and at last alighting upon the curtains of the bed—a little gray harbinger of Spring, who sat and looked about her with the confidence of one sure of a welcome. She alighted presently on the ottoman in the window, and was easily caught by the hand and put under an open-braided basket, to be safe for the night from the un-winged familiars of the house ; but, oh the interest of the story and the bird together, for the children in the morning ! Could any mortal persuade *them* that there was no meaning in her visit ? They watched the little feathered bosom with its throb of watchfulness, and mused upon its midnight coming with child-wonder ; and it is laid away, for life, among their vague thoughts of things supernatural. Such are waking dreams that need not be interpreted to be felt to have a meaning. When the little warbler flew forth again—released into the morning air—it was, even to my world-worn belief, an angel on his return.

The difference between city and country life, or their respective wayside influences and sympathies, has been brought to my mind very strongly within the last week. At the door of a house which I passed daily in my ride, some two miles from home, I had observed that the horse of our village physician was frequently tied ; and, though not acquainted with the family, I naturally stopped him, when one day coming out as I passed, to inquire who was so ill. It was an only daughter, a child of eight or nine years of age, not expected to live from hour to hour. A fever had struck upon the brain. I rode on, thinking of the distress of such a calamity, of course, and blessing God that the blow had not fallen upon my own home, not far off. The next day, passing again, I met a neighbor just beyond the house, and he stopped me to speak of the dying child near by. He knew her. She was a most interesting and intelligent little creature, he said, and her mother's darling. He was going to see whether she still lived. We parted, with his sad-toned words of the dreadful loss it would be, staying in my ears as I went once more upon my way. Coming home two days after, I rode behind a wagon for some distance, and, by a chance lifting of a white cloth by the wind, I saw that it covered a child's coffin. I knew where it would stop. The girl was dead. As they turned in at the gate, it was impossible not to look up at that house, and know, by its one open window, in which room she lay, and picture the coming of that fearful thing that was to enclose and hide her—the laying her into it—the night that must follow, with her straightened limbs motionless in that still chamber, and her pallid face waiting for that turned-back lid to close upon it forever. To look around, at my own home, an hour after, upon a table surrounded by healthy and happy children—beloved ones still spared, still uncoffined, and with a probable to-morrow of happiness and play instead of that dread certainty of a last going forth together and a return alone—was to thank God, once more, with a profound feeling that no levity could have evaded.

But houses are closer in the city, and they have their deaths in them, like this. And we pass daily along the street, under the windows of sick chambers, and close to thresholds that lead in where hearts are breaking, and beloved forms coffined, and waiting to be borne away. Nothing comes to our knowledge. The brick wall shuts in their sorrow and its lesson. Sickness and Death speak but to those whom they take away—to them and those who have loved them.

It is common to compare city and country life, by advantages of health and convenience. This is reasonable enough ; but the better air that the soul necessarily breathes, where the fibres of neighborly recognition and sympathy have life and room, should be considered, as well. Nature has her sad but needed lessons, which she gives us thus incidentally and unsought, in a life not too crowded and artificial. You hear them in the country, always—in the city, almost never.

LETTER LIV.

A Newfoundland Dog and his Nature—The Beauty of a Brook as a Playfellow for Children—Country Life's Opportunity to cultivate Intimacy with Children—Local Protection against East Winds—Mechanical Alleviation for Night-Coughs, &c., &c.

April 22, 1854.

THE kind of dog that loves water most, loves man most—confirming the chemical solution of a human being, viz. :—"five and a-half pailsful of water stirred up with forty-five pounds of carbon and nitrogen." Our recent acquisition of a "Newfoundland" seemed to take but the same space of time to become acquainted with the pond in the glen and the Five-and-a-half-pailsful that he was particularly to follow and obey. Idlewild has no inmate more joyously at home. Certainly the happiest of dogs is a water-dog, as the happiest of elements seems to be water. And the prevailing temper of humanity—which chemistry thus shows to be hydropathic—is, I am sure, of the same natural sparkle and brightness. Oh, how merry the brooks are now—in April ! How smilingly people in the country meet and exchange knowledge as to the April rains, and the grass and grain starting with the semi-human touch of those little reminding fingers !

Of all playfellows for children there is nothing like a running brook. The childish love of power may be gratified, perhaps—they can do so many things with it, and its changes by rains and droughts are spoken of with so much interest, at the same time, by those they look up to—a grown-up affair, in fact, of which they can have the control. But there seems something more than this in the charm of it. They find an accordance with their own natures in the way it flows and sparkles—in the careless abandonment to all that can lead hither or thither—in the brightness and music resumed after every check, and the joyousness never wearying, never ending. With our larger stream too much of a torrent for the greater part of the year, the smaller one, which dances into the meadow from another glen (Funnychild brook we call it), is our household's playfellow of playfellows till it dries up with mid-summer ; though, even then, its revisitings after the heavy showers are hailed like a beloved schoolboy's coming home in vacation. What variety there is in the games with it, to be sure ! The racing of boats, the building of dams and bridges, the digging of viaducts and canals, the gathering of wonderful pebbles to bring home, the chasing of minims and tadpoles, the finding of moss-seats along the banks, and tracing back of tributary springs—each day's adventures and achievements wonderful to tell. This lesser and coy little glen, so out of the way, and open only to the South, has been the haunt of Indian children before mine, probably, for my boy has brought in two of their small stone hatchets this Spring, found in the brook bed ; and some implement or other of their chiselling, is always turning up. Children should be free to play there till the world ends ! The life-feast—begun with the appetite of childhood and ended with the satiety of age—diminishing in zest and sweetness as we go on—is nowhere spread more invitingly than by such a brook. If I had a home to choose for a friend, there should be a brook in its grounds, whatever grandeur of prospect were given up for it.

Country life's *opportunity to cultivate intimacy with children*, seems to me a very important as well as agreeable advantage over life in the city. To be able to go out at any moment of the day when most convenient, and join a gay and loving little troop, and take share in their work or their play, unobserved by all eyes, is preferable to an opera, I think, as a relaxation from care and as a pleasure within reach. And there is fresh air with it, and exercise ; while its timeliness makes it serviceable to health. But the degree to which a man lives a stranger to his children, without it—understanding neither their minds nor their dispositions—can hardly be understood by those who have lived only in the city. There is no charm, for a child, like the presence of an elder person who takes an interest in his play ; and he loves and opens his nature to those who do so, as he loves and is frank with nothing else. To enter into the excitement of his occupations, and to listen and reply with habitual familiarity and earnestness to his questions and impartings, is to link his soul to you by an every-day strengthening of affection like the growing of a branch upon a tree. With his memories of these days—all golden and treasured—the parent who is the kindly companion out of doors is thus inseparably interwoven. Nature ordained such to be the intercourse between parent and child. It is seen in the instinctive fondness with which it is jumped to and clung to. And, while to daily life this gives a charm and a hallowing influence, it plants a flower of affection that will bloom when old age needs its fragrance of respect and tenderness.

With a Boston-bred horror of east wind, I sometimes get a "lively sense" of a geographical advantage of Idlewild, the wall of mountains between us and the east, and the difference of the weather where its pestilent wind gets a chance a little to the north of us. Quite inveigled by the stillness and softness of the air, yesterday—the children, complaining of the burthen of their winter clothes, and shaggy Don Quixote keeping his coat saturated by perpetual plunges into the brook—I started without an overcoat to get to Newburgh before the closing of the mail. I was very warm with the trot of the first two miles. It was like the air of summer. At a turn of the road, however, I felt a sudden change in the atmosphere, and, though riding before the wind, the check to perspiration started both our coughs—my own and my convalescent mare's. An accelerated pace soon quieted us ; but, in returning, the wind was so raw and disagreeable for half the way, as to make me note it for one of the most immediate transitions of weather I had ever experienced. On arriving at the same turn of the road where it had become suddenly cold, I felt the temperature grow summery again, and the rawness, which I thought was a sweeping change over the whole country, evidently had its limit at a certain mile-stone. Through the gap of the Highlands, it blew as through a funnel, and the almost perpendicular breast of the Storm-King mountain, was a corner to the south of which it had no reach or tempering influence. For the remaining two miles it was warm riding, as in June. For those who have a cough to find a home for, this geographical advantage of our neighborhood may be worth considering.

At the risk of being laughed at, by the way, I think I will be devoted enough to the invalid cause, to mention rather a funny discovery of mine in the way of cough alleviation. Of cough itself, I have long had an improving estimate. It is a removal of the material for diseases ; and the medicinal opiate which stills it is calling off the dog from the unexpelled enemy. The sleep one loses by it—an incidental aggravation of the cleansing process—is the only harm it can do, at least till it becomes itself a morbid irritation.

But, lying in bed one night, and wondering at the six or seven hours that Nature had been busy in pumping out the wrong secretions of my mucous membrane, I fell to speculating on its *hydraulic* action. From the fact that the fluid which it brought away was evidently turned upon an irritable portion of the stomach or lungs by the change of posture in lying down, the use of the cough must be to finish its up-hill progress to the mouth. It was a pump, the action of which was but the effort to overcome the remaining acclivity through a chest and head raised upon pillows. Would it be needed (thought I) if it were *down-hill* from the stomach to the mouth ? Why not save this hard-working cough the trouble by altering the level ?

I leaned over the side of the bed, and, with my hand rested on the round of a chair for support, tried the experiment. It aggravated the cough immediately—or, rather, it so increased its ejection of the mucous fluid that it seemed the result of a vomit. But, I was *tranquillized, and went to sleep immediately after*. In four or five minutes the *down-hill* cough seemed to do the work which, *up-hill*, would have occupied hours. It is somewhat for the same effect, perhaps, that most cough medicines are based upon ipecac. But the advantage of doing it by *posture* is, that the stomach is not weakened by medication.

I have a month or two of experience, on which to ground my recommendation of this alleviative to my co-pulmonary friends. I get through with my night's irritations of throat, now, habitually, by thus increasing and expediting them—one hour's work, or, oftener, a few minutes of violent and spasmodic coughing, instead of a slow and irritating bark for six or seven hours. The sleep after it has the lull of rest after fatigue. The cleansed tongue in the morning shows that the lining of the stomach had its airing attended to, while the lines around the eyes read a like certificate of reasonable sleep.

LETTER LV.

Snow-Storm in April—Newburgh to become a Seaport—Railroad from Hoboken, opposite Chamber Street, to West Point and Newburgh—Dutch Aristocracy—American difference from England as to Living near the Old Families, &c.

April 29, 1854.

THE third week in April, and the best of sleighing Snow covers all around us, averaging (to-day April 17th) eighteen inches in depth, say the farmers. It seems in no hurry, either. This is the fourth day of hard work on the road for anything but runners ; and the stifled sleigh-bells, dulled with the heavy flakes, make the out-door music, instead of the usual brown thrushes, with their "plant it—hoe it—weed it." The cold north wind is of a most uncompromising sharpness—(that last participle, by the way, looking so like un*corn*promising, as written, that the printer is very likely to commit a blunder with an improvement in it). Our cedars seem to be the principal sufferers. The usually erect shafts lie all around us with their stems doubled and their tops touching the ground—an overlading with the moist and heavy snow, which seems to happen to them with the seventh year periodicity of calamities to men. Some of the cedars (like some of us) recover their shape—some break under the pressure—many are to be seen, in all the country around, with their tall tops bent irrecoverably downwards.

Our second week of the present April was like the weather of the same week last year, mild and hazy as the days of the Indian Summer. On the same date as this cold snow-fall, however, I find chronicled, in my out-door journal of last year, a violent thunder-storm and freshet, followed by an opening and separating of the yellow bud-tops, that was like a sudden unpacking and exposure for sale of an arrival of French gloves. I chanced to cut out of a newspaper of last April, and paste in my weather-diary, as a remarkable fact, the following passage :—

> "A gentleman who travelled from Hampton to Kingston, Canada, on the 16th instant, says that, on some parts of the road, the sleighing was as good as if it were in the month of February."

This is followed, in my note-book, with a record of the weather at Idlewild when I read it—"April 28, hot as midsummer ; lilacs in full leaf ; several trees in full blossom ; willows out in leaves ; grass and clover up, and Nature recovering from her winter-swoon with a bright smile."

So vary those solemn customers, "The Seasons," that we rely upon with such faith and corresponding flannel, as they come round ! I should have confidently assured any pulmonary stranger, inquiring into climate hereabouts, that so lingering a winter as that Canadian one was never known in the Highlands of the Hudson.*

* * * * * *

We are wide awake, in this part of the country, with the idea of *becoming a seaport.* In the Report upon the great Diameter Railroad to and through the centre of the State (from NEWBURGH TO SYRACUSE, and so on to Detroit and San Francisco), *the Hudson, thus far*—to the broad expanse of deep water spread out before us, and which is encircled like a mountain dock by the Highlands—*is put down as an "extension of the Bay of New York* ; and Newburgh (continues the Report) is located most favorably on that Bay, with the finest of harbors. Ships of war and vessels of every description can lie securely at anchor there, and moor at her wharves." And this saves near a hundred miles of river navigation (to reach the railroad at Albany), and saves the forty days' difference between Newburgh and Albany as to clearance from ice, saves the shallows of the Overslaugh, and sixty-four miles of absolute distance to Syracuse. The great belt of thoroughfare from the Eastern States is to be clasped to the Western belt by this same mountain seaport—the main road from Boston to the West, which is far towards completion, crossing the Hudson from Fishkill to Newburgh.

But Chamber street, in the City of New York, is also to be extended to Newburgh, to meet this Diameter road—crossing directly to Hoboken, and then following the western bank of the Hudson—fifty miles of Chamber street ! So Idlewild will be on Chamber street, four miles this side of Newburgh. We shall thank Heaven and enjoy, not a little, the relief which this direct crossing, from our side of the river to the centre of the city, will give us—a relief from an *alternative of nuisance*, viz. :—the tedious horse-car-ing from Thirty-first street *down town* (from the depot of the Hudson River Road), or the hour's delay of jamming, crowding, dodging and vexing *up town* (from the Erie depot at the blocked-up and struggling Babel of Jersey Ferry). It is perplexing and dangerous work to get self and belongings to a hotel from the arrival-point of either of the two present roads. I have lost temper and baggage in the two last attempts I have

* My neighbor, the joyous Commodore, whose spirits and memory are un-damageable, tells me that there was just such a snow-storm in the latter part of the April of 1834—or, rather, a heavier one, as it quite buried his lawn fence, which was visible above the eighteen-inch snow of yesterday. It seems a twentennial affair.

made at it—old traveller as I am, and quite at home as I ought to be, in New York and its "dodges."

It is a curious thing that the Western bank of the Hudson River, for the first fifty miles from New York, is as much a wilderness at the present moment, as many a river-bank of equal length in the far West. While the Eastern shore is a close-linked chain of villages which makes it an extension of the suburbs of the city for fifty miles, and land all along this thickening and crowded line of railroad is selling for one and two thousand dollars the acre, the opposite river-bank from Hoboken to West Point is mostly a vague desert, of which the chance traveller knows nothing, except that Cozzens's caravanserai makes one break in its long stretch of *terra incognitia*. Most of the land has been, hitherto, comparatively valueless. And it has been valueless and unknown *only because no railroad gave access to it*. Yet—within an hour of New York, and with all the navigation-advantages and scenery of the Hudson—*a continuation, as it soon will be, of Chamber street to West Point*—what a magical change is to take place on that fifty miles of river-bank ! Villages and country-seats will multiply, we venture to predict, as they were never seen to multiply before. The "Report" expresses itself well on the general magic of railroad influence, to be tried here with such unprecedented opportunity :—

> "The effect of railways everywhere has been the same, greatly enhancing all property within their influences, and especially within twenty or twenty-five miles of them on each side. Hon. D. D. Andrews, in his report to Congress, says :—'It is estimated by the President of the Nashville and Chattanooga Road that the increased value of a belt of land, ten miles wide, lying upon each side of its line, is equal at least to seven dollars and a half per acre, or ninety-six thousand dollars for every mile of road, which will cost only about twenty thousand dollars per mile.' 'It is believed that the construction of the three thousand miles of railway in Ohio will add to the value of the landed property in the State at least five times the cost of the roads, assuming this to be sixty million of dollars.' 'The valuation of Massachusetts went up from 1840 to 1850, from two hundred and ninety million to five hundred and eighty million dollars, and by far the greater part of it due to the numerous railroads she has constructed.' Seventy-two towns, not enjoying railway advantages, did not increase in population during that period."

The extension-quill of Chambers street for fifty miles, with its feather of ten-mile breadth of farms, will cipher up the market supplies to balance the other statistics of New York growth and commerce ; but there is also a very possible SOCIAL RESULT, which is not likely to be put down with the cost and profit of the road, but which is as interesting a probability as it is purely a national one.

From the first settlement of the country, the Eastern shore of the Hudson has been a garden of Dutch aristocracy. It was divided up into the estates of "old families," from Manhattan to Albany—the Knickerbockers giving way reluctantly and grudgingly even to the well-paying intrusions of improvement ; and, even still, strengthening their fences around what they can afford to retain, and raising signs of warning to trespassers, with the jealousy of dignity invaded. Railway stations have been built, contrary to their protest and will ; villages have sprung up like mushrooms along the line of the opposed road ; country-houses, school-houses, and churches have thickened like bubbles on a canal break—*and yet they rule.* Those of the thousands of new residents whose beautiful houses are acknowledged to "belong to the first people," have propitiated the Knickerbocracy. All others live isolated amid their fresh paint and shingles.

But the most American feature of our time is the successful voting of such aristocracy to be "old-fogey-ism," and the being merrily independent of it—anywhere out of its immediate neighborhood. While, in England, a new-comer's preference for the site of a villa would be *nearness* to an "old family" mansion, in our country (conveniences being equal), the preference would be *distance* from it. In the natural rivalry for consequence, every self-enriched man prefers fair play and a fresh start to any hitchings-on or borrowings by subserviency. To genial Geoffrey, at Sunnyside, of course, any home-seeker in the Republic would like to be a neighbor—and an honoring and deferential one—but he is a Knickerbocker and himself beside.

"Old-fogey-ism," however, is a growth of centuries. While the *Eastern* bank of the Hudson has been *two hundred* years in settling and embellishing, the *Western* bank will start new and overtake it in from five to twenty. There will be "first people" everywhere. There is no help for it. But it is "a fair field and no favor" on the Hoboken shore. It will be so rapid a settlement of neighborhoods, too, that there will be no time for mould to cover up false claims to "gentility"—none impregnably the first by grave-yard iteration. As soon as this extremity of the great Diameter Railroad is completed—as soon as Chambers street is extended to West Point, for its first link of fifty miles—the home-seeking crowd, who wish to be within an hour of the city with the families they are enriching, will divide up this now desert riverside into estates and villa-grounds, while farmers and gardeners will cluster behind them in the valleys and on the hills—a Minerva-birth of a rich and populous range of country without infancy or weakness. This will be new, even in our newest of histories. The *social contrast* of the two banks of the Hudson will be without a precedent in the world's progress—"old-fogeyism" on one side of a river exclusively, and start-fair-dom on the other.

LETTER LVI.

Birds suffering from Snow—Answer to a Fault-finder—Preparing for Old Age by learning to live with Nature—Another Estimate of the Value of Farming—Common and strangely unvaried Idea of "a Villa"—Hints as to choosing and arranging a Home in the Country, &c., &c.

May 7, 1854.

WE should have a crop of music, this summer, if the sowing of dead birds would reproduce them, for they are scattered over the fields in great numbers—starved and frozen by the deep snow of a third week of April. We set the men to work and cleared a portion of our lawn to spread crumbs on a bit of bare ground for the singers of Idlewild, and it brought in such a troop of little mendicants as was curious to see. The snow still lies in spots all over the hills (April 26th, to-day), but the grain looks brilliantly green beside it. The farmers say that the wheat was hot-bedded and forwarded considerably by the week's covering from the air—Nature, like the Indian, finding warmth under a very cold blanket.

I am found fault with, a little, by a very pleasant writer in the *Horticulturist*—though scarcely with reason, considering that I have not yet occupied my premises a year, and considering that I have (among other things) set out, already, near a hundred fruit trees. Thus runs my homily :

> "In all parts of our country there is a new and constantly increasing disposition to shun the city and seek the enjoyments of country life. The question arises, What has given our people such a love of rural life ? Perhaps our own and other horticultural and the agricultural journals have done as much as any one cause to produce this result. Then the better cultivation of the soil, better and more tasty buildings, improved stock and beautiful gardens and orchards, have increased the attractiveness of the country, and thrown a charm around country life. The log cabin surrounded with stumps, was bearable ; it showed necessity, and adaptation, and gave an earnest of better things in the future. But, when this was suffered to go to partial decay, or substituted by an unsightly board house, surrounded with half-decayed stumps and tumble-down rail-fences, it was a picture by no means attractive to the man of taste. With this love of rural life has sprung up a rural literature. We have had 'Willis's Rural Letters,' 'Up Country Letters,' and now 'Up the River,' with many others of a somewhat similar character. We

> wish these authors knew more of horticulture—that they were familiar with fruits and flowers, and plants and trees—then their writings would be more interesting and profitable."

This occurs in a review of Mr. Shelton's delightful book, "Up the River," and *he* is especially called to account for his outlay of zeal and literature upon Shanghai fowls. But nothing so luxurious has been *my* hindrance to horticulture. Bridging streams, damming torrents, building roads along the shelves of precipices, shaping lawns and clearing underbrush, have been my first year's more pressing occupations.

But a prospective view of farming and horticulture, for me, is graver and fonder than the reviewer would be likely to have thought probable. I am looking forward to farming, or *learning to live actively with Nature* (patient and company-supplying and occupation-giving Nature), in case old age should befall me. With my present loosened hold upon life, the chances are against needing her kindly lap, except to sleep under her green apron without waking ; but, with any possibility of outliving the period of life's fullest reciprocities, the lack of this one and (it seems to me) *only* refuge for the superfluity we become, would be a calamity indeed. Books are something to the old, but the mind's relish lessens and shortens : they are tools to the weakened hand—tools with which no more work is to be done. Friends are something—but, ah, the dread of being "in the way," even of those who love us ! Indoors, with its open window or fire-side, is a place of repose—but one that grows more and more like a prison, as we are thought "best off" there, and "disposed of," and at liberty to be forgotten. From old age in the crowded and busy city—old age anywhere unemployed—may God in his mercy deliver me !

But the overseeing of a farm, even without labor, may be one man's efficient employment. An habitual exercise of acquired acknowledge in agriculture—exercise in directing and observing the culture of familiar soil—is no fatigue. An old man may do it as well as a young man. The master is hardly wanted for more than to be always out of doors. His oversight secures industry and correctness, and his mind, with its unvexed leisure, plans and arranges while he walks over his fields and among his men. On his horse or in his wagon he saves one man's labor in errands to the village, or to the blacksmith, or to the neighbor for exchange or sale of crops. Till crippled, or blind, or bed-ridden, he fills a full place, serves those who belong to him, and cumbers no spot of earth, no heart and no pocket. The farm never tires of his society. Nature keeps prodigally responding with her fertility and beauty to his demands—as cheerfully ready to bud and flower and bear fruit for him as for his handsomest grandson. With his laborers, and his horses, his herds and his fowls, all needing him, and calling for more time or thought, if he had it, he is never lonely. And is he anywhere likely to be so unenvied, so respected, so suited with tranquillity, and so mentally and bodily *well ?*

Of the seventy acres that I hope to be "out of the way" upon (if, as I said before, old age should befall me), thirty or so are arable, and in terraces rising one above another from the meadow on the Hudson. With the one or two acres of black muck, five feet deep, in a corner of this meadow, Professor Mapes would be delighted. I have studied the lectures and essays of the practical and learned Professor on the use of it, and my horses have been, all winter and spring, drawing it to the uplands, while the rocks were being blasted to give it clear space and a chance at the sub-soil. We look for a handsome corn crop this year, to begin with,—but hereafter we humbly hope to "pile up the progress." It is a matter of sanguine anticipation and preparation, and an excitement of most joyous alternateness with literary labor. Literature, in fact, is irksome work in comparison—keeping *me* in doors many an hour when things in which I am more interested are going on in the open air. The days when I can be nothing but a farmer will be days in which I shall be *that much more* at liberty to be happy.

By the fruit-trees of all kinds that have poured in upon Idlewild, from friends and readers at a distance, I seem to be generally booked for horticulture,—and I shall try my hand at it certainly ; though not to the hindrance of the more breadthy farming for which we have the room. The rich gentlemen on the "estates" around me say that nothing can be made by it,—but their estimates are rather to be put down to their fashion of *haughty*-culture than to the grain raising of more humble industry. And yet it is odd that these wealthy ruralizers do not find farming well worth their while. With house and land, "any-how"—barn, cattle, and fowls, "any-how"—horses that need exercise, "any-how," and spare time of their own, "any-how"—they have that number of advantages to start with, which need not fairly be reckoned in the outlay. And, if the *amusement* were taken into the account, the price of an opera box for the season might be put down among the profits of a fruit-garden, over and above what were sold and eaten. Farm produce is rapidly rising, however, and that may bring even "lordly manors" to the plough.

I have often thought of preaching a sermon on the *one stereotyped idea* with which city people select and model a *home in the country.* From the numbers who call on and write to me for information as to the sites for residences hereabouts, I am, perhaps, more in the way of knowing what is usually sought. They all want a *villa*, or its capabilities :—parks and lawn ; beautiful view from the portico ; barn and outbuildings out of sight ; gravel-walks and flower-garden, groves, avenues, and a fountain. And this is all very well, for those who still retain their home and occupations in the city, and who come to the country only for three months of idling in the summer. With money enough to tear down and build up, such improvers of the landscape are large contributors to the general welfare, and should be thanked and admired. But is there no other class of seekers of new homes in the country ?

My own sympathy is rather with a place that *looks like a farm*, an old one. A new building is rather a drawback. I would rather take any house, of whatever shape, and, by a few very easy and un-costly alterations, make it look *picturesque-ly homely*. Additions to the edges of the roof to make them project, stoops of the largest kind to the side and front doors, perhaps a portico where comfort and taste would combine to wish one, and frames and trellises for vines and creepers, are simple and cheap changes that would make the most angular and unsightly house look pleasantly enough. And (without going so far as the Havanese nobility, who keep their carriage in their front parlor), I like to see barn or stable close enough to *group in with the house and orchard*. The guest should see the shed he can tie his horse under, and the tree or bush where he can find the plums or the berries. And it should be evident to any passer by that the owner can go to his barn a dozen times a day, without hat or boots, and shake down hay for his cattle, or harness his own wagon for a drive. No man either looks, or is independent in a country home, who has not his stable completely under his eye—himself the first to know when a horse wants shoeing, or a wheel wants greasing, and hindered *never, and in no manner of thing*, by the absence or neglectfulness, or unwillingness of the "hired man." For me, aside from the convenience of it, there is a certain "*animal* magnetism" which makes the company of my horses and cows very agreeable.

Yet there are those who have lived all their lives among brick walls and sidewalks, and who, finding themselves able to give their children a home in the country, and yielding to a long-suppressed yearning of nature to allow to themselves this luxury at last, are still likely to make irreparable mistakes from inexperience and lack of counsel. Such a one would, perhaps, build his new cottage on the summit of a bare knoll for the sake of the view, rather than under the shelter, and with the background of a wood, ready grown. He might cut down trees because they stood irregularly, or forget how the spring water or the winter winds were to be managed, or neglect altogether to foresee the incidentalnesses of up hill and down, rain-washings to the road, frost-heavings to walls, etc., etc., etc.

In talking to one of my neighbors the other day, I told him he ought to make a profession of *giving a start* to exactly this class of new-comers to the country. It is all very well for the wealthy, who purchase estates and build villas, to send for a *landscape-gardener*, and pay high for a plan of grounds, and the layings out, plantings and embellishings, such as taste may dictate, without reference to cost. But counsel that is both cheaper and more practical than this, is wanted by the home-seeker of more moderate means. The neighbor I speak of (Mr. Chatfield) is one of a kind that should belong, like a carpenter or blacksmith, to every neighborhood, for this very use and employment. He is an uneducated (or rather a self-educated) and working man. But he has passed a life of rural industry and economy, is a most successful raiser of fruit, and a skilful gardener, knows everything about buildings and farms, and their wants and conveniences ; and, to the very best of practical good sense, he adds a taste and a knowledge, and a love of scenery that are quite above his condition in life. For a moderate compensation, I presume (though I write this entirely without his consent or knowledge), Mr. Chatfield would go and pass a week or more at a spot chosen for a residence, and tell all its capabilities, foresee all its difficulties, direct its location of buildings and garden, and planting of trees and orchards, and, in short, give the wisdom *beforehand*, which could otherwise be got only by a costly and somewhat mortifying experience. A beginner at anything *in*-doors—singing or painting, beard-growing or poetizing—may be his own teacher and adviser, and keep his failures to himself. But the *choosing and arranging of a home* is an *out*-door matter, of any mistakes in which the "people round" are most annoyingly aware.

LETTER LVII.

Remarkable Land-slide—Woman nearly Buried—Our Gateway Stopped—Ravages of Floods—Embellishment of a Neighbor's Grounds by a Landslide, &c., &c.

May 13, 1854.

THERE are odd surprises, occasionally, to wake us out of sleep ; but one of my nearest neighbors was aroused in the dead of last night (April 29) with a remarkable interruption to her dreams—a quince-tree from her garden entering her bed-room, followed by a neighboring hill ! The cottage, at the same time, began to move from its foundations ; the chimney and rafters tumbled in ; the weight of the earth which was pouring down upon her bed crushed it to the floor ; and her "old man," who slept in the room above, came through the ceiling. As the reader will have easily divined, it was the overwhelming of a cottage by one of the *land-slides* of the late unprecedented ruin.

But these first waking surprises of Mrs. S. were followed by rather a terrible half-hour. In bed with her was her daughter-in law, whose nearness to a critical period was the occasion of sharing her room ; and, by the sounds of gasping and choking, she discovered that this poor young woman was buried under the liquid mass of earth which was sweeping them away. With the bed broken down, the floor lifted to a slope, and the ruins falling in around her, she was guided through the terrible confusion and darkness by nothing but the sound ; but she found the head of the struggling sufferer at last, and was only able, with her hands, for a long time (she says "over an hour") to scratch away the mud from her daughter's mouth and keep it clear enough to enable her to breathe. The weight of the earth accumulating on the coverlid effectually prevented the extrication of the buried woman, and, as the neighbors were long in being summoned thither in the dead of the night, the struggle probably seemed as interminable as it was awful.

You might almost throw a stone from Idlewild lawn upon the roof of this cottage, and, of course, such an event was a stirring morning's news to us. In my daily ride along the beach, I pass their door ; and, from wayside chat with the "old man," as he chopped wood or hunted up his vagrant cows and pigs, I could not but feel the calamity to have happened to one of ourselves. Sympathy, notwithstanding, however, there was a ludicrous expression about the Sunday morning look of the little building—standing, corner-wise to the road, with its after-part cocked in the air, the peach-tree, which had checked its course apparently, sustaining its intoxicated posture with difficulty, and a quince-tree leaning with its buds out of the front window ! The tipsy-looking cottage was one of half a dozen humble dwellings built under the lofty river-bank which rises to the general level of the country ; and the two or three trees before it, and the small garden behind it, filled the narrow slope between the water's edge and the well-grassed ascent. Other buildings—were carried away by the slides, a mile farther down, but no lives were endangered that I could hear of.

One of our own hills of Idlewild took a walk at the same time ; and, by stopping to take breath in the middle of the road, has so completely altered the shape of our nearest corner to Newburgh that we shall be compelled to remove our main gate and make a new entrance altogether.* It is a pity, because it shuts us off from an avenue of full-grown hemlocks, and forces us to follow the public road outside of them. No small outlay of contrivance and labor has been expended to wind in the approach by those beautiful and stately evergreen trees—now to be exchanged for a new and unshaded gate through an open wall ! I must own to finding this hard to bear—much harder than such casualties as labor will restore. That one of our glen bridges was washed away, our upper dam torn to pieces, an acre of green meadow covered with gravel, a beautiful river-slope stripped of its sod, and unsightly channels cut in the brook-banks, right and left, are lesser and more remediable damages, for which we may easier find comfort. Our neighbors at the Moodna paper-mill, who are damaged to the amount of two or three thousand dollars, and will not get to work again probably for five or six weeks, tell us *we* have "got off pretty well !"

It will be a month before some of our choked-up public roads will be re-opened, and the swept-off bridge across the Moodna (a mile from this), and others along the various streams around us will be much longer in rebuilding. But the worst of it is the *continuance of sluice-way* that will follow every one of these slide-brakes in the hills. The raw sand-and-clay chasms are too precipitous to hold vegetation, or even to be re-sodded, if the expense of that could be borne. They are eye-sores and trouble-makers henceforward. We shall see what June verdure and foliage will do, to out-conspicu-fy the ugliness of them.

It has been a great flood ; but that heavy snow of the third week of April did the work—just holding on to a previous flood (as one of my men says) till this one could hook on to it. The trouble was the country's being called upon to get rid of two floods at once. Every inch of ground was saturated with water—snow having held it back unmelted for a week—when this heaviest of Spring rains commenced. The streams were already at their

* This gate has since been restored.

highest when the new freshet began. (And so accumulate and give way hearts and patiences sometimes !)

The newspapers (May 2d) have come in with accounts of disaster by flood, showing that we were bearing but our share, this time, with the country at large. This has a certain consolation in it, for our previous water-spouts and avalanches have been so local, that I had felt the romantic picturesqueness of Idlewild to be, like beauty to a woman, a dangerous gift, after all. Burthens are lessened by more shoulders under them. One of my wealthy neighbors, by the way, is indebted to a land-slide for quite an embellishment to his grounds. His lawn, skirted with magnificent forest-trees, abutted directly over the Hudson—a landscape table-land, like the level summit of a mountain pushed to the water's edge. A portion of this, with ten or twelve full-grown monarchs of the wood quietly *settled* thirty feet nearer to the river level, with its vast oaks, elms, and tulip-trees, standing perfectly unaltered in their erectness ; the grass unbroken between them and around their roots, and the general aspect of the greensward exactly the same. The whole area now forms the lower *steppe* or terrace, graduating, very beautifully to the eye, the descent to the beach below. A private wood-road ran under the precipitous bank, and, curiously enough, the descending mass acted like the weight of water in a pipe-curve, lifting this road, which lay forty feet beyond, to about the height of ten feet above its former elevation—the dropped lawn not having changed its place, except by vertical descent. "The hills" are certainly making a move in consequence of water's getting the upper hand, though whether the Maine Liquor Law will claim it to be a "leap for joy," we are waiting for some orator to let us know.

LETTER LVIII.

Immense Freshets—Islands in Solution—Curious Slides—Brickyards along the Hudson—Irish Laborers, and the Contrast between them and Native-Born Country People—The Infusorial Cemetery, &c., &c.

May 20, 1854.

THE Hudson, just now, is thick with yellow earth—the vagrant dilution of hundreds of honest farms, inveigled away from their homes in the mountains by the Lurley of the waters ; but, unlike the Mississippi, which is the pathway of the same sort of truants, our North River has no Delta at its outlet to receive and reclaim the wanderers. Usually as clear as crystal, the Hudson has been, for the few days since this unprecedented succession of floods, a current of creamy thickness, and so closely strewn with brush and flood-wood, besides, that the fleets of steamers which are doing the work of the interrupted railroads, have been inconveniently impeded. What a pity that such a group of lovely *islands in solution* should be passing New York and Hoboken, without a precipitate to "dump" them along the Jersey shore ! Thousands of acres of fertile mountain-soil passing those Jersey *"flats"* unthought-of and unarrested ! And it is the best part of the mountains, too—the mellow stream-slopes and leaf-packed meadows within reach of the torrents. Whole banks of May-flowers and forget-me-nots have gone from Idlewild—and daises and violets, that we had waited for, and found, and loved, this very April ! Well, the sea, with its vast forgetfulness, is welcome to them. Or, they can be sweet on some far isle where their roots may be thrown, without telling who has loved them before—only there will be wasted sunshine for a while, where the warm rays used to find them, and awake their fragrance and beauty.

Nature, like "great minds," which, Emerson says, "have nothing to do with consistency," is sometimes as funny as she is disastrous with her ravages. While lamentably disfiguring the grounds of one of my neighbors, she has slipped money into his pocket, hand over hand—not only disclosing a bank of the richest blue clay, by a land-slide, but furnishing the brick-yard where it could be worked, by extending a platform of earth and trees into the river ! From what was a straight gravel beach under a wooded hill, a few days ago, there is now a projecting point of thirty feet, with the trees on it to "log it in" for a wharf, and the loose brush ready mixed with the "filling in" of mud. Directly behind and above it is (in the place of the loveliest of groves shading the river bank) a broad hill-face of most unadulterated blue clay, worth much more for bricks than the scenery was worth for beauty. The promontory, by the way, of which this is the river front, is probably the most commandingly picturesque spot on our portion of the Hudson. It was once a mountain island, just off the shore at the mouth of the Moodna ; and, to Idlewild, it is the middle ground of our river landscape—half a mile of Moodna-water between us and its grove-shaded point, and the two-mile width of the Hudson extending beyond. With the large mansion upon the summit, and the park-like slopes of woodland and lawn, it forms the loveliest feature of the northern view from our windows—"to be continued," fortunately, as the brick development is on the opposite side. Our friend and neighbor mourns, as we do, the inroad upon the loveliness of his home—but, of the blocks of New York houses that might now be dug out of his side, he, of course, pays the rent while refusing to sell the clay to the brick-makers ; and it becomes a question between grounds *less* disturbed, or *more* property for children.

Brick-yards are our eye-sore, in the scenery of the Highlands. They will be, till the bank of blue clay along the edge of the river is entirely exhausted, leaving a terrace-bank, more suited for improving and beautifying than the original one. For the present—say a forty-year hegira of bricks—the traveller is expected to be blind to our "lower story" of landscape, just as, in Yankee architecture, the model of the house is entirely independent of the "kitchen basement." You do not trouble your critical taste about the cellar of an Italian palace ! Very well. Then merely allow *us* Americans the very trifling additional indulgence of having our cellar open in front.

In the drives along the upper road (one to two hundred feet above the river) we overlook, of course, the brick-hives along the water's edge, and among my wealthy neighbors I find there has lately been a "strike" as to "commuting" any longer upon the lower turnpike—all combining to ignore it, disgusted with the increasing obstructions and disfigurements ; and, with time and carriage-horses to spare, preferring to make a habit of the longer and cleanlier upper route for their daily drive to Newburgh. But, unsightly as they are, these miles of brick-yards are studies in their way. It is a loose and lively Irish fringe to our quiet American neighborhood of sagacious and thrifty farmers. If a Yankee condescends to be among them at all, it is in the capacity of teamster or "boss"—brick-yard-ing labor for day wages being a peg below the pride of a boy born in the country. Paddy likes it because there are so many of the b'hoys to work with him—farm-labor being quite too lonely for his liking—and because he is at home in the mud ; and there is no restraint on his dress, manners or morals ; and rainy days and Sundays are "rale holidays," with no barn-work, nor cattle to look after, nor other hindrance to his going to

Newburgh, where there are promiscuous attractions. If not the cleanest and best behaved of wayside population, however, the Irish are a variety that comes in well for contrast and invigoration to the musing and half conscious picture formed upon the eye during a drive. In the stout legs and arms, rosy cheeks and honest proportions of the women who belong to, and trudge with them, or lodge near and group around with wash-tubs and children, there is a supply for the lacking bulk and bloom of our American race, which it is a comfort to see on the same day with the slender-limbed intelligence of farmers' daughters, and the pale-faced pride and respectability of farmers' sons. It is an admirable graft—the Hibernian stock upon ours—for it acclimates and improves admirably, if left to itself for a generation or two. Ireland is the California whence comes the specie for our health-currency ; and the precious ore, though unsightly till refined and coined, looks fairer than other dirt when its value is remembered. And, may I confess, at the same time, to a certain relief in a mile or two of jolly and careless faces, such as the Irish on our lower road to Newburgh, after the miles of unsmiling responsibility of countenance and persevering anxiety of demeanor through which one runs a gauntlet of low spirits before arriving at that part of the country ? Every car in our American train is so sure to be a locomotive !

I see that one of the daily papers mentions the line of *mud discoloration*, from the river freshets, as extending far out into the harbor of New York—a descent of country cousins, or fresh water and its belongings, which must have temporarily driven the finny loafers of dock and wharf very nearly out of sewer-reach and soundings. At the meeting of salt water and fresh, there is an *infusorial cemetery* (Professor Johnson tells us), the myriads of insects which belong to each realm of the element dying with the touch of the other, and precipitating at once to the bottom—thus producing the twenty-five per cent, of animal remains found in the mud of all Deltas at the mouth of rivers. Whereabouts is this death-line on the Hudson ? The water is brackish even as high as West Point ; but there must be a broad margin, a mile or two in extent, where the full tide of the sea meets the perpetual down-flow of the stream—an insect "valley of the shadow of death" hitherto unrequiemed and un-named. Insects are Universalists, I believe, and there must be a heaven for both "beyonds"—Sunnyside, perhaps, the Elysium opening from the Infusorial Cemetery of the Sea. Mr. Irving should be "in *spirits*," all the time—or perhaps the down tide and the up impregnate the air by turns with dirge and Hallelujah. Tell us of your unaccountableness, dear Geoffrey—your tears and smiles which you have never yet attributed to the rise and fall of the river at the edge of your lawn—and let us trace to these unconscious influences of another world, to this changeful poetry of entomology, the sad and gay thoughts we find woven in your style's sweet alternation.

From my window, as I write, I can see a hill-side, from which an acre at least of thickly up-springing young *cedars* have slid away with the freshet—a contribution of monumental trees which might well be stopped at the death-line of the Hudson, and planted round its cemetery border.

LETTER LIX.

Distinctions of Rank in Vegetables—Splendid Outburst of Spring—Chivalry among Fowls—A daily Steamboat Luxury for this Neighborhood—Philosophy of Visits to the City, &c., &c.

May 27, 1854.

THE potatoes are going into the ground like reluctant dollars this week—the farmer, with the late marvellous rise in the price, and the increasing uncertainties of the crop, feeling as if he were making an investment of more ready money than he can spare, and for a return that is too skittish for his peace of mind. The once humble potato, meantime, that was a staple necessity, the stand-by for the farmer's table and cattle-trough, is now a promoted luxury, hasty-pudding and corn cakes occupying its familiar place. I noticed that my farm-tenant yesterday spoke of the potato-*garden*—that same modest acre having been hitherto known as the potato-*patch*. So bud and flower distinctions and titles, even among the vegetables of a republic !

We have had a week of heavenly Spring (the middle of May), and the belated flowers and leaves have overtaken the season with a jump. The fields and woods are—oh, how beautiful ! With such mornings, noons and evenings coming round, one is reminded of those globe-animalculæ, idle and blest, who, by mere and unconscious revolving, are brought in contact with what they require. Happiness seems but the time of day, in such weather—so sure to come and so naturally making a part of everything. To breathe and be abroad is heaven, in country-life just now.

* * * * * *

With the sudden outburst of this belated Spring, the foliage is of a singular brilliancy of tint, in the valleys around us. This morning, May 20, shows like a gala-day of the emerald, so festal is the dazzling brightness of the green, and so joyous is the effect of the new leaves among the bronze-tinted tassels of the evergreens. A thousand tables set with alabaster cups could not glitter more festively in the sun than the level-spread blossoms of the dogwoods, spotting the acclivities of Idlewild just now, and with the rainbows of wild flowers scarfing and carpeting the grove and meadow, the merriment in the fuller streams, the bustle of the building birds, and the intoxicating vitality of the air, it seems as if one must oneself revivify and grow—somehow or somewhere—to belong to this continuation of Eden. Such Springs cannot be all for vegetation. There must be a *soul*-Summer to come after a May like this—wakened by its warmth and music, color and fragrance—even if the root-reaching juices of the earth are not for our dulled pulses and fibres.

I had an amusing proof, this morning, however, that we belong to a world of many spheres*—all life by no means responsive to the same promptings. With a half-hour to spare, I had set it to thought-music by opening " Rural Hours " (that charming book by the daughter of Fenimore Cooper), and the following passage particularly arrested my attention :

> We American women, certainly, owe a debt of gratitude to our countrymen for their kindness and consideration of us generally. Gallantry may not always take a graceful form in this part of the world, and mere flattery may be worth as little here as elsewhere ; but there is a glow of generous feeling towards women in the hearts of most American men, which is highly honorable to them as a nation and as individuals. In no country is the protection given to woman's helplessness more full and free—in no country is the assistance she receives from the stronger arm so general—and nowhere does her weakness meet with more forbearance and consideration. Under such circumstances, it must be woman's own fault if she be not thoroughly respected also. The position accorded to her is favorable ; it remains for her to fill it in a manner worthy of her own sex, gratefully, kindly, and simply ; with truth and modesty of heart and life ; unwavering fidelity of feeling and principle, with patience, cheerfulness, and sweetness of temper—no unfit return to those who smoothe the daily path for her."

* With the chance that the reader may not be altogether "booked up" as to the ladder of existences of which ours is but a middling round, I will quote what the Rev. Mr. Graham, in his Lecture on Spiritual Manifestations, says of the steps *above* us, though my present comment is upon a manifestation of a step *below* :

"There are seven spheres in and around the earth, in which man is said to pass his existence preparatory to entering into heaven. The earth is the first : from this man passes by death to the second, which is above the atmosphere, a height of six miles. The third, still above, occupies about forty miles in height ; the fourth, yet further off, occupying a Space much larger ; and so on in geometrical ratio until you come to the seventh sphere, whence we are all eventually to pass by a kind of second death into heaven. In these different spheres dwell the spirits of the departed, studying the alphabet, if need be, learning arithmetic, and so on, up to fluxions, if they have not studied these on earth. They have their pet dogs and birds with them. They are all clothed as upon earth ; if rich, according to taste. One supernal theologian tell us that many of the females wear a plain robe confined at the waist by a girdle. A large portion of them wear their hair in flowing ringlets. Men dress as their taste inclines ; some in Oriental style, with turbans and Persian trousers ; others in the fashionable attire of the day. Most of them wear all of the beard. They but wish for dress and have it. They are taller or shorter than when on earth as they may choose to be. They cannot well see through opaque bodies as walls, nor beneath the earth's surface ; nor can they pass through solid substances, or a small space. They want doors and windows opened to pass through, and seldom deign to descend a chimney. We have no knowledge of a spirit having visited any of the planets."

Laying down the book at this complimentary tribute to our sex, I stepped out upon the lawn to speak to a gardener at work on one of the gravel walks, and found the man leaning on his spade and watching a domestic drama of somewhat different feather. A large turkey-hen, the widowed survivor of a pair that had been sent us from Carolina, was just getting the upper hand, in a fight, with a powerful dung-hill cock. It had been a long skrimmage, the man said, and he had "never seen a *she*-thing show such pluck"—but, just as the compliment was uttered, a new combatant appeared. The widowed bird had been coupled with a Northern turkey-cock, at the disappearance of her Carolina mate, a few weeks before, and this second husband now mingled in the affray, taking sides, however, with the rooster that was well nigh beaten, and *against his own wife and kind*, the mother of a troop of his own well-begotten turkey-lings, feeding at a little distance. It was an atrocity that I had thought too mean for an instinct—quite below barn-yard-fowls, at least, who strut and have a sense of ostentation as spouses. But there raged the fight—a husband and a bully against a crestless female—who, still, proved to be a match for them, and was showing no sign of knocking under when I ran to her rescue. It was a pleasure to have read Miss Cooper's tribute just before, and remember that there was a different inspiration, in the American air (for male breathing) a sphere or so higher. According to Theodore Parker, this marks our rate of progress in civilization. He says :–

> "The savage is always and everywhere a lazy animal ; but yet he must get work done, and, for this purpose, he subdues woman, and makes her work for him. The first thing that man conquered and annexed to himself was woman. The superiority of man lies in three things—First, in having the largest brain ; second, a stronger arm ; and third, his harder heart. In this triple superiority, man compels woman to do his drudgery. He kills a moose, or a deer, or a large fish, and the woman must drag it home, cook and prepare it. In all savage lands, woman is the slave of man. The boor of Germany rides home on his horse, and the daughter and wife walk home beside him."

* * * * * *

The lady inhabitants of this neighborhood have a summer convenience, which (partly by chance, perhaps) is more fitly arranged for their luxurious enjoyment, as to time and management, than would seem to belong to such a shortcomingdom as this our life. Breakfast leisurely over, somewhere about nine o'clock, a joyous bell rings across the bay, and the largest, swiftest and most sumptuous of all the day-boats on the river, the steamer Alida, comes swooping down the mirrored shore-line from Newburgh. You are invited (madam !) to go to town in a floating palace, pass four hours in Broadway, or where you please, and be brought back through the Highlands, in the enchantment of sunset. As you *go*, the shadows of the scenery will be thrown with artistic effect towards you, for it is morning, and the boat's course is South and East. As you *return*, the same accommodating shadows will fall with rosy tints of twilight, the other way. Both ways you will see the river in its utmost beauty. There is an upper and a lower forward-deck, luxuriously provided with seats, where the motion of the boat secures a breeze, though the river be breathless. Or, there is an elegant public saloon and a private one, daintily cushioned and mirrored, where you may read or chat, with the comforts of your own drawing-room at home. On the chance of your wanting all your time in the city, so that it might not be convenient to dine, a hot lunch is served a half-hour before reaching the wharf, and you may start for your shopping or calls with the freshness rather of town-gadders than of country-folks who have come sixty miles down the river. The stopping-place being the foot of Robinson street, directly opposite the centre of the Park, you may be at Stewart's in five minutes, without hackney-coach or confusion. At 4 P. M., you return to your floating-palace, and glide away towards your home again ; and, while you pass the first twenty less picturesque miles, perhaps, in lying down upon the cushioned seats of the private saloon, recovering from your fatigues, the ten-mile labyrinth of the Highlands is getting ready to present you with a panorama—a sunset extended through a river-tangle of zig-zag-ing mountains, the splendor of which, if seen for the first time, would make any day memorable. From the class of people whom it mainly accommodates—the occupants of the villas on the Hudson, and the summer visitors at West Point and Cozzen's—the Alida seems rather to be making an excursion of gaiety than a passage of convenience. Leaving Idlewild, as I did, a day or two ago, after breakfast, and getting home to tea—chatting with a large party of friends either way, and seeing an enchanting variety of effect in river-scenery—it seemed scarce credible to me that I had *also* travelled one hundred and sixty miles, and taken advantage of four hours for leisurely attention to my business in the city. "If Mahomet," says a Persian poet, "had lived long enough to know the pleasures of Shiraz, he would have prayed God to make him immortal there." And, without wishing to be an immortal passenger in the Alida, I doubt whether there was ever half such an immortality's-worth, as her trip up and down of a summer's day (Broadway and all) offered to the sinners and shoppers of Shiraz.

One goes to the city, at least an individual—a lump of sugar or a slice of lemon—but the feeling of being suddenly *lemonaded into insignificance*, on plunging into that busy stir, is common, I suspect, to those who land from a steamboat and walk towards Broadway. Without caring to be more seen or thought of by others, there is still a valuable sense privilege in having an atmosphere of one's own—the difference between a fig in a drum (city life), and the purple and gold fig, as it gives fragrance and drops honey from (country life) the tree. It would be a question, of course, whether the world is large enough to let every fig have room to show shape and color. Most men can only come to the thumb and finger of their destiny by the close packing where they are thought of by the thousand. But the instinctive preference for the *space and liberty to be an individual,* is at the bottom of the arrived-passenger feeling, spoken of above, and I presume the general dignity and self-respect of the human race are increasing with the improvements in steam and railroad which are putting country life within reach of a greater number. Figs and physiognomies alter alike, as to beauty and character, by too close indiscriminateness of pressure—though the meaner look is sometimes more valued as being more metropolitan.

LETTER LX.

Newness of Junes—Effects of the Eclipse—Cows embarrassed—Nature's Caprices—Visit to West Point—The Salute to the Visiting Committee—Cadets' Mess-Room—Professor Weir and the Gallery of Drawings—Parade—Stature of the Present Class of Cadets, &c., &c.

June 10, 1854.

THE poet said to his ——th lady-love, what one has felt like saying, perhaps, to every June as it came round, but certainly to this :—

"I feel that I have loved before,
But worshipped ne'er till now."

So prodigally beautiful and new, and so beyond April expectation, has been the outburst of foliage and flowers, that the inferiority of previous Junes seems the only way to account for the intoxicating novelty of the impression. Nature, clad previously in textures of silk, seems now in almost overburthened sumptuousness under "velvets of three-pile." We must guano our dictionary to chronicle such a summer as should follow.

The two twilights of an afternoon, that we had last week, proved that Nature can scarce give us a surfeit of her beauty. The regular "close of day" was a resplendent one in itself, but it was like the luxury of an encore in an opera, following so immediately upon the bird-roosting twilight of the eclipse—a sun of full brightness briefly intervening. Chancing to be taking one of my favorite rides during the progress of the phenomenon, I was glad of the opportunity to see a large extent of familiar scenery in a new light—the Hudson and its Highlands dramatised, as it were—for the effect, throughout the gradual obscuration, was that of an atmosphere of pictorial contrivance, such as a Claude Lorraine might give to a copy of the landscape from memory. Occasionally in England I have seen something of the same tender middle-tint in the first decline of the afternoon ; but, to our unpicturesque transparency of climate, the sweet room thus given to the imagination is rare. The shadows were uncertain, the distances and elevations very much increased, and, the river being tranquil, each mountain was doubled by reflection, and looked like a cloud peaked above and below. I shall remember it like some wonderful painting.

Among the lesser influences of these disturbed parallaxes and semi-diameters, I noticed that neighbor Smith's cows, who gipsy up and down two or three miles of road during the day, started for home with full faith in twilight No. 1, doubtless very much perplexed at seeing the sun blaze forth again over their hope deferred swill at the door-step. It saved the old man his usual tramp to "hurry home them critters," though the milk-pail might show that there was a loss of a half-pint's-worth or so, of grass-plunder prematurely suspended. The birds of all kinds I observed were in quite a flurry—their flights short and disturbed, and their notes expressive of distress. On the population along the road the effect was less reverential than I should have anticipated.* A bit of smoked glass was in almost every hand, but the joking and fun were universal—partly caused, perhaps, by the drolly emphasized and accented look of the general physiognomy, every nose of man, woman, and child, for five miles, it seemed to me, having a black tip from a rub of the lamp-smoke. A jolly Irishman, at one of the brick-yards, twitched off his hat as I came along, and raised a great laugh among the Paddies by taking a look through it at *me*—but he forgot, that, for an eclipse of the Sun or any other gentleman, there must be a lady (fair Dian) between him and the world. And, by the way (to ask a Woman's-Rights question), is it a mark of the superiority of our sex, or not, that the Sun may have four eclipses a year and the Moon only two ? What does it argue, that, among celestial bodies, as in good society on earth, they are thus twice as strict with the ladies ?

As a nail whereon to hang some of our unaccountablenesses, an eclipse is useful. It is owing to the eclipse, of course, that the oak and cedar seem to have a disease this year—buds blighted and both families of trees leafing very reluctant and poor. The hemlocks, on the contrary, with their unprecedented profusion of glittering tassel-tips, look as if gold had rained on them. Corn has had no chance with such a cold Spring—potatoes and turnips, on the other hand, profiting greatly by it. There are those who have had unexpected blessings, those who have had unexpected calamaties—all alike owing to the eclipse. According to Gloster, in *King Lear*, however, it is only evils that can be thus accounted for. He says :—

* Of the popular impression of an eclipse, exactly two hundred years ago, Francis Berneir, thus writes, quoted by Southey :—

"Some bought drugs against the eclipse, others kept themselves close in the dark in their caves and their well-closed chambers, others cast themselves in great multitudes into the churches ; those apprehending some malign and dangerous influence, and these believing that they were come to the last day, and that the eclipse would shake the foundations of nature and overturn it, notwithstanding anything that Gassendis, Robervals, and many other famous philosophers could say or write against this persuasion, when they demonstrate that this eclipse was of the same nature with so many others that had preceded without any mischief, and that it was a known accident, foreseen and ordinary, which had nothing peculiar."

> "These late *eclipses* in the sun and moon portend no good to us : though the wisdom of nature can reason thus and thus, yet nature finds itself scourged by the sequent effects. Love cools, friendship falls off, brothers divide : in cities, mutinies ; in countries, discord ; in palaces treason, and the bond crushed between son and father."

We certainly have had more violent freshets, slides, tempests, and irregularities of nature, hereabouts, within the last Winter and Spring, than the oldest inhabitant remembers the like of. Almost every operation of season and weather seems to have been either stronger or duller than usual—hardly anything in the old familiar way. But the wonderful rapidity with which June has overtaken and surpassed the lagging season, within a week, shows that the compensating influences are at work. The eclipse is over.

* * * * * *

Fifteen minutes from Idlewild to West Point at 9 A. M., by the swift Alida, on her way to New York—the grand annual review of the Cadets, with their military music and cannonading, for the Government Board of Visitors, to come off at twelve—the Alida, on her return, to bring us home through the Highlands, at sunset, in fifteen minutes of still more splendid parade of sky and water—and all on the first of June, that one day of the year when it was never known to rain since the memory of man—no ! there was no refusing, to a bold little pleader of six years old, the promise that I *"would go."* He was happy. But that was not all of it—for so was I. The sweetness—oh, the sweetness ! of an excuse to be a child again for a summer's day.

As usual, June the 1st dawned like a morning of Eden. It was one of those days when the curse of Adam's fall (industry or no happiness) was suspended, or altogether optional. In such weather there was no need to have anything to *do*. To *be* was enough. Calm, cloudless, elastic, pleasant in the sunshine or out of it, balmy to breathe and brilliant to look around—may we say, unprofanely, that we trust God for the like, after death ? It would be almost impious, it seems to me, to pray for "another and better world" on such a morning.

The Alida came along, loaded with Quakers on their way down to the Annual Meeting of their Sect of Peace—a chance parenthesis to my day of military curiosity, which I felt to be a (?) as to the propriety of thus sowing a filibuster-seed in the imagination of my boy. Fifteen minutes is short time to repent, however. We were at the wharf, with a soldier on guard, before I had looked the idea fairly in the face ; and the triumph of military engineering, which had given us a new road, like the Simplon, up the front of a cliff, made its beginning of the day's warlike captivation. That new pier and its road, joining the highway of the river, instead of the old wharf so inconveniently round a corner, are in accordance with the open-door spirit of the day—the policy at West Point having hitherto been, to entrench and seclude it from public access. The proposed road along the river-bank to Newburgh (to bring the military town within reach of a market, and open its parades to the drives of the surrounding country) was smothered by Secretary Marcy on the caterpillar policy, I believe ; but we look to him for its resuscitation, now that he is through with his chrysalis, and thinks a little more farsightedly, on the wing.

An omnibus did the climbing for us, to the summit-level of the parade-ground ; and, from that omnibus door, as we gradually ascended, the view down through a crowd of mountains, upon a river with a fleet of sloops threaded by the flying Alida * * * *

But we came to see soldiers, and I will try to say nothing of scenery. Only—if one's unlimited delight may speak a word as it goes to its dungeon of silence—the reader should run no risk of dying without a visit to this spot of Nature's most wanton extravagance of beauty. Leave no love nor wonder, no tenderness nor taste at home, dear reader ! You will want all you can be, do, borrow or imagine, for exquisite and enthusiastic delight and appreciation, at West Point on a summer's day. Oh, the * * * *

And now that the key is turned on that intoxicated gentleman, let us have a cool look for a cadet, or something with which Nature has nothing to do. This range of cannon (the passing officer tells us) is to fire a salute, presently, for the Board of Visitors on their way to the public buildings. And here comes a file of cadets from the college, to man the guns, and we will take a seat upon this big rock and see the manœuvering.

The tight, little gray coats, with their epauletted captain, had a few minutes' exercise in wheeling, advancing and loading the pieces of ordnance, and then the nine gentlemen in plain coats whom the powder was to honor, were seen coming from the hotel, escorted (and, as a matter of mere visibility, contradictorily eclipsed) by the Colonel in command and the military Professors. The heavy guns were handled like playthings by the cadets, nothing going wrong but two or three of the percussion-caps that missed fire—possibly from opposite politics, to the Nebraskan party under salute. (Or, the percussion might have been Democratic enough, and the powder Whig—a failure of a gun to go off by disaffection of party, which would never occur, of course, with shot in the charge or anything to hit.) The echoes, I presently discovered, were the answers to those pulled strings for which my wondering little companion gave the Captain the most credit. They reverberated back from the mountains in three peals, the last coming from the Storm King with a long, low roll like the most distant thunder (as measured by the watch of a gentleman who stood near us, two seconds between the first peal of echoes and the second, ten between the second and the third). Those cannons' voices impressed me curiously—as the first time I had ever heard our familiar mountains adequately spoken to ! It was, certainly, the first time I had ever heard them *answer*. Human utterance does not seem to corroborate our claim as lords of creation, stoutly as we assert it ; and I shall have my own misgivings on the subject, I fear, now that I have heard these twenty-four-pounders, until I can speak to the mountains and get some sort of civil answer, as they do.

The cadets' mess-room (for we had several friends among the professors, and had fallen into the procession of visitation) is in a very imposing new building of Norman architecture, which "tells" admirably on the scenery in which it is placed, and is heightened by it, in turn, with most embellishing foreground and background. The interior looked simple and serviceable. Table was laid for dinner, and we took a guess at the weight of the singularly massive china plates that were set—manufactured especially for cadet use and contingency. One professor thought a plate might weigh two pounds, another three. But if intended, as it probably was, to show what the supporter for a soldier's food (or the bottom of his stomach) should be like, it is certainly of sturdy promise for a campaign. The small round seats of cast-iron were of similar significance. War, if these are to be believed, needs tough stomachs and unsusceptible sittings down.

The library, the laboratory, the lecture-rooms, and gallery of drawings, were duly visited, and the public knows how serviceably and skilfully complete are this admirable institution's practical machineries of knowledge. The drawings *only* were a complete surprise to me. I knew how essential it was, of course, that a soldier should have a true eye, and understand distance and effect, size, action and color ; but it had not occurred to me, that, in learning these scientific steps of art, he must needs follow the progression of an artist. The framed drawings by the cadets, in that gallery, while they show a most thorough schooling of the eye, would do credit to any school of artists in the world. Professor Weir, himself a master among painters, has satisfactory proof thus to offer of the zeal and efficiency of the science he teaches ; but it is also a most pleasant evidence of his inspiring such a zeal in his pupils as to accomplish even more than the mechanism of art—its taste and ornamental execution.

Soldiers have to learn to be a great many things—chambermaids among others ; and the Representation of the Government, in whose train we had the honor to be walking, were to judge, of course, of the proficiency of the cadets in bed-making and general Pollyology. The "barracks" are a handsome new structure, and divided into those "bed-rooms for two," of the comforts and crockery of which, the undergraduate heroes have the exclusive care. As the colonel and his staff, and the honorable visiters walked along the entries, doors were thrown open, and the auto-broom-handling and slop-see-ings-after, as executed by the one of the two young soldiers who was the alternate Polly of the morning, were offered to official inspection. We looked in, with the rest. Really, neatness and order could no farther go ! I noticed but two peculiarities—(in addition, I mean, to a most martinet scantiness of superfluities)—first, that by male and military chamber-maiding, no coverlet petticoats were allowed to fall over the naked iron legs of the bedsteads, and over the one pair of shoes that stood in solitary readiness for action under each bed ; and, second, that the mattrass, as an article that could have no possibility of day-duty, was rolled snugly up to the bolster, out of temptation's way. Altogether, one gets the impression that glory is more tidy and scant than he had supposed, in looking at this as the training of it. I had expected two towels to a hero, at least—among other disappointments. And, as for Monterey and Buena Vista on one tooth-brush ! but these are considerations for the honorable board's more statistical Report to Congress.

Visits over, the parade came off at noon. How beautiful it was, on that green plateau, with sunshine, music, and June leaves, mountains and ladies looking on, Cuba and Canada in the distance, and a sumptuous collation expecting us at the colonel's house, immediately in the rear—I leave to the reader's fancy, with thus much of mention. A word or two only, before closing, upon points which my child-companion probably did not take in—with his ice-cream at the colonel's, and his bewildered delight and astonishment, swallowed immediately before.

Stature seems to go by periods. There was an age, the histories tell us, when all the great heroes and statesmen of the world were small men. The cadets, at West Point at present, are, it is said, unusually tall. They are, of course, nationally thin. But the contrast between their agile and wiry look, and the bluff and plump aspect of the cadets of Addiscomb in England (whom I remember from having once passed a month in the neighborhood of that military college, seeing the parades and exercises every day), would foreshow a natural and trying antagonism between the two. To my eye, the personal build and bearing of our own young graycoats could scarcely be improved upon, for endurance and action. They came here, doubtless, by that pick for the profession which ensures that they were the best among their playfellows for the appointment—but a more indomitable and reliable-looking a set of young customers for the enemy, need not be kept ready. And there is a singularly cool and thoughtful absence of swell and filibuster about them. It is the quiet manliness of air which belongs to fearlessness, with skill and knowledge. Their model is a high one—the Commandant, Colonel Lee, being, certainly, in feature, mien, and manners, the perfection of what they should study for a soldier. He (with the family of Washington whose honors he inherits) is well represented, by the way, among the cadets themselves, his son, a well-built and gallant-looking fellow, being at the head of the graduating class.

I had something to say of Weir's studio, which we visited in the course of the day—and of the charming drive to Cozzens's which we took with the agreeable gentlemen of the Board of Visitors, towards evening—and of Roe and his paradise of a summer hotel—and of the sunset return by the Alida, which came duly along with her usual crowd of well-bred company on board, and among them the far-famed Lieutenant Strain, and Headley the vehement historian—and of my boy's gradual digestion of his day of transcendent novelty and happiness—of these and some more things I could be communicative, possibly instructive. But we will let the reader draw breath. To one of the omitted topics, at least—Weir's beautiful pictures—I shall please the reader by promising to turn, hereafter.

LETTER LXI

Adventure with a Snapping-Turtle—Wild black Cat, and other quadruped Bandits—Visit to a Revolutionary Soldier—Venerable Companion—Privations of the Army—Washington's features, &c., &c.

June 24, 1854.

How we become acquainted with new neighbors is sometimes an event to ourselves. Coming home from a long gallop, yesterday, I had gradually drawn rein (to prolong the luxury of the last mile in the heaven of a June sunset), when, by the communicative ears of my mare, I was informed of something worth noticing in the road. I looked ahead. So near home, one is a little slow to be astonished ; but Lady Jane had not pricked up her telegraphic signals for a mere feminine love of news. There was a monster in the way. A moving house, with the six members of its family hanging clear out of the windows—the head, tail and legs of a *tortoise*, of the like of which I had never before seen a specimen, with its belongings all outside like Barnum's elephant, whose legs and trunk may be seen for nothing, though he walks from town to town with a barn around him—stood directly in the track. A *common* turtle my friend Morris had mercifully removed from the carriage road, near the house, a day or two before ; and the children every day bring in those little unresisting Quakers, with their toes and fingers drawn in to wait our pleasure—but this was a very different customer. The broad rim of my hat would not have taken in his entire outline, and his big shell might have stirred the envy of an alderman—evidently a bony paunch which he had the power of vacating altogether of its vital organs, to make room for his dinner. It was a *snapping-turtle*, in fact—but, let me anticipate a little, by quoting what Natural History says of the species :—

"The snapper (*E. Serpentina*) has been separated by some authors from *emys*, on account of the small size of the sternum which *serves very imperfectly to conceal the head and members*. It is found from New England to Florida, is very voracious, and destroys great quantities of fish. The shell is more or less tricarinate ; the head, neck, limbs and tail are very large, the latter strongly crested. From the form of its body, it is called, in the Southern States, *alligator tortoise*. It bites severely, and will seize anything presented to it, and sometimes will not let go its hold, even after the head is severed from the body. It attains large dimensions. Individuals have been met with, exceeding four feet and a half in total length."

The difference of a piano-forte, with or without its legs, was the difference between my previous impression of a turtle and the one before me. The shell of the animal, which was about two feet in length, stood well lifted from the mud, and he would apparently walk over an egg without breaking it. The head followed my movements, the little green eyes venomously intent on me, and, as my restless mare fretted around him, his tail acted like a scull-oar, assisting his legs in working about so as to keep head on to the enemy.

It appeared, as I looked at him, that a wheel of some light vehicle had left a mud-mark across the reptile's back, and, by his continuing in the road, he did not know enough to profit by his experience. He was in a fair way to be run over again, and by a heavier wagon ; and it was but neighborly, of course, to put him beyond danger. I dismounted and turned him on his back, by a sudden lift with my foot, but he whipped over on his legs again with the quickness of a torpedo, and, by a second jump, seized me at the ankle. I just felt the scrape of his toothless mandibles ; but, though my skin was not included in the bite, my boot and trouser were ; and, for a moment, it looked as if I must cut loose with a penknife or mount and ride home with a pendant snapping-turtle for a spur. He loosed his hold to prepare for a snap at Lady Jane, however, who was prancing dangerously near his toes meantime, and so I stood clear—once more reminded of what are this world's reciprocities for acts of kindness and mercy.

This kind of turtle is good eating, and, on my arriving at home and mentioning the encounter to Bell (my lesser-anxiety man), he started on a full run for the spot, anticipating a delicacy for his supper. But the gentleman (or rather the *lady*, for he said it was doubtless a female on her way up from the marsh to lay her eggs in the bushes on the hill-side), had made the best of the ten minutes to get away. I asked him how he would have brought her home without a weapon first to dispatch her ; and he said (what I think it may be useful to record for inexperienced captors of snapping-turtles) that he should have watched his chance to seize her by the tail. Once lifted clear of the ground, the jumping animal may be carried as easily as a carpet-bag.

I find that two of this same family were dug out from our muck-meadow last year, and eaten without mention ; so that Idlewild has probably its tenantry of snapping-turtles—awkward vicinage, perhaps, for such stray poets as throw themselves

"Prone on the grass in rapturous reverie ;"

particularly, as the reptile, half buried in clover and buttercups, would look very like a flat stone whereon to rest an elbow or sit dry. Brother scribblers and idlers are hereby cautioned against unexpected hostilities in places of rest.

Our veto upon guns and hunting-dogs has multiplied the game to a wonderful extent within these wild limits, but I find that animals of prey (perhaps snapping-turtles among them) are attracted to the spot by the same immunity, or by what it protects. The glen is a fastness of caves and precipices, and (the house barely overhanging its depths), there is but an easy scramble of two hundred feet between the fox's hole and our poultry yard. Turkey after turkey has disappeared, leaving but claws or bloody feathers to tell the tale, and a rabbit's foot here, or a squirrel's tail there, shows daily that our sacred asylum for these innocent and happy races is stealthily profaned. Among other quadruped bandits, curiously enough, is a black cat, who has been tempted by the abundance of the birds and other game, and has evidently abandoned kitchen dependence and civilisation, to live a savage life altogether in the glen. We get glimpses of her every day, in rambling about, and, occasionally, she passes very near, not at all disturbed by human approach ; but, after seeing a brilliant oriole in her claws the other day, I mentally pronounced her an outlaw. We must have a fox-hunt before long, in which the doom of the black cat must be included.

* * * * * *

Our Highland neighborhood prides itself on the *mastodon*, disinterred among its hills, and the memorials of Washington, so long here, and at such a trying period with his army. Science and history must take us in their way. Perhaps even Mr. Barnum, too, would give us a reconnoitering call, if he should *hear*, that, among other belongings of the Father of Independence, his *"usual nap"* still survives among us, as well as his tea-kettle and arm-chair. Such is the fact—if the ear alone is to be trusted with a word. Usual Knapp is the curious name of the only surviving member of Washington's Life-Guard, an old man of ninety-five years of age, here resident, and still hearty and active. And the circumstance with which he is commonly mentioned gives a promise of his still lasting longer—a habit, which he has kept up for the eight or nine years that he has now been a widower, of celebrating his own birthday by a call on all the widows of the country round about.

The portrait of this venerable "revolutionary," which hangs among the relics in the old mansion known as Washington's Head-Quarters, at Newburgh, had started a question as to his whereabout ; and we were surprised to discover that he was residing on just the other side of the mountain which we see from our western window—a brother farmer, within ten or twelve miles of Idlewild. This was startling vicinity for a still unsnapped link with an age gone by, and to drive over and see the old man on the first fair day, was the promise of an excursion that might even lay a rose leaf on the full cup of a June morning.

I have spoken once or twice in these letters of our venerable next neighbor, Friend S., the quaker, whose white locks and soul-calm tranquillity of mien and features are among the most precious and beautiful of the accustomed pictures in our secluded grounds. To him also it was a surprise to learn that so interesting a person as Usual Knapp was still living, and within visiting distance, and he willingly agreed to make one of the party. His company had the additional value to us, that it would bring together *two* whose eyes had been familiar with the form of Washington, Friend S. (now eighty years of age), having been a boy in the neighborhood when the head-quarters were here, and seeing the great man almost daily.

The rural township to which we were bound is called Little Britain, and the atmosphere, on the morning of our excursion (June 16th), was of that occasional summer haze which gives our hard and clear landscape the softer effect of that of England. There would have been a third reminder of the parent country, in the sign of the old tavern, representing General George Washington leading the British lion by a chain—but that remarkable painting is now removed. The highly cultivated fields of this part of our county of eggs and butter, looked very English, in the veiled sunshine. The cattle *were* English—Devon cows in every pasture. A belonging of our own native scenery was suddenly missed, as we descended from the gap in the ridge of Snake Hill—the thick *cedars* which line the walls on every road of Highland terrace. With the change of the soil, in passing the bowl-rim of mountains that shuts us in, the nourishment for this invaluable tree evidently ceases, and I had not realized before how fortunate we are in having such superb spontaneous avenues for the public roads, on our romantic ten-mile terrace.

At the gate of a small and unpainted farm cottage, on the side of a hill, I tied up my warm ponies, and, as the front porch showed no sign of life, we took the garden way to the back-door. Here we were met by a middle-aged lady, whose face we could but partially see, for she had on one of those *smotherers*, or hoods, which all our country girls wear till they have got through with their work in the morning—this useful article hanging, for the rest of the day, on a nail by the kitchen-door, ready to be slipped on whenever there is an errand to the barn, or whenever the hair is to be protected from dust, or the features from unwished for observation. Probably no passing stranger ever saw the face of an American girl while she was milking the cows, or weeding the carrot-patch.

The parlor blinds were thrown open, chairs placed, and the kindest of welcomes given us, by this disguised lady in her smotherer, and then, saying that her father would be in presently, she disappeared, to be seen no more for that visit.* The old man was at work in his garden, but his slow steps were soon heard, and he entered the room, throwing his hat upon the floor at one side of the threshold, and his stick at the other. With a smile on his face and both hands open, he came forward to greet the strangers. He was tall and bent, but evidently of the lithe and symmetrical build which was likeliest to attain his present age of ninety-five. His head and features were exceedingly fine. A sculptor would have modelled a Cæsar from them, a half century ago. Frankness, cordiality, and self-confident simplicity, were marked in his expression of face, voice, and manners.

Very deaf, he drew our chairs very near him ; and, with his right hand on the leg of Friend S., and his left hand on mine, he made himself acquainted with our names and professions. The group chanced to be a curious ladder of ages—my boy of six years of age, his father, and his grandfather (Mr. Grinnell of New Bedford), the octogenarian Friend S., and the almost centarian we had come to visit—five stages of a century, in a circle intent upon honoring and listening to the oldest. And what a wilderness of deeds and dinners, to fill up the interval between the first round of that ladder and the last ! With all the success and honor of the three rounds above me, I must say it seemed rather a *climb*. My conscious likelihood of not coming to the next had a relief in it, like the crossed-out item in a bill.

The two old men, with the long gray locks of their two beautiful heads laid close together, soon got to comparing their reminiscences of Washington—the subject we were the most interested in bringing about. Friend S. related how the boys used to be called out of school when the commander-in-chief was seen to be coming along the road on horseback, and how dignified and noble he looked, as he rode past with his hat off, courteously returning the low-bowed salutation of the lads. He said also, that he now lived in the house Lafayette occupied at that time, at the junction of the Moodna with the Hudson ; and then they refreshed their memories with the story of the Irishman who undertook to carry the marquis across that stream on his back, and dropped him into the water—a possibility of an intention to drown the popular officer, which made the Irishman so detested that he was obliged to leave the neighborhood.

But the old sergeant's description of the parade of the life-guard every morning before the mansion of headquarters, and the look of the general as he slowly walked up and down the portico, "straight as a dart and noble as he could be," was the most glowing of all. They "had the three

* In a drive over which I have since taken, to give my wife the pleasure of seeing the honored veteran, we had the good fortune to see one of the ladies, and were very much delighted with her inheritance of countenance and manners. She is, indeed, a worthy daughter of a sire such as republics depend on.

best drummers in the army," he said, and "they made such music that it took you right off your feet." It entirely straightened the old man's spine to talk of it. He sat bolt upright, and the squeeze of his bony fingers upon my leg could not have been much looser than the one with which he "charged bayonet" at the battle of Monmouth. He said he remembered a verbal order Washington gave him, at that time—not to present arms or take notice of him when he was alone. "He was a man of few words," he said, "and never familiar with anybody." He repeated a story he had once before told to Headley the historian, of his having seen Washington dodge a spent ball that passed close to his head on the battle-field, and his smiling immediately, as if at his unsoldierlike weakness in doing so, and turning to his officers with the remark, "Ah, the frailty of poor human nature !"

Of the General's dress he gave us a minute description. Mrs. Washington, he said, was with him at Newburgh, but "she was older than the General, and not a handsome woman." Of General Knox, who was stationed at West Point, and of the wonderful beauty of Mrs. Knox, his mention was very enthusiastic. Knox was a "large splendid man." The sergeant was often employed to go with a boat to the Point, and bring General and Mrs. Knox to dine with General Washington. He was once ordered by the imperious officer to land at a certain place where he knew it was too shallow. He remonstrated, but Knox insisted. So they obeyed and ran into the mud, and were obliged to sit in the boat till the tide rose to take them off ; and the delay was very provoking at the time.

The old soldier gave us a thrilling description of the privations of the army in its forced march to the South. It was the wettest season ever known, and he had not a dry thread on him for weeks, but he never took cold. The rations were next to starvation—often a dried herring a day, and no bread. At the battle of Monmouth every man in his company was shot, he himself received no wound then, or in the other actions he was in, during the war, except a slight graze of a ball on the back of his left hand. The old man's feelings got the better of him once or twice in narrating the stirring scenes in which he had borne a part, and he "choked off"—but it evidently gave him great pleasure to recall them. He said he had no memory for things, *now*, but he could remember everything that happened *then*, as if it were yesterday. He enlisted at the age of sixteen, and was in the army six years. Since the disbanding, at the Peace, he has been a farmer, taking no part in the war of 1812. His wife died eight years ago, at the age of seventy-nine, and his two only children (daughters, one of whom assists in the support of her father, by dress-making), live with him. His pension of ten dollars a month is much too little—for his merits, I should think, as well as for his wants.

To see those two men, to whose eyes Washington's living features and form have been familiar—sitting together, and talking of him with their eyes bent upon each other's faces, yet each seeing the memory-picture of the great man, as he talked or listened—gave a strange impetus to the imagination, a new one to me, for the conceiving of what Washington was, as he breathed and acted. It was the Present turned back to the Past, in the magician's mirror. As we drove home, I felt as if we were returning from a place where we had seen times gone by,—though my horses, by the unusual length of the drive and the delay in their dinners, doubtless thought it more like a stretch into the Future.

LETTER LXII.

Celebration of the Fourth of July by Children—Procession through the Grounds of Idlewild—Song by the Children—Their Pic-nic in the Grove—Speeches, &c., &c.

July 8, 1854.

On the morning of the Fourth of July, A HUNDRED CHILDREN, chanting a hymn, walked in procession down the hemlock avenue of Idlewild, led by their Sabbath-school teachers, and followed by their parents and friends. They were bound to our shaded meadow-glade (at the outlet where the two glens, Funnychild and its wilder brother, run their torrents into one), to celebrate the day with a pic-nic on the grass. It had been intimated by our friend Mr. Roe, the principal teacher, that it would gratify the children to be received first at the house, taking our family into their musical procession as they should afterwards go upon their way ; and hence the beautiful picture which we now saw across the lawn—the long array of children along its rising curve making the centre of a landscape, with the Storm-King and a summer-sky lifting beyond, very much as the glowing pencil of De la Roche would have contrived and painted it.

The hymn ceased as they reached the portico, and we welcomed the gaily-dressed troop, distributing them about through the four or five open rooms, and enjoining full liberty upon their feet and eyes, with such access to pitchers of water as would sustain their Glorious Fourthification till the more substantial refreshment basketed in the meadow below. Pictures and statuary were new to most of the little mountaineers, and our wilderness of trifles (more rococo than costly) seemed to fully absorb their curiosity—one bright boy, whom I noticed, standing with open mouth before a marble shepherdess lying in nude slumber beside her crook, apparently pleased, though surprised, to find that the loveliness of unclad innocence was a matter of drawing-room admiration. A hundred children cannot but have a thick sprinkle of beauty ; and, standing in our central hall, and looking around upon the four rooms crowded with their joyous faces, I could not resist that sort of submerged feeling—the kind of emotional half-drown with which the soul gets out of its depth in sudden admiration. Nature prepares so many, to be beautiful and noble ! The children of the poor are so apt to look as if the rich would have been over-blest with such !

Alas for the angel capabilities, interrupted so soon with care, and with after life so sadly unfulfilled !

A very old woman, leaning on her long rough stick, and drawn from her bed of rheumatism by the stir of the day, had hobbled in among the rest ; and the large troop of the children's friends numbered several gray heads, and two who were eighty years of age—so that we had no lack of such contrast as artist and moralist equally admire. The half-hour to which the teachers had limited the visit was to me a magical revealing of what our mountain-scenery hides among its rocks and leafy woods, and I shall see the broad sweep of the landscape with more understanding eyes hereafter. We know now what life is astir in the covered pulses of those romantic hills.

The procession re-formed in the pine grove which overhangs the glen, in the rear of the house ; and, as we, and the city guests who chanced to be with us, fell in, they took up the song of "Little Things"—a very touching one, by the way, which, though much thumbed in Sabbath-school literature, is well worth copying for the more general reader. Thus sang the hundred child-voices, as they wound away :—

Little drops of water,
  Little grains of sand,
Make the mighty ocean,
  And the beauteous land.

And the little moments,
  Humble though they be,
Make the mighty ages
  Of eternity.

So our little errors
  Lead the soul away
From the paths of virtue,
  Oft in sin to stray

Little deeds of kindness,
  Little words of love,
Make our earth an Eden,
  Like the heaven above.

Great things have less stirred pine-tassels and me !

With a moment's interruption from a sudden onslaught upon the procession made by Don, our wilful Newfoundland, who poured his thundering bass into the treble chorus as they neared the stable (following it up with his excited legs and tail, like a mad organist carried away with the music, and plunging over upon the congregation to add himself to the swell of the *dogs*-ology)—with this brief interruption, the many little singers wound their way down the ravine. All gayly dressed as they were, in white and bright colors, it was a startlingly new and bright thread drawn through that winding road, and gleaming in and out among the trees and around the precipices and rocks—probably more beautiful to our eyes from our being accustomed to it as a solitude. It was a stage whose lifted curtain had hitherto shown us a brilliant scene, but to which were now added the figures of the play. Human beings improve scenery—spite of the geologist's theory that mankind are incidental, and not necessary, to the destiny of this our planet

Upon the steep instep of the mountain's projected foot, which divides the two glens of Idlewild and Funny-child, the children grouped themselves under the trees, as if among the columns of an ascending gallery, while the old people and the visitors and friends reclined beneath the spreading hemlocks of the meadow-glade below. Architecture could scarcely have contrived a better arrangement of a congregation for seeing and listening. The long table covered with eatables, in a darkly-shaded thicket on the brook-bank, promised to "bring down the gallery," when the services should be over, and the unfenced perspectives under the trees, stretching away indistinctly on either side, offered labyrinthine rambles to any who should choose solitude after the feast. It looked like a picture of a Happy Valley—so happy, at least, as to be altogether out of harmony with that cold hymn to Indifference :—

"Half-pleased, contented I will be—
Content but half to please."

The address and prayer by the village clergyman were followed by a Sabbath-school song, and then came the reading of the DECLARATION OF INDEPENDENCE—that faultless language-temple of Liberty, which brings the soul to its knee with the mere recognition of its truth, strength, and beauty. What thoughts, and what language ! It should be written on school-walls, and graven on entablatures behind the platforms for orators, and be largely legible wherever public assemblies must gaze and read—for, till its rock-hewn sentences are forgotten, not to be free were to be ashamed.

Our venerable neighbor, Friend S. (whom the children love, far and near), stood up with his white locks, and was eagerly listened to, for a few minutes ; and our guest, Mr. Charles Butler, made a brief and very effective address ; and Mr. Roe, the principal of the admirable boys'-school near by, went straight to the child-level of perception, with his usual tact, in a playful speech. One general hymn wound up the *gravities* of the day.

The history of the *gaieties*—the subsequent descent upon the ginger-nuts and sandwiches—is too active for my contemplative pen. The subject outruns me. In fact, my own dinner was awaiting me, about that time, on the precipice two hundred feet above ; and, though the echoes of the shouts and merry laughter came to our ears as we sat at table, and we could see the glimmer of the white dresses and gay ribbons among the far-down trees, looking out of our windows, from time to time, during the afternoon, I did not again join the merry little republicans. They were happy. And they associated that happiness with the celebration of their country's great day of Liberty. They will remember the one by the other. And, certainly, Idlewild can be no better honored than by an acceptance of its welcome—next year and thenceforward—to celebrate, under the shade of its spreading trees, the festival so full of blessing and meaning.

LETTER LXIII.

Government of the American Homestead—Republic in the Country, but not in the City—Aristocracy of upper Servants not tolerated—Each Individual's Self-Esteem to be cared for—Irish lad in his progress in Americanizing—Difficulty of other Servants allowing a Head Man, &c., &c.

July 22, 1854.

THE oligarchy of a small homestead is not without its questions of embarrassing policy. The children and the other members of our little Government at Idlewild are at a stand-still, which the White House at Washington could scarcely show the like of, discussion having come to a momentous crisis as to the social position and destiny of Don the dog.

The first act of this Quixotic Newfoundland—attacking the vast water-wheel of our neighbor the miller—was indulgently attributed to a rustic ignorance. But his subsequent conduct has shown it to have sprung from an eccentricity of character unsusceptible of domestic discipline and obligations. With all the majestic beauty of his race, he is strangely deficient in their usual docility, and particularly in their attachment to children and much prized inexhaustibleness of patience. He has repeatedly bitten his little playfellows, and with each repeated chaining-up and whipping, we have hoped it would be the last transgression. But, a week or more since, a friend from New York called upon us, with his two boys who are at a school in the neighborhood, accompanied by a son of Professor Weir, who is also a pupil. Don walked into the group, as they sat upon the portico, and, while young Weir laid his hand confidingly between the open jaws of the dog, one of the other boys gave a sudden twist to the tail. A furious growl and a savage mangle of the hand in his mouth was the immediate consequence—the fine boy showing where he had been cradled (at West Point) by keeping an unchanged smile upon his face, and contending for the extrication of his hand like a little gladiator.

Now, though small dogs are comparatively irresponsible in the country, big dogs have their rural "fire and brimstone." The treadmill churn of the nearest farm is open to transgressors—many a pound of fresh butter in Orange county being the work of sinner-power thus exemplarily turned to account. I had a soft place in my own heart for the Don. He had made me the one object of his affections from the day of his arrival—a preference he would never be fed, nor coaxed, nor whipped out of—happy only under some window where he could hear me cough, savagely jealous of my horse, and drawing happiness enough through a crack, apparently, if permitted to lie all day outside my study door. Whichever way metempsychosis might make room for the imagination—whether I had once walked upon four legs or he upon two—there was something in this mysterious affection which tended to modify my sense of justice. I was not quite dead to being inexplicably loved. But he had bitten a friend's son ; and, with children about, dog-days coming, drought prophesied, and possible hydrophobia—no ! the weakness in the judge was overruled. Sore-footed butter-making was the culprit's doom.

But my farm-tenant here put in a plea. We should have no peace with trespassing hogs, if that big dog were once out of sight ; and he could be taken to the farm-cottage, below the hill, and regularly broken in, as a pork-patrol ; and Bell warranted, with a little discipline, he himself would soon be the dog's sole master, and that strangers and the children should hear no more of his caprices. Agreed to. And, with a rope around his neck, the astonished Quixote was led off, to lay aside his gentleman instincts, and be numbered among the exclusively usefuls.

Dogs have stomachs with opinions in them, however, and the Don rebelled at the immediate difference to which he was called upon to accommodate himself in his drink and diet. With his rope gnawed off and dragging after him, he returned and returned, looking thin and unhappy, and resumed his picturesque postures upon the lawn, his large eyes eloquent with expectancy of his accustomed bread and milk (for strangely enough, he has an unconquered aversion to meat), and his sides hollow with dismay at the possibility of more bones and water. The cook melted to pity. Nurses and chambermaids declared the dog a victim. The children shared their suppers with him. And so we stand—Idlewild divided, but a majority of our little oligarchy strenuous in favor of a repeal of the pig compromise, and a complete restoration of the handsome dog to his former privileges and perambulations. Questions of state policy have been kept pending before now, with less conflicts of principles and partialities.

In fact while a family *in town* may be governed and held together mainly by money, there is a republic within the ring fence of a *country residence*, which is not kept comfortable and respectable without high principles and careful statesmanship in its daily administration. In America, at least, the rights of every living creature, from men and women servants, to horse, cow and dog, *had better* be well understood and watchfully respected. The master is the first and worst sufferer, otherwise. And this is a call upon the character for its better qualities—injustice, discrimination, self-restraint, dignity, and willing recognition of others' wants and deservings—which makes country life a school for the mind and heart. There is said to be danger of self-confidence in the dictatory habit of having a little world like a rural household to control. Men are sometimes thought to need the elbowing and insignificant-izing of cities. But it seems to me that the immediateness of responsibility to the opinion of a country neighborhood, is even a better check to conceit than the rebuke of mere overlooking by a crowd too busy to notice us ; and, while every dependant and every animal must thus be, at least, kindly and rightly treated, the calls for good qualities in ourselves are much too grave and wholesome to have any inflating influence.

The complaints as to servants, in American country-houses, are loud and many ; and it is probably rare, if not altogether impracticable, to have the order and comfort of an English manor-house, in our republican atmosphere. The attempts and failures are driving many back to a division of the seasons between watering-places and town life. But, with a willingness to forego a point or two of the show, and unlearn some little, both of the dependence and the unapproachableness of the English system, an American country household may have all its comforts and (philosophically speaking) be at a worthier and more natural level of every-day life and reciprocities. A lesson or two which I have picked out of my experience at Idlewild may be instructive, on this point, perhaps.

Servants are natural republicans—whatever their nation or color—and a country-house is easiest managed, I have more and more come to believe, where each individual's capacities are carefully recognized and respected, and where the general opinion of the household is allowed to have the natural influence of majorities. With higher wages, of course, servants can be made to stay, *anywhere* ; but, as justice to neighbors requires a conformity to the common standard in this respect, the difference between "places" is mainly that of treatment and incidental agreeableness. The great difficulty in an American country-house is to *make servants stay*—the perpetual renewal of them, and the uncomfortableness of strange faces and unaccommodated habits, being, at present, our national difficulty of country life.

A great source of trouble is removed, in the first place, if the aristocracy of "upper servants" is done away with—no American kitchen being willing to "stand the airs" of people between them and their employers. A housekeeper, a dandy coachman, a head-gardener (or *haughty*-culturist), and a butler, form the class not tolerated in the country-life of a republic, If the mistress of the house shows that she understands the cook's work, and the chambermaid's and nurse's, and gives her own orders with equal regularity to all, the tempers below stairs find obedience wonderfully easier. But the coachman is the most common trouble-maker. He dresses better, has more display and pleasure in his particular services, uses large privileges as to irregularity of meals, and usually ranks himself above other servants. This aristocrat may be got rid of, by having the vehicles so constructed that the master can do his own driving ; while the stable work, as well as the garden and farm work, may be very harmoniously done, if the master takes the trouble to be the one who gives the orders and knows most about it. The understanding of horse-management and daily overseeing of stable and garden, furnish interest and occupation, which, I think, quite compensate to a gentleman for any *style* he may thereby forego. And it is no trifle, besides, to be so able, "upon a push," to harness, feed, doctor or drive one's own horses, as not to be at the mercy of a coachman's caprices or misrepresentations.

Servants are human beings with different individual characters, however ; and there are chances of their not remaining contented, even in thus much of a republic, unless their self-esteem is reasonably cared for, and unless they are made to feel that their health, comfort and morals are subjects of responsible oversight on the part of their employers. It is an attention to these particulars in the *country* household, which must compensate to servants for the distance from amusements and other differences in favor of *town* service. But without generalizing farther, I will give an instance or two of what has been the "salt upon the tails" of such of these flitting birds as have stayed longest at Idlewild.

Riding along the road one day, when first here, I met a rosy-cheeked Irish lad of eighteen or twenty years of age, with a stick and bundle on his shoulders, whose open blue eye and bright smile, as he asked for "any sort of job," took my fancy at once. I set him to work with a shovel. He and his bundle were soon at home. Too newly from Ireland to dodge his work, however, he was an unconscious reproach to two or three of his countrymen whose wills and backs were more Americanized, and to whom half his day's digging was "the dollar's worth ;" and, for the first month or two he was somewhat unpopular, and likely to be plotted or worried into a change of place. His excessive good nature overcoming this, he became a fixture, and worked on very steadily for a year.

But there was another rock ahead. The eighteen or twenty words with which he asked and answered common questions, constituted apparently his whole capability of language ; and, in some other respects, he seemed to be what is called half-witted. Among five or six colored servants, in-doors, who could read and write, and three or four field hands, whose intelligence had made them prefer farming to the mere drudgery of brick-yard labor, Tim naturally became a butt. They laughed at him, while they liked and made use of him. But this was gradually sapping his contentment ; and there were signs that his drooping self-esteem was looking for a more favorable climate elsewhere, when, by chance, I discovered a new quality in him. Forgetting to stake out a curve of road upon which he was digging, I found that he had done even better without me—cutting the bend most correctly and artistically with his shovel. He had, what laborers are most deficient in, an eye for beauty in a line. With this he could lay out garden paths and build stone walls, a change of work to which I was not slow in promoting him. By warm praise and calling of attention to the cleverness of his labors, I soon made him think better of himself, and, with that change, vanished all disposition to "quit." Treated with sufficiently more respect in the kitchen, Tim has stayed on very contentedly for another year—though, having lately been surprised into matrimony, by an old girl in the neighborhood who is considerably his senior, I anticipate a stammering announcement, before long, of a preference of some "place for two."

A very handsome and bright table-servant, a mulatto lad, for whom his city mother is very ambitious, would not be a fixture in our secluded household, probably, but for one or two incidental privileges. With the younger children, who have their daily lessons from their mother, he is an admitted pupil of the nursery, and fast progressing in the rudimental education which he needed ; while, with our country life and its errands, he is picking up health and horsemanship—three advantages that, for some time to come, may induce old Sylvia, his mother, to let him "stay," though she looks forward to seeing him a Broadway hair-dresser, at least, before she dies.

But the most threatening torpedo, among the sparks of our kitchen cabinet, is the maintenance of an un-republican luxury of my own—what the men stigmatize as a "second boss," and what I deprecatingly defend as a lesser-anxiety-man, indispensable to one of my profession and state of health. Several hands have "quit" rather than "stand Sam Bell" any longer ; but I must really exhaust measures and compromises before I dispense with his vice-*boss*-idency. It is difficult, I find, to make working men, particularly Irishmen, understand my little mud-puddle infirmity of never being intellectually clear after I am once "riled" in the morning. What writing I am to do in a day, must be done before my thicker sediment is stirred up—the pellucid reflecting of stars and butterflies being, for me, a simple matter of tranquillity after settling over night. But there are orders to be given before breakfast, according to the wear, tear, and weather of each day—hay cut or muck carted, horses shod or cows hoppled, fowls killed or fences mended, feed mixed, stray pigs caught, harness cleaned, and wheels greased—contingencies by the dozen, which require each morning's separate ordering and arranging. The "Missus" can't do it. Messages and overnight arrangements are nothing but confusion. There must be a "boss" on the spot, weather-wise and plenipotential, and of undisputed omniscience as to the befallings of pasture, pig-stye and stable.

Now, Bell, though he would be the very perfection of a premier under a monarchical Government, is, it must be owned, a little stringent and imperative in measures and language for a vice-boss in a seventy-acre republic. I found him on the spot. He was the tenant of the small farm-cottage on the river-bank, paying his twenty-five-dollars-a-year rent, but otherwise independent—a shad-fisherman in the season, a boat-builder in the winter, a hand on board a river-steamer now and then, a famous dambuilder, quite a horse-doctor, a complete farmer, and enough of carpenter and blacksmith to make anything "do for the present." The neighbors were so sure that I should not agree, for three days together, with "a chap of that temper," and warned me so against him as a permanency, that, in re-letting the cottage to him, I reserved the right of ejectment at will ; but, up to the present time (now nearly three years), I can make him out to be nothing but a downright Truth on two legs, with the Yankee variety of accomplishments above enumerated. To be sure he wears his hat in the parlor, sometimes, and drives the ladies to church with his coat off or his leg hung out over the side of the driver's box (to be comfortable) ; and he speaks his mind like a pump, to me or anybody else that stirs the handle ; but I would call upon him to-morrow, sooner than upon any other man in the world, to break his neck for me, or tell me the truth about a horse ; or see the last of me with the plague, or swim the river for a Doctor, or corner a rattle-snake, or kill a mad dog. And as such possibilities make one value a man, I have a partiality for Bell which makes me spare no pains to make him otherwise popular. He will make no compromises himself ; but in various trifles, I bring the compensatory policy to bear. By putting the horses and wagons entirely under his control, the cook or chambermaid has to ask Bell if she has shopping to do, and wants a ride to Newburgh. The men know, that, if they wish anything extra, a day's holiday or any indulgence or change of labor, Bell's kind-hearted reason ableness is easier worked upon than mine. He is the dispenser of all favors, and, so, forgiven for many a sharp look and blunt word. The fact is, that the kitchen majority are always in favor of his harsh honesty and his certainty of being right, though the individual sufferer may rebel and "quit." And as Bell's wages are no higher than the other men's, and he certainly out-works any one of them, at any sort of job, his boss-ocracy cannot rightfully be offensive to their republicanism.

With our cities getting overcrowded, and country residences becoming more and more desired as railways make them more and more accessible, it is well to show, with some particularity, what difficulties are in the way. A system of *household republics*, is worth perfecting and MAKING NATIONAL—at least until we *aristocratize* sufficiently (which I think we shall never do) to have an unthinking and unthought-of class for our domestics, and household service a mere matter of obedient machinery. The display that we must necessarily forego, and the more personal and immediate share that employers must necessarily take in the duties and sympathies of their dependents, to carry out these little rural republics, will not be differences from European life which we need very greatly regret.

Gossip for Invalids only.

LETTER LXIV.

Invalid Wishes for Letters on their Class of Subjects—Boston Physician and his Alkaline Treatment—Experiment and its Failure—Consumption and its Alleviations, &c., &c.

August 5, 1854.

It would be natural to think that nothing new could be said to invalids. And, probably, nothing can. The invalid appetite for *more*, however—based, doubtless, upon the desponding heart's communicative craving for sympathy, rather than from expectation of learning any untold secret of cure—seems to continue lively. I had written, I thought, as much as the modesty of print would bear, of my personal experiences in struggling with pulmonary disease—dating, with a certain degree of justification, from a home in the Highland Cheltenham, to which sufferers under this our country's prevailing ailment are medically sent. But letters, asking opinion as to medicines, systems of cure, climate, &c., thicken daily upon me, and, as a large proportion of these are from clergymen (the class oftenest stricken by consumption), I still have, perhaps, in my experience and multiplicity of kind counsel from others, a casting weight to throw. On one point, certainly—my own rash experiment of a new system, with disastrous effects on my progress and condition of health—I can speak instructively.

With the letter from a Boston physician, published not long since in the *Home Journal*, I presume the invalid reader to be familiar. Coming from one who was a stranger to me, it was written in a spirit of Christian kindness that inspired immediate confidence ; while the ability, good sense, directness, and novelty withal, of the medical advice, was like the sound of a trumpet to the army of despairing consumptives. Letters requesting to know the name and address of the writer have poured upon me from a continuous multitude of those wishing personal consultation, while the newspapers of the country have so generally copied the theory and its brief directions, that the knowledge of it, at least, must be almost universal. I have heard of very numerous cases of experiment without farther counsel than the perusal of it.

To my grateful expression of thanks for this kind physician's interest, I received a second truly admirable letter, accompanied with the requisite internal medicines and directions more minute. As my homœopathic aids to convalescence had, for some little time, seemed to have weakened or changed in their action upon my system, and my friends warned me that I was losing ground, I was the more willing to try the new remedy—misgiving, however, that, in a certain passage of the doctor's letter, where he mistrusts the wisdom of "prescribing for a patient at Idlewild and *his* fingers at Boston," there was a difficulty I should first remove by going to him. And that misgiving was my good angel, to whose "still, small voice" I gave too little heed. So skilful a physician would have said probably, at once, on seeing me, that his prescription was based upon very different phases of disease ; *and it is to inspire a much needed caution on this point, that I have now resumed the subject.* Invalids are so apt to clutch, as I thus did, at a remedy, without first making certain that it is *their* form of disease to which it is suited.

With my unconquerable night-coughs and hemorrhages for the groundwork of his theory, the doctor, it will be remembered, says :—

> "In all cases like yours the skin does not perform its office. * * The system is surcharged, overflowing with *acidity.*" * * "Admit these facts, and what is the conclusion of the whole matter ? It is this :—Take a warm alkaline bath, say twice a week."
>
> * * "Next, but not second in importance, night and day surround the chest with a *soap-jacket,* made of flannel and spread with the darkest brown soap (being strongest with the *alkali*), melted to the consistence of a thick paste with a little boiling water. * * "Use a simple, pure *alkali,* internally, to neutralize the acidity already there."

It was the latter part of May, and the very warm weather was already commencing when I entered upon the *alkaline treatment.* The "soap-jacket," of course, could not be worn without a second flannel shirt over it, to keep in its paste and moisture, and here was my first trouble. So excessive was the perspiration, night and day, with the impermeable closeness of the covering, that I was sensibly weakened and distressed for breath, while exercise was nearly impossible and every puff of air seemed to give me a cold. My voice weakened, by the third day, so that I could scarcely articulate, my head seemed crammed with an hourly increasing catarrh, I felt the return of some old rheumatic symptoms, the muscles of my face and eyes showed rapid exhaustion, and my family, much alarmed, insisted on a stoppage of the treatment. I thought it best to make a fair trial of it, however, and strictly followed the directions till the eighth day—when the "internal alkali" had so completely deadened the coats of my stomach and destroyed the tone, that I feared I should be unable to take the nourishment necessary for life. I had the sensation of being *tanned inwardly to sole-leather,* scarce able to taste the differences in food and drinks, and palpably burthening nature with every morsel I swallowed.

And, as in all my previous illness I had never before failed to have appetite proportionate to exercise, and had known no feeling of discomfort inwardly except from the convulsion of the cough, I was sure that the internal effect, at least, was injurious. My hemorrhages, meantime, grew more profuse, and, as I persisted in my rides, the least motion of the horse beyond a walk brought the blood to my mouth abundantly.

With the giving up of the alkalis on the eighth day, I found myself more ill than I had ever previously been. There was no sign that the antagonist *acids* had been encountered, or that anything but poor weakened Nature herself had received the deadly ammunition of the *alkalis.* With the resuming of my former un-medicinal system, however, I began to rally again. The vigorous use of flesh-brush and crash-towels before and after cold baths in the morning, a more generous diet, and a free horse, brought me gradually up ; and, now (after seven weeks), I am once more where the alkalis began with me. Another patient who made the same experiment (a distinguished officer of the army who had brought consumption home from his campaigns in Mexico), but whose first result from the alkalis, unlike mine, was a relief, has since died under the treatment. With the publicity which I have unexpectedly given to the *"alkali cure,"* and a confidence thus indirectly expressed in it, it is but just, perhaps, that I should declare my own belief that it is likely to be wholly misapplied, and, in any case, dangerous without the best of medical counsel and supervision.

Of the unusual professional frankness of the writer of the letter, and of his high moral and intellectual tone of study, sympathy and duty, no one could doubt, who has read it. The proof is the universal confidence it inspired, and the numbers who have since sought him out with great eagerness for advice. With personal knowledge of a patient, the danger of his theory, I doubt not, would be obviated by his conscientious making first certain of its fitness to the case. It is not wonderful that all manner of sick people do not get the full attention of the overworked best doctors, and that this same *making first certain* is somewhat rare. It is for this reason that a physician as an intimate friend is invaluable—one who will make an untiring enthusiasm of your cure—while one who gives you ten minutes and one or two looks and touches, and a little uninterested listening, at a professional hour, is *a risk,* to say the least. Fortunately, nine out of ten of the medicines for every disease are prescribed by Nature—fresh air, exercise, control of habits and appetite, etc., etc.—but it is not too much to add, that nine points out of ten of *medical advice also,* are given by Nature. The utter faith with which the sick receive and follow the hasty opinion of a doctor, and the utter inattention to the complainings and promptings of their own pain-taught and truth-telling nerves, organs and senses, is a giving up of the whole business to a tenth committee-man, who, by rights, should only be one in a consultation. "It has surprised me more than anything else," says a very sensible man, writing his experience in consumption, "to find how many *different opinions* I have received, in regard to the seat of my disease, from physicians of high standing." In fact the five-minute omniscience that is expected of doctors is expecting too much. It would be much wiser to go *first to a careful lawyer,* who will sit down and cross-examine you, put your symptoms into condensed and comprehensible language, reconcile your contradictions, sift off your reluctancies and superfluities, and take the side-evidence of your friends and attendants ; and from this prepare a *digest of what you yourself know* of your case, which the physician can read while he looks at you and feels your pulse for the professional corroborations. In no shorter way, I am inclined to think, will any common patient get the best advice from a "physician with extensive practice."

And now shall I stop ?—or may we, dear invalid reader, safely gossip away another half-hour upon our theme of sympathies ?

I think there is a grain of truth for us in almost every theory of cure—something in hydropathy, something in "kneading and pommelling the stomach," something in "inhalations," something in raising the siege of the disease by counter-irritation, or by dislodgment and change of action with homœopathic alternations, etc., etc., etc. By judicious care and counsel we may combine a self-treatment from two or more of these "positive cures for consumption,"—particularly, from such as involve no use of violent medicines, or are mainly alleviative—thus keeping prudence awake and encouraging hope, even if we do not stumble by chance on the specific for our particular case. In homœopathy, however—as administered by a prophet in its secrets like Doctor Gray of New York—I may express my individual "settling down" of faith and preference.

But consumption, mourned over as it is, seems to me a gentle untying of the knot of life, instead of the sudden and harsh tearing asunder of its threads by other disease—a tenderness in the destroying angel, as it were, which greatly softens, for *some,* his inevitable errand to *all.* It is a decay with little or no pain, insensible almost in its progress, delayed, sometimes, year after year, in its more fatal approaches. And it is not alone in its indulgent prolonging and deferring that consumption is like a blessing. The cords which it first loosens are the coarser ones most confining to the mind. The weight of the material senses is gradually taken from the soul with the lightening of their food and the lessening of their strength. Probably, till he owns himself an invalid, no man has ever given the wings of his spirit room enough—few, if any, have thought to adjust the ministerings to body and soul so as to subdue the senses to their secondary place and play. With illness enough for this, and not enough to distress or weaken—with consumption, in other words, as most commonly experienced—the mind becomes conscious of a wonderfully new freedom and predominance. Things around alter their value. Estimates of persons and pursuits strangely change. Nature seems as newly beautiful as if a film had fallen from the eyes. The purer affections, the simpler motives, the humbler and more secluded reliances for sympathy, are found to have been the closest-linked with thoughts bolder and freer. Who has not wondered at the cheerfulness of consumptive persons ? It is because, with the senses kept under by invalid treatment, there is no "depression of spirit." With careful regimen, and the system purified and disciplined, life, what there is of it, is in the most exhilarating balance of its varied proportions. Death is not dreaded where there is, thus, such a conscious breaking through of the wings of another life, freer and higher.

LETTER LXV.

Affection for our Doctors—Excellent Letter from my Friend of the Alkali—Taboo upon Tea—Letter from an Allopathic Physician—Doctor's Visits, &c., &c.

August 26, 1854.

WE love our doctors. It is a question whether they do not get more than their share of human affection—more, at least, than they can very well know what to do with (for doctors, like other "great guns," have their *bore*, showing what they can "carry"). Just now, indeed, I am beginning to think one of them a whole castle, with a battery of patients* to defend him—the last few mails fairly bombarding me with letters in vindication of the Boston physician, of whose "alkaline treatment" I had ventured to announce my own unsuccessful experiment. With his personal advice and supervision, it seems (by their loud report) to be a very different thing. They speak most enthusiastically and gratefully of it and him. That he is a very able and purely philanthropic man, we are very sure that no can one doubt who has read his letters ; and his practice, professionally, seems to be as effective and fascinating as his pen. There is, by the way, in the second letter which he so kindly addressed to me, upon my own complaints, a passage full of valuable suggestion for invalids, and, with the Doctor's permission, we will share it among us. He says :—

"The alkali which I commonly use is soda ; a saturated solution, impregnated with, rather than containing, some preparation of *iron*, generally the carbonate. Why the Creator placed both iron and soda as constituent elements in all healthy blood, I need not inquire. It is sufficient to the medical man that such is the fact. And, in cases like yours, where as you admit, there is an excess of acidity in the system, I need not demonstrate that the blood must necessarily be deprived of these to a greater or less extent. An acid will neutralize and destroy an alkali. If deprived of them, the blood must become thickened. If thickened, will it, can it, circulate as freely in the extremities and smaller vessels ? If not in these, must there not be increased congestion of the large vessels which are on the chest and brain—in the more vascular

* A distinguished literary man is among these, and also the brother-in-law of one of our ablest Professors. They both recommend a publication of their statements of having greatly benefited by the personal advice and prescription of this physician, for whose name they had applied on reading his letter in the *Home Journal*.

parts of the system ? If undue pressure there, would there not be increased tendency to hemorrhage, whether once a month or once in two months ?

"But it is in vain that you attempt to correct this, unless acids, and all articles which become acid in the stomach, are strictly, rigidly avoided. Every individual has his dietic idiosyncracies, so to say : and the old proverb is that 'a man at thirty, as to his diet, is either a physician or a fool.' What may become acidulous with one, may not with another. But a patient should notice his own peculiarities, and make his diet conform to the rule given. Generally, I advise to avoid all acids, vinegar in all its diguises—pies, cakes, preserves ; puddings, except sago, tapioca, arrow-root, etc., and these to be used without sweet sauces—all fruits, whether foreign or domestic. If once or twice in the season the rule is relaxed to freshen the memory with these articles, it is in favor of a few ripe whortleberries, or a ripe sweet peach at breakfast. And last but not least, I forbid *tea* and *coffee.*

"Of the necessity of this last, it is often very difficult to convince patients. It is no argument to say, 'all the world uses them.' I answer, 'to the pure all things are pure,' and to the healthy all things are innocent in a measure. It is the system in a particular state to which I refer. But patients say, 'tea or coffee makes me feel much brighter !' I know they come with a soothing promise. I know Abdel Kader said of coffee :—'It is the drink of the people of God !' And I often think of the description of tea, said to have been given by an ambassador of the 'flowery kingdom,' on introducing it at the court of Thibet :—'It is,' said he, 'a beverage which quenches thirst, and mitigates sorrow !' And, to the student, especially with a sensitive organization, and one whose susceptibility to stimulus has not been vitiated by a resort to more potent *stimuli,* its first effect is so *spirituelle,* so refreshing, so delightful ! But, to a disordered and enfeebled digestive system, they impart no more permanent strength, than the whip and spur give strength to the jaded, worn-out racer. I should strenuously advise you to *exorcise the tea.* I am aware that Liebig has advanced the idea that tea may possibly increase the secretion of bile, and, in this view, you might think it perhaps beneficial in your occasional bilious derelictions. But we all *know* that it contains *tannic acid,* and my experience is, that it is injurious where the vigor of the digestive system is at all impaired, and where it is used *warm.* As a substitute, you have iced milk, if your stomach will tolerate it ; or, better still, the antediluvian beverage, *cold water.* Aside from everything else, I should urge *cold fluids in all cases where there is a tendency to hemorrhage.* And the water, depend upon it, will give a more substantial, reliable vigor for the day's work, than tea or coffee. If, remembering whom I have the pleasure of addressing, a line of poetry in a medical letter, would not be out of place, I would add, that there is as much scientific truth as poetic beauty in the words which say of 'a cup of water,' that

'Its draught
Of cool refreshment, drained by fevered lips,
Will give a shock of pleasure to the frame,
More exquisite than when nectarean juice
Renews the life of joy in happiest hours.'

"The *horseback exercise*, though I do not believe with Sydenham, that, 'with bark, it is a cure for consumption,' yet it is excellent for exercise—nothing better."

The taboo upon *tea*, in this passage of dietetics, touches invalids upon a tender point. Without tea the desponding sick man is a monotone indeed—his life one note (and that *b* flat) from morn till night, and from night till morn again. If the spirits need to be medicined as well as the body (as sometimes they do), may there not be a natural want of some such preventive against *mere platitude* ? The Indian, in his journey through the wilderness, climbs once a day into a tall tree, to get the range of his weary steps, and keep acquainted with the sky and the horizon—overlooking, for that brief moment, at least, that which overshadows his path and confines his view. To be able to *see far and generalize, once a day*, is, experience tells a man, a necessity—in this be-littling world, even with the best of health. In sickness, it is often a necessity—always a compensating luxury and consolation. The grateful stimulus of the tea-cup need not be taken in excess. With the system made delicate and sensitive, a very weak tea serves for the elation of the spirits—what is commonly called the "English breakfast tea," the most innocent as well as full-flavored of these precious leaves of the Orient, being (for me at least) stimulus enough. Without assenting to Dr. Johnson's punning demand, in his parody of Horace :—

"TEA, *sole oriente,* TEA, *decente, requiro,*["]

the *morning* cup might be safely insisted on by the invalid—though the *"te"* of the Latin poet was probably more agreeable at evening.

From his inexorability on this point, and the trenchant unsparingness of his favorite theory of soap-cure, I fancy that my Boston correspondent is a *young* man. Another physician, equally a stranger to me, but animated by the same genial sympathy and kindness, writes to me with the prefatory remark that he has been twenty-five years a practitioner of medicine, and his opinion as to dietetics, seems to have grown more indulgent with experience. I must quote a passage from his letter (though, like the other, intended for a private one), the professional liberality and well-acquired convictions with which he writes, making it of value to all invalids :—

* * "You should banish from your mind, if you ever entertained it, all notion of *specifics* for your malady. Such do not exist for consumption, nor for any disease. The most that drugs can do is to palliate till Nature can relieve. The cure is to be sought in other influences ; such especially as promote the functions of digestion, assimilation, and absorption. The course which you first adopted, of horseback exercise, cold bathing, friction, and free exposure to the air, was well adapted to these ends—especially if connected with a nutritious diet, chiefly of animal food, and aided by good malt liquor, such as London

porter, or Calton ale. The cod-liver oil I should have wished you to continue, at the same time, and I should have prescribed, also, ten or fifteen grains of tartarized iron, to be taken three times a day. If this course, persevered in, would not avert your disease, I doubt whether anything would. If the appetite and digestion continue good, however, there is always strong encouragement that the disease may be overcome. Sustain the appetite and digestion by outdoor exercise, friction, cold baths, etc., and hope confidently for restoration. An issue in the arm, or below the clavicle, would be very likely, in such a case as yours, to afford considerable relief by its revulsive influence. If malt liquors do not agree with you, use a little pure brandy, or sherry or Madeira wine."

It is easy to see why we love doctors, when they discourse to us so cheeringly and earnestly on what concerns ourselves only. In fact, sickness has its pleasant compensations. It is one end of a completing circle of experience that very nearly touches the other. Many a day of health is less happy than many a day of sickness. A faithful joy-ometer, could we keep one, might surprise us with its comparative average of the rise and fall of contentment's varying quicksilver, when well or when ill. Could any possible morning call equal the interest of the doctor's visit ? And convalescence ! The happiness of *that* is among the experiences of life which it is wonderful should be unsung. To how many, has the month of convalescence been the month oftenest remembered and wished for again—health and honeymoons forgotten while this is thought of !

LETTER LXVI.

Chat upon Invalid Indiscretions—Dietetics of the Soul—Forenoon on Horseback—Use of an Errand in a Ride—Steel Pens, and the consequent Decline of Penknives—Fatigue after Pleasure, &c., &c.

September 9, 1854.

SHALL we chat of our indiscretions of appetite, this morning—I giving you (with invalid freedom to digress, if temptation offer) the history of a dietetic irregularity of mine ? Nature "breaks diet" occasionally, with a freshet, and it evidently does Nature good—clearing away the insensible accretions, and reaching the dull deposits in otherwise inaccessible corners. Even with the flow of the daily life-stream hopelessly diminished, it is still pleasant to know where *was* the channel, and where *once* reached the bubbles—is it not ?

My "spree," I should premise, was not a violation of the dietetics of the stomach. To these I have found no great trouble to be constant. In fact, with salads and lobsters, champagne, pastry and pickles, gravies, garnishings and "good things" generally, I closed my mortal accounts without a sigh—possibly with an eye to business, in my resignation, however, as I found that the "single dish" of the doctor's prescription made its way much quicker, without company, to that finger's end that picks adjectives and pronouns. Industry of *pen* increases by what might lessen industry of the *plough*.

A German physician, Ernest Von Feuchtersleben, has written upon the "Dietetics of the Soul." The book has passed through seven editions, in the original, and is now just translated and published by Francis and Co., in Boston. It shows us how we "break diet" (too often) with our sins of passion and imagination, and how we may care for our bodily health, and obtain convalescence and cure, by strict regimen of the temper and the intellect. I mention this to justify what might seem like a fancifulness on my part—the speaking of other dietetics than those of meat and drink. Von Feuchtersleben (to plunder an idea for the gentler gender as we go) even thinks *beauty is attainable or recoverable* by this fancy-pathy. He quotes from a celebrated German lady, who says :—"Persons like ourselves can only become healthy by feeling the greatest disgust at illness, and placing implicit reliance on the axiom that health is most lovely and loveable."

But, *not to have my will of a whole day of summer*, is the dietetic that has troubled me most. You know how it is, dear pulmonary brother ! The appetite for out of doors, with free abandonment to the chances of idleness, keener and more appreciative as its relish has become—is still lessened in the *time it can sustain itself*. It must be a *short* walk, though with exquisite enjoyment of sunshine and air—a *brief* ride, though with exhilarating sense of pulses quickened by motion. The eyes tire and the soul shuts, in the very middle of a study of a landscape *at* which the first glance was enchantment. A whole morning is a meal for a man in the glory of health. A sunset with a long summer twilight—*that* is a feast which must have been prepared for by abstinence ; by late rising and a forenoon of in-doors. And the over-tasking of the powers of attention, I find—fatigue of the sense of beauty, or a surfeit of agreeable people—acts immediately on the bodily health. It starts a hemorrhage. It aggravates a cough.

There came a forenoon, however—(those who know the differences in forenoons understand how there might be such a one)—altogether irresistible. It seemed like an improvement in the article. No first fig, in the opening of a new box, ever seemed, to a child, sweeter than all that are gone before, than the smell of that nine A.M. to my sensitive nostrils. It was during the cool week we had, in the closing of July—if you remember—or, rather, it was the coming round of the South wind again, after coolness a little unseasonable, and with fragrance and softness that had been, meantime, ripening like wine. Of *such* a feast, to take a taste of half an hour, and then turn away to an easy chair and books ? To save appetite for an evening, with *such* a morning spread out to tempt one ? Saddle my mare, on the contrary !

Forenoon exercise on horseback—temptingly delicious as it is in a breezy summer's day—is a forbidden fruit to invalids, for two or three incidental reasons. First, as I have already explained, it exhausts the stock of elasticity for the twelve waking hours of which it is the beginning. Second, it irritates (often into profuse bleeding from the mouth, in my case) the comparatively empty stomach, which needs the cushioning of food for its half-healed membranes. And, third, it renders later exercise impossible—thus depriving the night's sleep of the immediate lull which follows fresh fatigue, and substituting for it the wakefulness of exhaustion, prolonged through a long day into nervousness. "The doctor's orders" are not accompanied with this satisfactory explanation, usually ; but it is for these or similar reasons that the docile patient takes his ride only with the lengthening shadows of the afternoon.

But life—the wine of the life of this world—is in the morning air. Breath for the pores, exhilaration for the blood, newness and freshness for the worn senses and fibres, are the over-runnings from the cups of the *ascending* dewdrops. The *descending* dew of evening may be purer, but it is not fragrant yet with the breath of the flowers it is on its way to.

The earth-tried and recalled—the dews laden with perfume and exhaling reluctantly through the forenoon's warmer hours—are the tempters for senses still mortal. For flesh-and-blood consciousness of existence, the intoxication is in the just full glory of the day.

The drought had stilled Idlewild brook, and the parting steps of my mare's dainty feet, as she picked her way down the windings of the precipitous road, were not set to music as usual. But the leaves rustled and the birds sang. And when we left the closed gate behind us, and galloped off upon the level bank of the Moodna, it was with a sense of health that had a one-horse power—the animal at the end of my spine, and subject to my volition, being as much a part of me as the smile I could bridle on my lip—as the tear subject to the lashes of my eye. God has thus, in the horse, given us limbs we can put on and leave off—lungs we can borrow for more speed—strength we can incorporate with our weakness. Not to have a horse in familiar and daily use—to the degree which embodies the generous animal and his powers into your consciousness of forces and faculties—is to be less of a being by that much.

There is a point, in the pleasantest ride, when one feels that an errand would have made it pleasanter. The invalid, particularly is apt to draw rein (without an object in his ride), and start too soon on his return. By a caprice of irregular spirits, exercise is thus shirked, sometimes, when there is no beginning of weariness of the body. So flourishing a town as Newburgh, four miles off, and to which there are four different and pleasant roads from Idlewild, is quite a treasure to me in this respect. It is hard not to have an errand there ; for, failing everything else, there is almost the certainty of a letter at the Post-office—many of my correspondents being quite oblivious of my address of *Moodna, Orange Co.*, and directing (with wonderful faith in propinquity and postmasters) to the largest place they can think of in the neighborhood.

But, upon this "spree" of a forenoon-full of out-of-doors, I gave myself a special errand to Newburgh (to make sure of getting there, though I should go round by Mortonville, the wildest and longest way), and as the errand in question reminds me of *an appeal I have long thought of making to manufacturers*, for the benefit of a certain class of suffering authors, a digression to it will perhaps be excused by invalids—a redeeming feature of *utility* being very necessary, occasionally, to make the strong and hearty feel kindly towards our sick-room gossip.

The "improvement of the age," in which, I presume, no one can take a share who has any feeling for grace in a line or freedom in thumb and finger, is *the steel pen*. An invention of wooden shoes, of the same size for all human beings, would be for me a very similar economy and convenience. The use of the article has become very general, however—a circumstance which, in all probability, has accidentally taken a census of the mechanical-fingered and angular-brained of our highly free-and-equal population. There is a remaining class to whom the steel pen is an inconvenience of the most positive kind—poets and writers on imaginative or delicate subjects, whose grace and ease of style are at once paralysed by a nib so unsusceptible and stiff, and, indeed, at whose invitation of ink, with such misrepresenting angularity of scratch, no playful or tender sentiment will pass from brain to finger. I presume it has always been true, that, if it were not for geese and the more pliable medium they give us, poetry and fancy would be cut off from communication with the world.

But goose-quills (and here comes the tight place) require penknives of the best quality ; and even as first-class statesmen and patriots have died out with the universality of middling politicians, so, first-rate penknives have disappeared with the universality of tolerable pens ready-made. The *brick*-ifying movement of the age—making all men and things of a size—leaves no eminences of *day* (such as Henry Clay) standing around us ; and with *steel pens, and no "Rogers's best penknives,"* poets will soon be "as like as bricks," if heard of at all.

In galloping up the ascents of the tangled valley of Ring's Mills, where the Moodna ties a love-knot of scenery among the abrupt hills and rocks so magnificently wooded—feeling (horse and all) as strong and swift as was any man's share—I had the *new penknife* in my mind, which was the morning's errand to Newburgh. The old one a cherished double-blade which had long bridged over, for me, the uncertain chasm between brain and white paper—had been called upon (like the Hon. Mrs. Norton) for duties a little beyond the strength of its fine edge. A slate-pencil had been sharpened with it. For a week or two I had tried honeing and stropping, and struggled to believe in the renewableness of temper so unyielding hitherto. But the nibs that were to be re-pointed were only crushed. The readers of the *Home Journal* will remember the articles in which the conveyance of my meaning was painfully clumsy and imperfect. Nobody could write with such a penknife.

Brown's, in Newburgh, is a hardware store worthy of Broadway—a museum of usefulnesses and positivities, which, I have found it a refreshing change from modern poetry to make a lounge of—and I was soon, by permission, behind his counter, lost in an inviting wilderness of little brown bundles, each with its tempting specimen outside under the twine. Oh, the pleasure of opening one of each, trying its edge upon the round of the hand, and imagining the adjectives and pronouns, the similitudes and sentiments, for the passage of which it could make a quill once more inviting to the capricious brain !

But I was disappointed. Calling for a quill, to make a final experiment before choosing (not compelled, fortunately, to take it for better or worse without trial), I found the edges of those polished and showy looking things untrue. The tempers had not been prepared for such work. Pen-making being no longer among the duties in a knife's destiny, owing to the common use of steel-pens, the blade is now only fitted to cut threads and to clean finger-nails.

I called on my friend Mr. Brown, and explained my difficulty.

"Oh, my dear sir," said he, looking unencouragingly at the tall shelves with his assorted wilderness of cutlery, "penknives are not what they used to be. You'll not find one, I am afraid, in those new parcels. But" (he continued, putting his hand in his waistcoat pocket and pulling out a plain old article, such as we used to see in the days of Tom Hood and Elia), "here is one that I have carried for years in my pocket—a Rogers's best—and I will make you a present of it."

It was a flower flung on the ebbing current of my forenoon ! (for, by this time, and, with my strength tied by the bridle to the post outside, I was beginning to exhaust and be dispirited), and I mentally thanked Mr. Brown for a kindness that chanced to be as timely as it was frank and flattering. I needed both the knife and the tender thought.

Of all the kinds of sadness which an invalid knows (to resume our Idlewild gossip), the most leaden and prostrating is that of fatigue after a forbidden pleasure. One becomes, in a long illness, a luxuriast in sadness—discriminating between its moods, as a mourner between plaintiveness in music. The brain—as I have elsewhere said—has its lift and scope, strangely independent, sometimes, of the weaknesses of the body. "I have often observed myself with attention," says the author of the "Dietetics of the Soul," "and found that even when the head is most bewildered, thought remains pure and free, like some force which has retired unscathed to its stronghold before the enemy." But—(for our dignity as immortal spirits, let it make us grateful to remember)—there is no escape from the depression of self-reproach. Not even the oblivion of a reverie will beguile fatigue that was imprudent and needless.

Of my nervous and weary afternoon, dear brother invalid—of the sunset hour and twilight, lost because Unappreciable after the forenoon surfeit and exhaustion—I need give you only the moral. Suffering, which makes us dwell upon our failure in constancy and resolution, is very different from the suffering which elevates us—elevates us, because, while it brings us nearer to what is nobler and purer, it seems to be only detaching us from the coarser life which prevented our being part of it. I should like to feel that my extravagance in a truant forenoon—which gave me a night of illness, as well as a day-penance of irredeemable depression—may have made palatable, in the gossip which confesses it, a lesson of prudence for some fellow-sinner of an invalid.

LETTER LXVII.

Sufferers from Drought—Our Hyla or Tree-toad—Cure of Jaundice—Abuses by Telegraph-menders, &c., &c.

September 16, 1854.

THE lungs of ten thousand trees, invalids every one, are suffering from the drought, in the woods of Idlewild. We are a pulmonary wilderness—they and I. The *yellow pine* is the single exception—healthier and brighter than I have ever before known it, doubtless from the more arid and Southern atmosphere which has taken possession of our Northern latitude. (So will there be no plague without some to thrive better for it !) Our willows look "in the last stages," however. Elms are of a reconciled yellow, waiting for autumn. Oaks and chestnuts have dropped their superfluous leaves from the ends of branches too luxuriant (laid aside their dissipations, as it were), and hold on for the deferred rains with a confidence in re-invigoration yet possible. The evening wind walks through our hospital with a fallen-leaf cadence in its sigh—the medicine of its dews of small avail.

But we have one apparent sufferer by the excessive drought, who has been the object of some superstitious tenderness at Idlewild—his fastidious preference as to a room in which to be sick, and his obstinacy as to putting us to inconvenience, having engendered the idea that it was a human soul in the habit of having his own way, though at present, probably, in a very purgatorial stage of downward transmigration. This, our in-door guest by his own choice and invitation, is known in Natural History as a *Hyla*, and in common mention as "a nasty tree-toad." And that opprobrious adjective is so invariably prefixed, by all who see and name him, as to seem a penal retribution of Providence for sins in another existence ; though as *we* have not joined in thus stigmatizing the outcast, but as, on the contrary, our family sympathies have converted him into an object of respectful interest and attention, it looks a little as if purgatory may not be altogether without its chances of pity.

The intelligence manifested by this little reptile may be well worth recording. His first appearance was a jump that he made from the long neck of a goblet of earthern ware, used to keep drinking-water cool through the night, and which stood upon a wash-stand in a dressing-room. With the upset of his hiding-place, to turn out a tumbler of water, he sprang to the wall, clinging to it by the mucous tubercle on the toe which forms his peculiarity. The servants were summoned, and he was caught and thrown out of the window—finding his way in again, however, before morning, and again and again ejected and returning—four times—till at last he was taken to the window at the rear of the house, and pitched roughly upon the gravelled area at the kitchen door. My wife, whose visitor he was, presumed this to be the last of him ; but, strangely enough, his protuberant eyes looked at her from the neck of the water-jar, as usual, the next morning ; he having found his way around the house, passing a dozen windows within which water was equally accessible, entering between the slats of a closed blind, and taking possession once more of that particular vessel—certainly a less convenient one (with its narrow neck through which he could hardly squeeze himself) than the bath-tub and water-pitcher near by.

Curiosity was, by this time, grown thoughtful, however. We all remembered having heard, as long as we had lived at Idlewild, the gurgle of a tree-toad's song, from the side of the house upon which the window of that dressing-room opens. His voice, and a night-owl's, apparently from the same tree overhanging the precipice, were the music familiar to all who walked at late hours under our roof. He was an out-door one of us—driven to take shelter within, by the unseasonable weather and sickness—it was now acknowledged, by all, and with regret at the tardiness of the recognition. But, from that time he has been tenderly treated. My wife cares for Hyla as others care for nightingales and goldfinches. He jumps to the window-ledge or to the wall, apparently for air and exercise, once a day—the maid, meantime, changing the water, into which he returns, to sit hydropathically immersed. His bead-like eyes twinkle, and his curtain-like throat swells and throbs with his breathings, when he is approached, but he does not stir. He believes in us—a faith in those who once misunderstood him which has its lesson of humility. For six weeks he has now been our inmate.

In these days, when the "places that know us" seem struggling to reveal that they know spirits also, we look inquiringly upon all that announces a new presence. Of this trusting tree-toad's errand and quality my uncertainty is at least respectful.

* * * * * *

I do not know whether, among our invalid public of readers, there are any whose complaint is the jaundice ; but the German cure for it—sudden stir of the bile by an arousal of the indignation*—is to be found in the

* My brother, the nervous and delicately organized Editor of the *Musical World*, called in a physician when prostrated with the jaundice in Leipsic, Germany. The Doctor left, promising to send in his prescription. Meantime an old woman entered, who accused my brother of stealing, spat in his face and ran out of the room ! This was the medicine—immediately effectual—for with the vigorous start of the bile commenced a rapid recovery.

highways about Idlewild, its efficacy likely to be tried upon you, indeed, let your complaint be what it will. I speak of a one-horse wagon, with two men and an axe and a ladder—telegraph-menders who pass to and fro, periodically, and who feel at liberty to cut down, without leave or consultation, any beautiful tree upon the roadside, the waving of whose branches may interfere with the wires. Lined as our Highland roads are with bird-planted cedars, and the telegraph track being compelled by law to follow the highway, here is a plump conflict between utility and beauty. I saw two cedars cut down yesterday, and their spires of luxuriant foliage thrown into the ditch like weeds or thistles, and twenty years would not restore the lovely like of them to the border of my daily ride. What news their delicate branch-tips may have tampered with, or what friend's lightning-sped message, sad or joyous, was likely to be modified or hindered by the leaving our highway shaded and beautiful, of course was not taken into immediate consideration. A jaundice would have time enough to be cured, before most human tempers would remember friends or news enough to neutralize such an irritant of the bile. But (dear Directors and Companies !) is there no way to give your wires room enough, without cutting a track for them through the shade-trees under which beggar and invalid, traveller and laboring man, bless God for common and free shelter from the sun ? A tree in a field is one man's. A tree in the road is the people's—sacred to the wayfarer and the weary. Would it not be better—(greatly lessening the distance, at the same time)—to change the law restricting the telegraph to the highways, and run them, in a bee-line, across fields, from city to city ? The question is an open one, at least ; and let us hope to find, by discussing it, that our country can be "fast," and yet have the beauty and comfort for the many—in such matters, for instance, as the only trees whose shade is without money and without price—kindly and thoughtfully respected.

LETTER LXVIII.

Difficulty of knowing what cures Us—Od-ic Influence—Letter from an Artist, introducing and describing an Od-omatrician—His Letter—The Experiment—Table-movings, &c., &c.

September 23, 1854.

OUR sick brother Summer is "picking up again." The two months' drought has been broken at last by rains ; and, though the hectic upon the hills still flushes in the cleared air (their slopes looking like strata of fossil rainbows, with the prematurely discolored leaves) the washed evergreens look bright and the grass-tips are lifting once more green and beautiful in the pastures. Possibly to give me the advantage of a sympathy with the equinox, my doctor has followed Nature's treatment of the sick Summer ; and, by a sudden change to sustained and powerful tonics, has brightened me into such a promise of my regular October, that, with casual observers, it passes for my time of year—a dropped leaf here and there, but not more sad than seasonable. We shall see how we stand the letting down of the Indian Summer ; but, if there is no pull upon our juices by a second drought, and an autumn of reluctant invigoration, Summer and I may consider our chasm bridged over.

One of the puzzles of illness, however, is, when getting better, to know what has cured us. One secretly tries a thing or two that has been recommended by kind friends, not telling the doctor, perhaps, till he comes to rejoice in the success of his prescription. I fear that Homœopathy and my friend Gray must divide the agency of my improval with a certain mysterious power called OD-IC INFLUENCE, exercised upon me through four white-wood wands which I received from a stranger, a week or two since, with directions as to the employment of a power with which he had impregnated them for my cure. But, as all I know of the matter is explainable on paper, and as the directions are so full and satisfactory as to be easily followed by those who wish, it is a fair contribution to the Invalid treasury to make it public—premature though, perhaps, it may somewhat be, as a mist from the spirit-world whose once remote atmosphere seems drawing closer around us.

But, to the story.

Hand-writings have their physiognomy ; and, on opening a thick package among my letters by the day's mail, and laying aside an outer letter and a pierced card through which were run four slender and dagger-shaped sticks, of sandal-wood color, and of the length from a lady's bracelet to her wedding ring, I was startled by the aspect of a manuscript in a strange, old-fashioned hand—four pages closely written, with upright and angular letters, and interspersed with curious diagrams and large black numbers. It was dated at a small country town of which I know something by hearsay, and signed with the writer's name—and, by retaining only the date and the name, I shall give all that those interested will need for experiment, while at the same time, I secure the privacy intended in the communication.

It will be as well to precede the manuscript with part of the introductory letter which accompanied it, and which gives some particulars of the habits and character of my mysterious well-wisher. The introducer is an artist, well known for his talents, whom. I once had the pleasure of meeting, and who is passing his professional summer in the romantic and secluded neighborhood of the odimetrician's residence, the old gentleman being a distant connection of his family. After, an explanation as to the inclosed manuscript, my kind friend goes on to say :—

* * "He (Mr. ——) is now sixty-six years of age. He is independent in his means, has never married, and has mingled little with the world. For the last forty years he has slept but three or four hours out of the twenty-four. He says he began the practice of sitting up late as a cure for suffusion of blood to the eyes, and has kept it up ever since. He rises at six, takes a walk of half an hour up and down a tracked path behind his house, of which the grounds are extensive, then eats a breakfast which is invariably of the same food and quantity—a small plate of minced meat, and a slice and a half of toast covered with pepper and lumps of butter. He remains in his study till a little before twelve, takes another walk, dines on an exact repetition of his breakfast, remains in his study till five, and then takes another walk on the beaten path. His supper is varied by the substitution of shad and potato for the minced meat. Coffee he drinks morning and evening He has made this his diet for forty years With another walk after his supper he goes to his study, where he reads and tries his od-imetric experiments till three or four in the morning.

"Mr. —— is very tall and of wonderful vigor and youthfulness of frame and feeling, though his hair is as white as snow. He attributes his strength to his absolutely regular habits, for, when young, he was thought by his father (who was a physician) to be dying of consumption. He sees no company, except myself, and as I sit at table with him, and listen to his conversation, exceedingly rich, varied and extraordinary as it is, I mourn that Dickens is not here to take his picture for the world. He is a rare specimen of the gentleman of the old school in his manners, very benevolent to the poor, kind-hearted and generous in all his impulses. I never expect to look upon his like again. By the neighbors, who are rather superstitious about him, he is considered deranged on religious and scientific subjects, and it is said, that he has for years taken opium, though this I think doubtful.

"The chance malformation of a double thumb on his right hand, in the form of a cross, is considered by Mr. —— as the mark of his high calling as a prophet. He believes himself the milennial successor of Isaiah, but says that England is the chosen milennial kingdom. He has written pamphlets in explanation of the prophecies, has had them printed, and is preparing another. If I had time I would tell you of his 'grand experiments' as he terms them (and grand they certainly are), accounts of which are to appear in his work. I wish you could see them. I have sat up with him many a night, seeing him perform his 'enchantments,' as he also sometimes names them, and really fearful they were to behold. The house is an old one, walls gloomy and dark, and there he would sit, dressed in a most unique as well as antique costume, hair white as snow, three or four lights shedding a dim glare around the apartment, and he, with his pendules, bones and machineries, going through a series of experiments as visionary as the dreamings of an eater of 'hasheesh.'

"Among his opinions, he says ninety out of every one hundred are possessed with a devil. He has the power of dispossessing, and dispossessed *me*, which he told me was the most serious event of my whole life. He considers cotton and women diabolic mediums, those who wear cotton being more apt to do wrong than those who wear linen, the Bible declaring that 'linen is the righteousness of the saints.' He writes poetry, and is certainly, aside from his idiosyncrasies, a philosopher and a highly cultivated and polished gentleman. He is also a musical composer. He sometimes walks around the house singing all night. His voice is admirable and of great strength. I have listened many an hour in wonder to hear the beauty with which he sings English songs, as well as sacred music, of which he is very fond.

* * "In a letter to him, after seeing by the papers that you were so ill, I asked him to send an od-ic to your lungs, distance being of no consequence, in his theory. The result was the letter which I inclose. He wrote it with a sincere belief that it was for your recovery. He afterwards proposed to me that he should pay all expenses, and that we should go to Idlewild, to see you and show you how to use the wands, &c. His regard for you is very great."

* * * * * *

And by this artistic description of the odimetrician by our artist friend, the reader is prepared for the odimetric letter itself, which follows verbally as written :—

—— , *August* 14, 1854.

"SIR :—I shall leave it to my friend, well-known as a poet, artist, and contributor to American literature, and who, I believe, is slightly acquainted with you, to forward this communication, with such introductory notes as may be proper. I am a subscriber to the *Home Journal*, and have been much entertained by the descriptions of your proceedings at Idlewild, and of the surroundings ; and have felt much sympathy in reading the occasional notices of your complaint. I had hoped till latterly, that you were recovering, and that the world would long have the benefit of the efforts of your brilliant pen. Two days since, I received a letter from Mr. Lawrence, in which he says :—'I see Willis is failing, and am very sorry. Please throw an odic into his lungs, and see if you cannot save him." This I should by no means feel at liberty to do, without your knowledge and consent ; although, as Mr. —— well knows, the distance would interpose no obstacle. But to explain :—

"I have for some time been engaged in a course of experiments on Reichenbach's OD-FORCE, and appear to have made some valuable discoveries ; among which is this :—That every different class of substances has an ODIC peculiar to itself ; that these ODICS can be detached and transmitted to a distance with the speed of the telegraph, and fixed permanently in other bodies, or any part of them, in living bodies, or upon any organ, &c. ; and that the odics of medicinal substances produce effects similar to those of, the substances from which they are derived, exhibited in the usual methods, but more ethereal. The Eclectic School of Medicine in this country, of which Dr. Buchanan, the discoverer of psychometry, is perhaps regarded as the chief, insists much, of late, upon the fact that an article of medicine, carried about the person, even in a glass vial hermetically sealed, produces on many sensitives, effects similar to those of the medicine, &c. These effects are not improbably caused by OD-FORCE, for there is no other element or principle, at present known, peculiar to any article of medicine, that could permeate the glass, &c. But this method of applying the OD-FORCE must be very unequal and uncertain. A method which I propose, and which I will directly describe, has the advantages, that an accurately measured quantity can be thrown permanently upon any organ or part of the system which may be affected, may be dispersed, wholly or in part, renewed, &c., at will. Accompanying this, you will receive four WANDS, which are supposed to possess very considerable odimetric virtues, which I will proceed to specify ; but first, as to the method of using the wands.

"It will be necessary, in the first place, to find one in whose hand a pendule will traverse spontaneously. A pendule is a gold ring or other light weight, suspended by a thread five or six inches long, and held in the right hand, over a motor. A slip of any silk stuff, or small piece of cotton or linen cloth, is a good motor. When a pendule is held (as above) over one of these, the mind being kept perfectly passive (if in the right hand) the pendule in a few seconds acquires a spontaneous movement : if over silk, rotary ; if over cotton, oscillating ; if over linen, rotary. Such an one being found, let him, with one of the wands in his right hand, point, with the lesser extremity, to the motor or basis, and pronounce mentally, with conscious purpose, this formula :— ' LET VIRTUE GO FORTH, —— DEGREES, INTO THE BASIS "—moving the wand slightly, at the close, towards the basis. If the blank be filled by the word seven, and if virtue have gone forth, the pendule will now refuse to move, the native and artificial odics being exactly balanced. Linen free from cotton, ten degrees. If a number greater than seven and less than ninety, be mentioned, the pendule will acquire a new movement. The wands, which I will designate, according to the marks, by the numbers one, two, three, four, will give, respectively, these movements. [Here follow diagrams which we cannot give in print, representing the movements.]

" To remove the odic, let the operator hold the wand by the lesser extremity, and pointing as before, pronounce this formula : 'Let —— degrees of the artificial odic be entirely dispersed ;' or, 'let the artificial odic,'&c. The basis or motor should thus be restored partially or wholly to its normal condition. Should this succeed, the operator can throw an odic into the person of another, or upon any organ, &c. The particular form of words is not essential, only a method is required to concentrate the animus, which is the moving force that—so to speak—hoists the gate, or throws on the steam, &c. The pendule and wand would, doubtless, operate in the hands of many (where they will not) were it not for their surroundings. A new garment of any mixed fabric, snuff or tobacco about the person, &c., will commonly prevent. The presence of others who are incredulous or unfriendly, produces much the same effect as in mesmeric experiments.

"Of the wands, number one is designed to operate directly upon your disease, the odic to be thrown in upon your lungs. Holding the wand as first above, and pointing towards your chest, let the operator say, "Let virtue go forth into the lungs of Mr. Willis —— degrees." It appears that twenty-five degrees would be a proper dose, though it might be well to begin with a less number. I have had no opportunity to try this ODIC upon one in your complaint, but have thrown it in upon my own lungs, when I had a cold, with excellent effect. Number two will throw an odic of hyoscyamus, designed to abate your cough. I think you mentioned that your cough was much worse at night. If so, it might be best to disperse this odic for the day, and to employ it only at night. The two can be employed together—twenty-three degrees being a proper dose of this.

"Number three. Many persons believe that, to a certain extent, and in a certain manner, the consumption is contagious. The odic of this wand is designed to prevent the effect of this contagion. There is a family in this region, the father of which, and one sister, have died of consumption, and another sister is sick. I threw this odic, at a distance of some dozen miles, into the lungs of the mother and two well sisters, and into those of a brother, last November. Another sister, subsequently. The effect appears to have been admirable. The brother's lungs were very considerably affected for a long time after the first sister's death. But now, though this sister has been sick more than a year, his lungs are affected very little—none in the ordinary sense ; he is in good health, and his mother and sisters continue well, including one who has been constantly with the invalid. Of her—the sick one—if space permitted, I could tell some remarkable particulars, tending to prove the efficiency of these applications. Suffice it to say, she has continued much longer than was expected, and is still surprisingly comfortable.

"Number four will dispense an ODIC that I have very considerable reason for supposing will be more efficacious in the treatment of your complaint than number one, but I have had no opportunity of making trial of it. The proper dose of this is also twenty-five degrees. That of number three, for a stout Irish girl, eighty-three degrees—for a lady of more delicate organization, fifty-three—for a little child, twenty-four. It will be understood that all the ODICS are to be applied to the lungs. The wands will operate as far as the limits of an apartment, or, in the open air, to a distance of ten feet. They will throw ninety degrees of ODIC at once, or any less number, and the process may be repeated at will. They will retain their efficacy for one year, or till August 14, 1855, when it will suddenly cease. Number four can be employed with number two, but not with number one.

"It has given me pleasure, sir, to prepare the wands, and to write this hurried and immethodical letter, prompted as I have been by Mr. ——, and hoping I might do some good ; but I shall neither be surprised nor disappointed, if you should not deem it prudent or expedient to employ applications so little known. Should you conclude to make use of them, I should be gratified to hear from you, but not unless you can write without the least inconvenience, for I believe all over-exertion in your complaint is very detrimental. With the best wishes for your welfare and recovery, I am, very respectfully

——."

It was a rainy afternoon ; and, of the five or six guests who chanced to be prisoned in-doors, at Idlewild, with the leisure for an experiment on their hands, the character was varied enough to give us an unusual chance of finding a good "medium." A Judge of the City Bench, two lady leaders of society (one from gay and inconsequent New York, and one from ethical and abstract Boston), a young lady just returned from Europe, a substantial merchant, and a successful author, were of the circle gathered around the *od*-ic wands for an experiment—and the last-mentioned (Bayard Taylor) was found to be the one in whose force of will best resided the power. The lady's gold ring we had borrowed, and, suspended to his well-steadied and motionless finger, by a silken thread, moved in absolute obedience—circling from right to left, or from left to right, backwards or forwards, or from side to side, stopping still or resuming motion, as the spectators requested, and as he accordingly *willed*. [Whether the same gold could be willed out of one pocket into another, was the naturally-suggested thought—but that degree of *od*-icity is probably millennial.]

Having thus found the "one in whose hand a pendule will traverse spontaneously," the slender wands were unsheathed ; and, Mr. Taylor assuring us that his "mind was perfectly passive," he took each wand in its turn, between his just-tested thumb and fore-finger, selected the degree, "pointed with the lesser extremity to the basis" (me), and pronounced the prescribed formula. The company were silent. The rain poured heavily. Our thoughts played pendulum between the white-haired *od*-imetrician, hundreds of miles away, and our friend the handsome viaduct through whom, at that moment, the magic influence must supernaturally pass. He commanded the "virtue to go forth." It probably did. Such transfers are vague, at best. What Taylor felt at his loss, he may tell us, perhaps, in a poem. I cannot say that I had any very definite sensation at the passing of his virtue into me.

But I am "better." Whether it is *od*-ic or physic, is, as I said before, the embarrassing point for my acknowledgments. Either way, however, I am not the less grateful to my venerable *od*-imetric friend, whom I respectfully and tenderly hope I shall yet see at Idlewild. His wands "retain their efficacy till August 14, 1855 ;" but my welcome to him will last longer—if I do.

I should add, by the way, that we had reason to wonder, that afternoon, whether the *od*-ic-opened door may not let in other unseen spirits besides the health-bringing ones, or whether these may not do more than they are bid. Perhaps it may be as well to caution experimenters, that, possibly,

"More water runneth by the mill
Than wots the miller of."

Our talk naturally led to experiments at table-moving ; and one of the wooden-legged quadrupeds—an ormolu table, hitherto of the most steady habits, standing in the centre of the drawing-room, began to prance with our Boston friend's laying her hands lightly upon it, and, the next moment (though she is a large and majestic lady), knocked her and my little daughter Lilian prostrate upon the floor, very nearly upset the Judge, and broke the arm of a lotus-crowned statue of Melancholy which was on a stand in the corner. It appeared that spirits invoked to heal lungs, may also assault ladies and children, damage furniture, and break objects of art—mischievous "angels of mercy," to say the least. Under the touch of one of our visitors (an invalid lady who could scarcely walk across the room), the tables, one and all, that evening, seemed particularly ungovernable. Two of our neighbors who chanced to come in (our venerable friend S. and a stout working farmer)—were obliged to hop out of the way, in the midst of their unbelief, to make room for the "possessed" mahogany, pirouetting under the mere touch of her slender fingers. No two of the men present could, by holding on with main strength, stop the one-lady's-will-power thus exercised—the table rising from the floor or gliding away, as if gentlemen-wills were the only obstacle. The faces of the scared servants, who were peeping in at the doors, would have been a study for Fuseli. The very tables they had bees-waxed every day !

Of course we *"believed"* nothing—any of us. But this was what we *saw*.

I may as well add, perhaps, that, to my own touch, the "possessed" tables were wholly insensible—as they were to the touch of all the gentlemen present. They danced only with ladies.

And all this from having a cough to cure. We must not be inconsolable, dear brother invalids.

LETTER LXIX.

Acquaintance across the Styx—Letter from our Friend the Od-ometrician, &c.

September 30, 1854.

I AM by no means sure that our invalid society has not proved attractive to unseen spirits. We have more to wonder at than we used to have, and nearer neighborhood, perhaps, may have brought us calls from "Styx's other shore"—as might be easily imagined from the results of our conjuring experiments with the *od*-ic wands, as recorded in the last number of the *Home Journal*. We are assured, by the poet, that *"parting* spirits see across," and there is abundant reason to believe that *parted* spirits cannot only see back, but make their eyes felt, over the ferry they have passed. *Looks*, from the spirit-land, rest upon us, every heart must, at times, have been made to feel.

But, to get *words* to us—they whose lips are shadows and whose tongues are air ! To the music without words, which is *their* voice—the voices of sweet influences unsyllabled—we need an opening through the flesh-coatings of the ear. If spirits speak to us, therefore, it is indirectly—through words borrowed from others—by tongues or pens which they "possess" to speak or write to us. We may be spoken to by friends, with words of counsel or cheer, when the apology is more literal than they think—"because the spirit moves them"—another spirit than their own, to whose promptings they have thus lent mortal utterance.

Oh, to bridge that gulf with our "belief in spirits !" That a child may be reached from heaven by its mother's love and watchfulness ! That love may follow thither—told of by the same chain of electric consciousness which brings their love to us ! Rather than retard the coming of a "mesmeric" millennium like this, let us be thought visionary and credulous. Life has arithmetic enough.

Of one of our invalid company who has died since we began to have a sick-room corner in our journal, I am made to feel something like the continued memory. These too careless gossippings were her pleasure in her illness. A stranger personally, she made such eager search along the shore of the Hudson, in her last journey up the river—wishing to see, before she died, the Idle-wild where those like her were remembered—that the broken heart of him who mourns for her turns hither with its sadness. His letters, far away as he is, seem to bring me with him to her presence. They are strangely touching, beautiful, and truthful. The pen should write reverently that sends vibrations to such strings.

With belief turned out upon God's large universe, however—exploring for discovery rather than fencing in from conviction—speculation tempts far. Let us try our wings once more with my friend the mysterious and venerable *od*-ometrician, who thus discourses to me, in a second letter, dated September 13, 1854 :—

"———

"SIR :—I will suppose that a former communication, of August 14, has been received. I cannot doubt, if so, that you have some curiosity to know more about the od-force ; and I propose—hoping it will amuse you—to give you some little account of its effects upon vegetation. Last fall I threw od-ics into the only growing crop, turnips ; and the result led me to the conclusion, that vegetation might be accelerated fifty per cent, in the course of the growing season. The experiments of the present season have more than confirmed this supposition. Of six cotton plants, side by side—circumstances all similar—the three that were od-icised the 1st of July, weighed, compared with the non-od-icised, August 25, in the proportion of 147 to 100.

"I have made another very interesting discovery. You are aware that some persons cannot bear cotton next the skin. It produces irritation, general uneasiness, itching, inflamed eyes, aggravates humors, &c. The number of those who are insidiously affected, is probably greater, beyond comparison, than of those who are affected palpably and unequivocally. There is reason to believe that it lays the foundation of various chronic and lingering complaints ; and I believe that the indirect (or direct !) moral effect is more to be deprecated than the hygienic or non-hygienic. A person who cannot wear cotton socks in warm weather, without such continual itching, that, as a natural consequence, the ankles and feet have as many galled spots as a first-rate patriot could expect at the close of an electioneering campaign, has worn, the past season, cotton socks that had been permanently de-od-icised, and od-icised with the od-ic of linen, of the normal intensity, without the least inconvenience. The cotton seemed entirely "healed,"—to be effectually linenized.

"Will you permit me, in this connection, to suggest a point of ethics ? If you have had the curiosity to look over one or two pamphlets that I have sent you, *on the prophetical Scriptures* (perhaps sent to the *Home Journal*), you may recollect that I have advanced the theory that England is the nation to which the kingdom of God was to be given (Matt. xxi. 43),—*the millennial kingdom*. Now, should these discoveries, *at first*, be generally disseminated, or limited, for a time, to the millennial kingdom ? I have called the above a point of ethics, but it is ethico-political—the ethical considerations at the basis. I do not wish you to give me an *ex-cathedrâ* opinion on the subject, nor indeed any opinion, unless it should come in your way to give an intelligible hint in the *Home Journal*. For many years I have been almost a recluse ; during which time you have travelled much, observed much, and reflected much.

"I am getting on as I can with a pamphlet on the subject of the *od*-force, which I hope to have in readiness for distribution by the middle of November. If you wish, I will send you a bundle of them for distribution among your friends.

'I take the liberty to send you two more wands. They are set as to degrees, etc., like the others. No. 1 throws a compound *od*-ic of bugle-weed and sugar of lead, designed to prevent hemoptysis. Dose, thrown into the lungs, twenty-five degrees, though I should recommend a smaller dose at first, and great caution. No. 2 throws a compound *od*-ic of French brandy (the real article, such as used to be in the market forty years ago), quassia, and the sulphate of zinc, designed as an appetizer and tonic—dose, forty-five degrees, to be thrown into the stomach. *According to my theory, the consumption makes little or no progress, so long as the stomach can be kept in tone.* Hence the singular benefit of exercise on horseback.

"Since commencing this letter, I have visited a *plantation* which I have at some little distance. There are cotton plants (which have grown, from the seed, under *od*-ometric influences) that are three and one-half feet high, and much the same in diameter. One of them is supposed to have some fifty buds, blossoms, and balls upon it. Some of the balls are, and will be, I think, matured sufficiently to produce acclimated seed for another year. I have learned much this season, and should judge from critical observation, that the Plant might be matured, another year, six weeks earlier. That it can, by selecting the earliest acclimated seed, and by continuing *od*-ometric influences, be acclimated in a few years, is, I think, little doubtful. There is also a magnificent growth of river rice, though grown on upland. The product of a single seed, in some instances, is a dense cluster of stems, as large as I can clasp with both hands—the broad rice-grass above, reaching in some instances, to the height of three and one-half feet. But, there is not a single seed-bearing stalk. The plants grew on a side hill, exposed to the full glare of the sun all day, but suffered less from drought than most other vegetation. I see no reason why the upland or dry rice may not be grown as well in New England as in Alabama ; and the river rice in water, as well as in South Carolina. At any rate, on the uplands, it would be exceedingly productive for feed. I held a wisp to Mulley (cow), and she almost dislocated my arm by tearing off a mouthful. It is very tenacious, in consequence of having little moisture ; and, for the same reason, the yield would be great. I should judge it would not lose more than half as much weight, by drying, as English grass.

"Should you happen to wish for other wands, for any specific purpose, please to write, and I will endeavor to prepare them.—I am, sir, with great respect, your obedient servant,

"———."

"P.S.—Some rice that I have dried by the stove, and just weighed, lost in weight but about sixty per cent."

The question in ethics proposed by this venerable student of mysteries, is too broad and difficult to be answered—short, at least, of his own scope and study in a pamphlet ; but I remember a passage which has a bearing upon it, and which I ran a pencil against, years ago, in a book of very high authority—viz. : *"That the world is not fit to be trusted with secrets, even concerning movements for its own good, is a principle acted upon by wise men, as well as by mysterious Providence."* Whether our friend himself is not on the scene-shifter's side of the curtain not ready to be raised, is a nice question also, I am inclined to think ; though the class who form the readers of the *Home Journal* are, perhaps, the best pick that could be made for the exceptions to see a "star in the East."

LETTER LXX.

Certainty of a *Genius Loci*—His Susceptibility of *Pique*—Curious Exercise of it—The Drip-Rock Parlor—Check to a falling Leaf—Farewell.

October 7, 1854.

SEPARATE a rural spot from the rest of the world, either by poetry or property—only putting around it the fairy ring of a thought-haunt, where your love and sadness are at home—and it is curious how you are made gradually conscious that there is a *genius loci*, a spirit, inhabiting just what you have fenced in with thoughts or rails. The almost inarticulate welcome that yon feel, as you enter the gate, or re-cross the limit after absence—the sigh of desertedness as you go from it into the world—show that it is a loving spirit, though (like an angel with a prudent mamma) it waited to see some definite habitation before acknowledging the preference. But we mistake, I think, if we invest it with any qualities that are inconvenient—any mystery or majesty, that is to say, which would inspire awe, or make us any way uncomfortable. It is a familiar spirit. Its demonstrations are very human—playful and capricious, when not called upon to be sympathetic and tender. Our table-movings last week, I more than half suspect were mere bits of fun by the Spirit of Idlewild.

But, that the "spirit of a spot" is *susceptible of pique*, was a discovery of mine a day or two ago—more interesting as being another step in the mortal-ward progress which the spirit world is making (or which is thought to be shown in the spirit world's behaving as men and women would very likely do in the same circumstances, or out of the reach of their ordinary amusements and occupations), and the new knowledge is therefore perhaps worthy to be recorded. The future historian of our age, with his increased responsibilities, may thank us—his business being with the events of things visible and a little way beyond.

The most precious natural treasure of Idlewild, as well as its most beautiful feature, had been left undescribed. At the farthest depth between precipices, hidden and romantically wild, lies a sanctuary of rock and water, which for various whims of reasons, I have never chanced to portray, in these my descriptive pencillings. It was partly because I wished for more leisure to sketch the spot well, partly because its coyness of privacy was a charm which the directing of attention to it might destroy—the common rambler through the glen walking over its rock-roof, and leaving it unvisited and unsuspected. And so the Spirit of Idlewild felt a sigh—her drip-rock parlor, with its overhanging eaves and cool floor, its lofty shading of trees and its deep-down basin, left all unpictured.

But, if *I* would not do it, *somebody else* would. Oh, the Spirit of the Spot did not depend altogether on *me !* If it could not bring another writer actually here to describe it, there was a first-rate one who could be made to see it in a dream ! And he would tell his dream ! What was my amazement to take up *"The Independent,"* last Saturday, and, in the midst of Beecher's, charming letter from his new home in the country, read the following abrupt digression—a sudden and most singular breaking away from his actual description of what was around him, to portray most graphically and exactly, this drip-rock parlor at Idlewild :—

> "I have always wished that there might be a rock-spring upon my place. I could wish to have, back of the house some two hundred yards, a steep and tree-covered height of broad, cold, and mossy rocks—rocks that have seen trouble, and been upheaved by deep inward forces, and are lying in any way of noble confusion, full of clefts, and dark and mysterious passages, without echoes in them, upholstered with pendulous vines and soft with deep moss. Upon all this silent tumult of wild and shattered rocks, struck through with stillness and rest, the thick forest should shed down a perpetual twilight. The only glow that ever chased away its solemn shadows should be the red rose-light of sunsets, shot beneath the branches and through the trunks, lighting up the gray rocks with strange golden glory. What light is so impressive as this last light of the day streaming into a forest so dark that even insects leave it silent ? Yes, another light is as strange—that rose-light of the afternoon, which shines down a hillside of vivid green grass, taking its hues, and strikes through the transparent leaves into the forest below, and spreads itself along the ground in a tender color for which we have no name, as if green was just melting into rose color, and orange color was just seizing them both.
>
> "But to return to the spring. In such a rock forest as I have spoken of, far up in one of its silent aisles, a spring should burst forth, making haste from the seams of the rock, as if just touched with the prophet's rod—cold, clear, copious and musical from its birth. All the way to the outer edge of the forest it should find, its own channels, and live its own life, unshaped by human hands. But before the sun touched it, we should have a rock reservoir, into which it should gather its congregation of drops now about to go forth into useful life. Thence it should have liberty of will to *flow where* it could not help flowing, through strong pipes into every chamber of the house. And it should be to every room copious as the atmosphere, so that one might bathe in molten ice every hour of the day if he chose, without fear of exhausting

the fountain, and in the joy of abundance beyond all squandering.* Just such a spring I have *not*, and cannot have."

And here he returns to *his own* Tempé—quite unconscious, probably, that, with his eloquent digression, he has been gratifying the jealous pique of the Spirit of *mine*—literary describing the beauty-spot I had neglected !

I have made what atonement was possible to the offended glen-fairy—showing her tall drip-curtain and its romantic surroundings to Wandesford the artist, who chanced to be staying with us, and who immediately picked out the point of view for his pencil of magic. He will make such a picture of that hiding-place of beauty as will stir pens more poetical than mine.

I called Wandesford's attention to a pretty little mock of invalid enjoyment of life, as he was sketching in another part of the glen, that morning. Cut off from conversation for awhile, by his wanting my broad-brimmed hat in the background, to give effect to his drawing, I was in the bliss of a summer morning's mere existence—gazing into the depths of the glen without a thought that had more grammar in it than the pulse in my wrist—when an object of unusual brilliancy and activity caught my eye. The rock I was "doing figure" upon was a seat half way down a hanging path in the side of a cliff, the broken light flickering through the gigantic trees overhead, and the furious cascades which were performing their accustomed sublimities far below, keeping a constant tremulousness in the air.

My eye had once or twice rested upon what I took to be a hovering butterfly, poised midway over the abyss ; but, with its humming-bird activity of wings, and its remaining unchangeably in one spot, my attention became gradually fixed upon it. It was a faded leaf, held by a spider's thread, but so poised that it revolved in the currents of air with the glitter and show of an insect. Wandesford left his pencils to come and look at it. The cobweb was invisible, and he was puzzled to see how it was upheld, or why, with its wonderful liveliness of revolution, it did not wear itself loose from a thread so delicate. But there it fluttered—checked half way to the swift current below, and lingering in the summer air, more moved with every passing breath than in its vigor of June. And there it lingers still. I have seen it since, morning after morning, in my ramble—waiting, probably, for the deferred winds of a gentle Autumn to loose it when the

* Making it a point to be literally correct in these sketches, I should here observe, that, though the spring flows "where it cannot help flowing," and so "to every room in the house," there is a circumstance which Mr. Beecher omits to mention, viz.—that this path to the house, being one hundred and fifty feet up a precipitous hill, it goes that trifle out of its way by the persuasion of a hydraulic ram—its own weight being made the propulsive force (the same as in the down-hill part of its journey), according to the principle of that most beautiful of mechanic inventions.

skies grow ruder. There is one fair lingerer, far West, who has written to number herself in the troop for whom we gossip, and she will find in this leaf her cheerful likeness. May her thread—and that of all to whom this invalid gossip has been the wile-time of a summer prolonged beyond hope—part before the storm would be too wintry. The falling leaf should not linger till ice would make its grave.

* * * * * *

And here the Letters from Idlewild come to an end. The author has thus long—not too long, he trusts—made the readers of the *Home Journal* guests at his home. He brought them here at first, because, confined to its seclusion himself, he felt that he might claim an invalid's privilege to be kindly visited. The friendly interest and willingness to listen have been shown in many ways, and have been, it need scarce be said, most deeply gratifying. The readers of the *Journal* have rapidly increased and are now, many indeed ; and if the author's friendship in the world may be thus measured, he can well afford to care little for its fame. He assures these kind thousands that the memory of their sympathetic listenings will be tenderly cherished in his heart, though the gate of Idlewild is here shut upon the pen that is their servant.

THE END.

www.ingramcontent.com/pod-product-compliance
Lightning Source LLC
LaVergne TN
LVHW050149080826
844660LV00002B/131

* 9 7 8 1 4 3 8 4 8 6 2 3 9 *